TAKE ME
TO THE SOURCE

Rupert Wright

Take Me
To The Source

In Search of Water

Harvill *Secker*
LONDON

Published by Harvill Secker 2008

2 4 6 8 10 9 7 5 3 1

First published in Great Britain in 2008 by
HARVILL SECKER
Random House, 20 Vauxhall Bridge Road,
London SW1V 2SA

www.rbooks.co.uk

Addresses for companies within The Random House Group Limited can be found at:
www.randomhouse.co.uk/offices.htm

The Random House Group Limited Reg. No. 954009

A CIP catalogue record for this book
is available from the British Library

ISBN 9781846550713

The Random House Group Limited supports The Forest Stewardship
Council (FSC), the leading international forest certification organisation. All our titles
that are printed on Greenpeace approved FSC certified paper carry the FSC logo.
Our paper procurement policy can be found at www.rbooks.co.uk/environment

Typeset in Fournier MT by Palimpsest Book Production Limited,
Grangemouth, Stirlingshire

Printed and bound in the UK by
CPI Mackays, Chatham ME5 8TD

For my parents and my children:
blood is thicker than water

Contents

Everything is water.

Thales of Miletus (attrib.)

Disclaimer

This book does not offer a solution to the world's water problems, nor does it travel the globe visiting places where once there was water, and now there is none. I do not believe that one day – soon – the lakes and rivers will run dry, the wells will be empty and we will all die of thirst. Anyone who has sailed or flown over the oceans will have noted that there is a lot of water about. Whether or not we can get our hands on it is another matter.

Prologue

THE AFRICAN SUN IS high, it's midday, and so it's strange that the young woman is not in the shade. The sun makes her skin shine like copper, but she does not sweat. She is young, no more than fourteen, and attractive, although it's difficult to see much of her face because it's covered by her arms. A light breeze ripples her short dress. Her legs are long; she wears no shoes. There are few features in the desert landscape, just an acacia in the distance, and overhead a few black dots that could be birds.

In his sonnet 'Le Dormeur du Val', Arthur Rimbaud, the French poet, describes a young soldier lying by a riverbank. It's a beautiful day, the sun is shining and the river is singing. The man is sleeping among the cress and the wild flowers. He is bareheaded, his mouth open. His feet are resting among gladioli, but their scent does not trouble his nostrils. His hands rest on his body. And then we notice that there are two red holes on the right of his chest. He will never wake up.

Another look at the young girl sleeping in the hot sun by the side of the well. Those birds are no longer dots. They are vultures and they are getting closer. The girl will never wake up. It isn't bullets that have killed her, but thirst. The well is dry.

What happens when you die of thirst? In 1906, W. J. McGee, director of the St Louis Public Museum, published *Philbrick*, which contains one of the most detailed descriptions of the ravages of extreme dehydration. It was based on the experiences of Pablo Valencia, a forty-year-old sailor-turned-prospector, who survived almost seven days in the Arizona desert without water.

When you don't have anything to drink, your saliva turns thick and foul-tasting; your tongue clings to the teeth and the roof of the mouth. A lump forms in the throat. Your head and neck ache. Your face feels like it will explode. Many people begin to hallucinate. Hearing is difficult, almost distorted. Then comes the agony of a mouth that has ceased to generate saliva. The tongue stiffens into what McGee describes as 'a senseless weight, swinging on the still-soft root and striking strangely against the teeth'. Speech becomes impossible, although sufferers have been known to moan like a pregnant cow.

This is just the beginning. Next is the 'blood sweats' phase, involving 'a progressive mummification of the initially living body'. The tongue swells to such proportions that it squeezes past the lips. The eyelids crack and the eyeballs begin to weep tears of blood. The throat is so swollen that breathing is difficult, creating an incongruous yet appalling sense of drowning.

The last stage is close to death. This was the state into which Pablo Valencia had fallen when McGee discovered him on a desert trail, crawling on his hands and knees. McGee describes how 'his lips had disappeared as if amputated, leaving low edges of blackened tissue; his teeth and gums projected like those of a skinned animal, but the flesh was black and dry as a hank of jerky; his nose was withered and shrunken to half its length, and the nostril lining showing black; his eyes were set in a winkless stare, with surrounding skin so contracted as to expose the conjunctiva, itself as black as the gums . . . his skin [had] generally turned a ghastly purplish yet ashen gray, with great livid blotches and streaks; his lower legs and feet . . . were torn and scratched by contact with thorns and sharp rocks, yet even the freshest cuts were so many scratches in dry leather, without trace of blood.'

At the heart of the ecological debate gripping the planet is a simple but complex substance: water. It is colourless, tasteless and odourless, which is perhaps why few of us pay it any mind. Most of us come into contact with water every day and generally it's a pleasant experience. We look forward to a shower, a bath or a swim. It's the most refreshing drink after a run; and wise dinner-party guests alternate glasses of wine with glasses of water. Water becomes apparent only when it is absent. If water rates a mention at all, it is as a footnote to the warning that unless we act to reduce carbon emissions, we will all be overwhelmed in a great flood, or face a drought so prolonged that the animals will be wiped out, there will be nothing to eat, and we must move elsewhere or die our own slow and terrible deaths. Is this true? The honest answer is that nobody knows. Scientists make great claims, but they have done that before, as when they predicted that there would be an Aids pandemic in the 1980s. For most of us, that didn't happen. An epidemic came, but was contained. To claim, as former US vice president Al Gore did in his speech while accepting the Nobel Peace Prize in 2007 that the 'earth is running a fever' is the worst kind of anthropomorphism. At times the earth has been hot, and at other times it has been unpleasantly cold. None of this had anything to do with human activity. It may well be that carbon emissions are affecting the climate and we should reduce them; but it has got hotter before.

While the debate rages, and aeroplanes take a fresh band of delegates to the next starry convention hall to decide nothing but the date of another meeting, the substance that should be at the centre of the dialogue is ignored. Never mind a future that may or may not happen. We have dammed rivers, drained aquifers and polluted water to such an extent that we only have ourselves to blame. While quietly, but insidiously, water kills around 6,000 people – mainly children – every day. This isn't water's fault. With the possible exception of arsenic contamination, which only occurs when it is extracted from boreholes, water in its natural state is pure and benevolent. But as man moves to cities – and at no time in our history have we done it so quickly as in the last hundred years – the basic needs, particularly of the poor, are not met. Water becomes unclean and contaminated. Cholera, once the scourge of great cities such as London, Paris and New York in the nineteenth century, has reappeared in places such as Luanda, Maputo and New Delhi. Why? Because of indifference, mismanagement, greed and corruption. And nobody really cares. Certainly, nobody wants to pay a realistic price for clean water. The general public wants as much of it as possible and baulks at the first sign of an increase in water rates; the farmers want to spray it in the air, and pay nothing for it; while industrialists are happy to use it and sometimes pay for it, although some of them try to dump the polluted waste in the rivers in the hope it will be washed away before anyone notices or complains.

It has been argued that the primary cause of the Iraq war, which toppled Saddam Hussein, was oil. Maybe. But if the war was fought for oil, it was lost by water. Iraqis, forced to live under a cruel dictator, were at least able to turn on their taps, cook their rice and vegetables and wash the dust from their hair. Under their occupiers, the Iraqis were reduced to visiting standpipes while soldiers in Humvees, sipping their bottles of iced Poland Spring, watched them carrying buckets. It shouldn't surprise anyone that the Iraqis found this an intolerable situation.

Without water, we suddenly become helpless, desperate

even. During the siege of the Beslan school in September 2004, the terrorists refused to give the hostages food or water for four days. It was the lack of water that started to drive them mad. One mother, who was breastfeeding at the time, allowed the children near her to suckle on her breasts. Later, when there was hardly any milk left, she eked out what she could and passed it round in a teaspoon. Marina Kisieva, whose husband and son died in the attack, can hardly bear to think about it: 'For the first two months I was completely numb. I didn't go out. I neglected the house. I wanted nothing to do with my daughter. I was completely isolated. I couldn't bear to turn the tap on, I couldn't bear to hear the sound of running water. Why didn't they let the children drink?'

After the Battle of the Crater during the American Civil War, confederate soldiers took out their anger on black soldiers on the Union side with savagery. Private Harry Bird noted that black soldiers, begging for water, were silenced by bayonet thrusts. General Robert E. Lee looked on and did nothing to stop the carnage. What makes this especially shocking is not just the callousness of the action, but that the injured were asking for water. To deny somebody that is almost a crime against humanity.

That September the children in Beslan were craving refreshment, I was watering my peach trees in the south of France. The water was fresh and pure. You could drink it straight from the hosepipe. The French family that we bought the house from had told us that we had our own water supply. I was delighted to hear this, but had absolutely no idea of the implications. I imagine I just thought that I wouldn't have to pay any water bills. Inside the house my wife was preparing dinner for our young daughter and me. The washing machine was churning away in the garage, my daughter was splashing in the bath. I was congratulating myself on my good fortune to have such a beautiful house in such a splendid landscape. It was eight o'clock, but it was still warm. There wasn't a cloud in the sky. Overhead the swallows performed Battle of Britain stunts. They would soon be leaving for Africa, but seemed as happy with life as I was. Then the hosepipe started to make a choking noise. The water turned brown, the hosepipe spat, and then the water stopped. My wife came running out.

'The water's stopped,' she cried.

'I know.'

Dr Water Gives Scientific Explanations

Banquo: It will be rain tonight.
First Murderer: Let it come down.
Macbeth, William Shakespeare

LIKE MOST PEOPLE I didn't think about water until I had none. Few people do, until suddenly it's not there, it's polluted, or there is too much of it and belongings are being washed away in a flood. As Jake Gittes, the main character in the film *Chinatown*, says: 'Before this – I turned on the faucet, it came out hot and cold, I didn't think there was a thing to it.'

The story of water is the story of Man – his invention, curiosity, ingenuity, stupidity and greed. Without his intervention, water would flow as it always has, ever since it was created. Its natural state is in the sea, where it makes up some three fifths of the surface area of the planet. On land it seems engaged in a permanent effort to get back to the oceans, either by running in rivers or sweating through animals or plants, turning into clouds, and raining down on the waves. Leonardo da Vinci described water as 'the driving force of nature'. Water cleanses, it purifies, it dilutes.

Man, however, seeks to control nature, to conserve and use fresh water. Water's history is that of civilisation. The major cities of the world were founded next to rivers, not just because of the easy access to water, but also because there would be watercourses or aquifers near those rivers. And they used the water not just for drinking, but also for transport, power and washing. Live by a clean river and you have everything you need, even fish for supper. London's existence without the Thames is unthinkable, as is Paris' without the Seine. Until the last century there were washing boats on the Seine in the heart of Paris, where the women would go with their laundry. The French even have a word, *le fontainier*, to describe a person who finds springs and brings water to supply fountains. In Egypt during the times of the pharaohs, taxes were set according to the flow of the Nile. Around June the Nile would burst its banks, covering the floodplain with fertile soil. When the waters had receded, the farmers would plant their crops. To measure the level of water, various measuring rods known as 'Nilo-meters' were designed, either in temples or in columns submerged by the river. The best known is on Elephantine Island in Aswan. This is on Egypt's southern border and also acted as an early warning system. If the water levels were low, the taxes were set accordingly. Too high, and the waters caused too much damage, so the taxes might even be waived. What everyone wanted – and what would determine the success or otherwise of a pharaonic dynasty – was what is known as a 'timely flow'.

Elsewhere, along the Indus, Mekong and Euphrates, civil-isations sprang up along the riverbanks. The people could grow crops along the river after the annual floods, and use the river to transport the goods. Because of the benefits – but also the dangers – of living close to the river, people were forced to cooperate. In *Oriental Despotism: A Comparative Study of Total Power*, Professor Karl August Wittfogel argues that what he dubs 'hydraulic societies' seized power in places such as Egypt, Mesopotamia, China, even Mexico and Peru. Wittfogel's main idea is that the cost of hydraulic construction and the maintenance of an irrigation system was so great that it required a workforce composed mainly of slave labour. This led to despotism. 'Those who control the [hydraulic] network are uniquely prepared to wield supreme power,' he writes. In other words, control of water became a monopoly that could easily be abused. If you discount the fact that not all the societies he describes were in the Orient, nor were they all despotic, it's a compelling argument. Control the water and you control society. In twelfth-century Paris, the water merchants, with the tacit approval of Louis VII, became one of the most powerful bodies in the city, with a monopoly of trade on the water, which involved policing their beat. By the time of Philip Augustus, who ruled from 1180 to 1223, they were granted control of weights and measures, and became the de facto city council, whose seal became the seal of Paris.

The modern method of water despotism is to raise water bills. To brag about their sophistication and green credentials, cities like to show how clean their rivers are. In the Dark Ages their waters were filthy, their rivers a convenient place to dump anything you didn't want to see again. Richard Cobb, the historian, described how in the seventeenth century, women who were abandoned by their lovers and disowned by their fathers were either dumped or jumped into the River Seine. More recently on 17 October, 1961, the same river ran red with the blood of Algerians. They had been protesting against the introduction of a curfew for all French Muslims from 8.30 at night to 5.30 in the morning. The French police fought with the crowd – estimates suggest there were up to 30,000 protesters – and anywhere between 70 and 300 Algerians were either killed and thrown into the river, or simply bound and thrown into the water to drown. At the time the authorities claimed that there had been only two deaths. There is now a plaque on the Saint-Michel Bridge commemorating this murky event.

Pontius Pilate was the first person in history caught washing his hands of a problem, but we all know the feeling. It's that sense of freshness you get when you rinse your hands after eating something sticky. 'I'm going to wash that man right out of my hair', as the song says. Death is washed away, while the living is celebrated, even if it's only a fish. There was much excitement around the Thames in 2006 when a bottlenose whale was found swimming upstream towards the Houses of Parliament. The whale died while being transported back to the sea, but there was widespread delight that she had managed to get that far – along with the inevitable jokes that, being female, it was no surprise that she had got lost. The mayor of Rosario in Argentina boasted in *Le Monde* that you can now swim in the Paraná River, which bisects the city, because it is no longer contaminated. In the 1950s the Rhine was the most polluted river in Europe, possibly the world, dubbed 'the sewer of Europe', home to more than half the world's chemical production. A hundred years earlier salmon fishing had been a lucrative trade, employing thousands of people, but now the river was dead. In 1987 the Rhine Action Plan was launched, with the goal of returning salmon to its waters. By the turn of the millennium salmon were found as far up as Mannheim, and the inhabitants had much to celebrate.

Rivers have always been boundaries, providing natural defences. The Roman Empire rarely managed to cross the Danube, and when it did the consequences were invariably disastrous. Augustus suffered the only major defeat of his career there and urged his successor to stay away. He didn't of course, but eventually the triangle formed by the Danube and the Rhine was abandoned to the Alemanni tribe. In Britain, when Julius Caesar reached the Thames, he found the Celts gathered on the northern side. Their resistance proved less impressive than the

Alemanni's. But if the Danube was a barrier to expansion, it was also a line of defence. When the end came for the Roman Empire, the invaders first had to cross the river.

The founders of Venice – surely the world's most watery city – comprised refugees from the Roman cities of Padua, Aquileia, Altino and Concordia fleeing successive waves of barbarian armies who had first forded the Danube to get there. The Quadi and the Marcomanni were the first invaders, followed

Lala Meredith-Vula's photographs explore the special intimacy of women and water

by the Visigoths in the fifth century and the Huns some fifty years later. The lagoon became a haven. It was only later, once they had built their great navies, that the Venetians became a major power. The first centre of Venice, named Malamocco, no longer exists. Some 800 years ago, the city, built on a sand dune, was washed away in a storm. Most people escaped to the Rialto – literally 'high ground'. The name of the city that became Venice is remembered in the port of Malamocco on the Lido. For some 600 years one of Venice's most important government bodies has been the Magistrato alle Acqua or the Magistracy of the Waters, set up to regulate the amount of water in the lagoon. Neither too much, nor too little. Originally the Grand Canal followed the route of the River Brenta, but the river was diverted to stop the canals from silting up. The latest scheme to stop high floods in the lagoon, the Mose Project, is running behind schedule and will be hugely expensive. How well it will work is a moot point, but the world is watching with interest. Landscape becomes character. The shifting sands and different currents have conspired to create a people who have adopted some of the protean qualities of the lagoon's water: attractive, slippery and not at all transparent.

Where there is no water, cities and towns die. The water source for the Byzantine city of Mistras in the Peloponnese was unable to cope with demand and in the nineteenth century the citizens moved elsewhere. The Indian capital of Fatehpur Sikri, built by Akbar the Great in the sixteenth century, was abandoned soon afterwards, not because his followers were disillusioned or diseased, but simply because there was not enough water. If a river changes course, the animals follow. In deserts, where it might rain only once every few years, flowers will bloom after an unexpected rainfall. But it is hard to move a city. Fatehpur

Sikri was capital of India for only ten years. Its beautiful red sandstone temples and buildings stand empty, the cisterns have filled up again with water but their only use now is as swimming pools for small boys during the hot Indian summers.

When man began to treat water as a commodity that you could beckon just by turning on a tap, something was lost. For different countries this transition came at different times, but generally it is linked to industrialisation. Is there, in our willingness to pay £5 for a bottle of Evian in a restaurant, a memory of how valuable water once was? Otherwise, we tend not to think about it. Newspapers love to run stories of toxic waste, of women sheltering from raging rivers and giving birth in trees, but once the mess has been cleaned up and the flood waters have receded, they find better things to write about. When there is enough water – but not too much, and not too expensive – there's no story. MAN GETS WATER OUT OF TAP AND RUNS BATH will not sell many papers. The only countries that seem to care about water are either those that have an excess – such as Canada and Sweden – or those that have precious little, such as Yemen and Egypt. Yemen and Egypt have elaborate plans and intricate mechanisms for storing their water supplies. Canada and Sweden organise conferences on 'blue gold' and send envoys around the world telling people how they should deal with their water. The Canadians in particular are vehemently opposed to privatisation. Some argue that they should be told, with respect, to mind their own business. What works for them may not be the answer to everybody else's problem.

For water is both the simplest and most complex of natural resources. James Joyce called it 'fresh cold neverchanging everchanging water'. So plentiful that it falls from the sky; so essential that without it life would not be possible. Both constant and yet transitory. Transparent yet reflective. You cannot live without it, but it can kill you quite easily. We need it for heating; in oil-and coal-fired power stations the fuel heats water that turns into steam and powers a turbine, while most nuclear power stations are located on rivers because water acts as a coolant. The Egyptians, Greeks and Chinese used water to power clocks, known as *clepsydra* – literally 'water thieves'. The mechanism was similar to an egg timer. The Greeks would use them to time the speeches in a courtroom. When the water had flowed out, the defence's speech had to close. Time had literally run out for the accused.

The phrase 'His name is writ in water' implies that fame won't last, as it might if it were written on paper, or stone. Yet water outlasts both. It is ironic then that this is the epitaph chosen by the poet John Keats for his tombstone, which you can find in the Protestant Cemetery in Rome: 'Here lies one whose name was writ in water.'

When Oscar Wilde visited Italy, he made a pilgrimage to Keats' grave, prostrated himself before it, and declared: 'This is the holiest place in Rome.' Proof, perhaps, that the fame of a poet, just like water, can be enduring, as well as ephemeral.

To understand the science of water, I thought I would have to travel to a laboratory, where people in white coats and goggles would swirl test tubes and demonstrate to me all its known properties. In fact, I discovered that there was a way of finding out all about it just by asking one man. That man is Dr Felix Franks. He has been nicknamed 'Water Franks'. I prefer to think of him as 'Dr Water'. There are a number of people known as Dr Death – including Jack Kevorkian, an Armenian American pathologist who helps people commit suicide, and Harold

Shipman, a British general practitioner and murderer. His final act was to kill himself. It's easy enough to be nicknamed Dr Death: all you need is a medical qualification and a number of dead patients. But as far as I know, Dr Franks is the only Dr Water. It is important to make sure you're not dealing with an impostor.

I found him the way we find everything these days, from books to washing powder to lovers – on the Internet. After an email exchange designed, I think, to establish my credentials and seriousness, he agreed to meet me in the British Library. When I was at London University, I wrote a thesis in the old British Library in the rotunda at the British Museum. It was a fantastic place to work, as Karl Marx discovered when he drafted *Das Kapital* there. But the sheer number of books being published meant that the city needed a new library, so the books and the librarians moved across town to a new building near King's Cross. It is not as charming as the old building, all red bricks and metal and glass, but it has a couple of nice places to eat, a bookshop, and every book you've ever wanted to read. At ten o'clock sharp, on a fresh January morning under a grey sky, I found a frail-looking man in his eighties sitting in a corner of the lobby, wearing a green anorak and grey trousers. His face was alert, the eyes bright, and the hair grey. It turned out he is not particularly frail, but had injured his Achilles heel on a walking trip in the Dolomites. With the aid of a stick, he walked with me to the café, where he spent the next three hours explaining a lifetime's work.

Water, this ubiquitous substance, turns out to be rather mysterious, scientifically speaking. For a start, we don't know where water came from, or how oxygen arrived on our planet. What we do know is that two extremely toxic elements – hydrogen and oxygen – that on their own are combustible, combine to create the seemingly benign, life-giving force we call water.

When the earth was still extremely hot the temperature was beyond the critical point for water, which is when a liquid ceases to exist and becomes a gas. For water, this is 374°C. Once the earth began to cool, H_2O would have dropped through the atmosphere and condensed on the earth – only to be boiled up again, because the temperature was still over 100°C. This process would have continued until the earth cooled sufficiently for water to remain on the surface in a liquid state. In a sense this was the beginning of the hydrological cycle, which continues to this day. All surface water on the planet is recycled – and has been since time immemorial. No water has ever left the atmosphere. You could still, theoretically, drink the same water as Jesus Christ, or stand in a rain shower and be hit by a drop that was once sweat on the brow of Cleopatra, provoked during a torrid lovemaking session with either Julius Caesar or Mark Antony. Or both.

Thanks to the heat from the sun, water evaporates, floats into the air as vapour, and then when the vapour cools, returns to earth as rain, snow, sleet or hail. The process starts all over again. According to Dr Franks' calculations, the sun's energy and gravity means this recycling happens thirty-seven times a year. Water is the ultimate sustainable resource: you cannot get rid of it, even if you wanted to. Boil a kettle, make a cup of tea, and the water will return to the atmosphere. Drink it, and some of that water will turn into sweat. This is why anyone who says that all the water is being used up is talking nonsense. What is true though is that there are more demands on it and more people using it every day. As people grow more affluent, they want daily baths and power showers; they cannot live without swimming pools; their cars must be cleaned and their dishes washed by machines; they demand gardens and lawns; and they want to eat more meat, which takes more water to produce than vegetables. Never mind your carbon footprint: what's your water wake?

As well as falling from the sky, water also gets into the atmosphere via transpiration, in which water moves up through roots in plants, up their trunks, and out through small holes in the undersides of their leaves. This is not an insignificant amount of water. According to data from the United States Geological Survey, an acre of maize releases 11,500 litres to 15,000 litres a year; an oak tree can produce 151,000 litres a year. Likewise, animals release water via sweating. The water keeps recycling.

As we sit sipping our coffee, he with a regular cup and me with an espresso, I ask Dr Franks what makes water so special.

'Its structure,' he says, producing a model of a water molecule from his briefcase. It is shaped like a triangle, with one oxygen particle and two hydrogen atoms. There are a couple of neutrons, but they count for very little, although they are not entirely unimportant. To his original model he fits another similar structure. Then he pulls them apart. In a normal chemical bond there is a sharing of electrons, which are provided by both entities. With water, electrons are provided by one of the oxygen nuclei.

'It is this structure, this loose-fitting bond full of empty space that can easily be broken; that is the basis of the whole story. Take ice for instance. When it melts, the space between the particles contracts. Freeze it, and the space expands. In any other substance, the solid form is denser than the liquid. But ice is lighter than water, so ice floats. If it didn't, fish would freeze in the winter when there's ice on the lakes, because the ice would sink to the bottom of the lake. Water shouldn't even be a liquid at ordinary temperatures, it should be a gas. The physical properties of water are crazy.'

They are certainly unusual. For example, at standard temperature and pressure water is in dynamic equilibrium between the liquid, gas and solid states. It is the only pure substance found on earth that is like this. A dynamic equilibrium is when two reversible processes occur at the same rate. If you were to fill a bucket with water and put it in a small closed room, the water from the bucket would evaporate, and the air in the room would start to fill up with water vapour. Eventually, the air would be completely saturated with water, and the level of water in the bucket would stop falling. However, water from the bucket is still evaporating. What is happening is that the molecules of water in the air will strike the surface of the water and condense back into the liquid water, while, at the same time, water evaporates from the bucket. This is dynamic equilibrium, because the rate of evaporation equals the rate of condensation.

He sits back and smiles at me as I struggle to understand and to take notes at the same time. I think of the D. H. Lawrence poem, 'The Third Thing':

> Water is H_2O, hydrogen two parts, oxygen one,
> but there is also a third thing, that makes it water
> and nobody knows what that is.

'It is the physical properties of water that make our life possible,' says Franks. I had always thought that life could not exist without oxygen. 'Not so,' he says. 'There was life on earth before there was oxygen. There are still beasts in deep-sea trenches to whom oxygen is toxic. Expose them to it and they will die. But once oxygen arrived, we were able to drag ourselves out of the sea.'

According to Franks, water takes part in just about every process in the human body. 'Our whole organism is attuned to

H_2O. For example, if you consumed heavy water, which is just H_2O with an extra neutron so that it is actually heavier, that would be lethal.'

We watched the people drinking their mid-morning coffees. I looked around to see if anybody was drinking water. It could be their last drop. If you combine different types of hydrogen with oxygen, you can produce something that looks like water, smells like water and is in chemical terms identical to water, but different in terms of radioactivity and mass. First there is deuterium, an isotope of hydrogen that contains an extra neutron, and is thus slightly heavier; and tritium, which is a radioactive isotope of hydrogen that contains two extra neutrons and thus even heavier. Normal, everyday water is 0.03125 per cent deuterium. But it is stable, totally natural and at normal levels, quite safe. Tritiated water, on the other hand, does not exist in nature. You can make it in a laboratory. It has a half-life of around ten years, after which it starts to decay, disappearing after about a hundred years, though it is possible that it has existed naturally at some time during the planet's life. It is toxic because it is radioactive. Encourage somebody to drink it and they would die relatively quickly.

Heavy water, or D_2O, is water with an artificially increased concentration of deuterium and is not radioactive, even though it is one of several substances used to make a nuclear bomb. Other substances include graphite, beryllium and ordinary water. They are used to slow down fast-moving neutrons released by nuclear fission so they have more time to react with the nuclear fuel. As you'd expect, heavy water weighs more than normal water, with a density of 1.108 g/cm³. It sinks in normal liquid water. It is easier to freeze, becoming solid at 3.81°C

(38.86°F) and boiling at 101.42°C (214.56°F) at standard atmospheric pressure. However, it is not stable. It could exist in normal conditions, but it would not hang around for long.

Heavy water is toxic because it changes the speed of chemical reactions in the body, affecting certain cellular processes, especially cell division, by the difference in binding energy in the hydrogen bonds needed to make some proteins. It is rather like the cancer treatment chemotherapy.

'I thought about writing a thriller in which the murderer administers nothing more than cups of tea to his victim,' he says. 'You see, the tea would be deadly. It would accelerate the ageing process and the person would die. But there would be no trace of any poison. The perfect crime!'

This shows just how sensitive life processes are to water. The extra neutron just adds a little weight, alters the vibration of the composition of water. But it's hard to acquire, and expensive, costing at least £150 per kilogram. And while it would take longer to kill somebody with it than tritiated water, it would be undetectable.

'A physicist would say that it's a trivial alteration,' he said. 'But it brings life to a standstill.'

As well as killing people, water could also be used to catch murderers. Forensic scientists in the United States now think water can provide the clue to where people have been living. Tap water in different parts of the country contains variations in hydrogen and oxygen isotopes; these same variations appear in people's hair. 'Police are already using this to reconstruct the possible origins of unidentified murder victims,' said James Ehleringer, a biologist at the University of Utah. It is not yet an exact science. It works like this: when water evaporates at sea, hydrogen and oxygen isotopes gather to form clouds, which are then blown towards land. As it rains, the heavier isotopes fall first. So people living near the sea, or in mountainous areas where it rains a lot, have traces of heavier isotopes in their hair. It's bad luck if you are suspected of murdering somebody in Hollywood and you've spent the last year in Laguna Beach; however, if you have been in Texas, you may have an alibi.

What else can water do? It has the ability to absorb heat. It has the ability to store energy, which is why it takes a lot to boil a kettle or heat a swimming pool. It is one of the key elements in keeping the planet cool – our very own air conditioning.

Water in its natural state does not exist in Dr Franks' neat model, with its two hydrogen elements, one of oxygen and a couple of unassuming but not unimportant neutrons. Wherever it exists, particularly in the liquid state, water mixes with whatever it touches. Thus water can and will contain particles of carbonate and bicarbonate, calcium, silica, sulphate, chloride, sodium, magnesium, manganese, potassium, phosphate, iron and nitrate. Pure water does not exist in nature. The minute a drop touches the earth, the same qualities that make it a universal solvent cause it to acquire tiny impurities from everything it comes into contact with.

Water also has refractive qualities. So when you try to spear a fish in the sea, or pick up something from the bottom of a swimming pool, you often miss. And it takes on the characteristics of its surroundings, like a chameleon. Thus it can look turquoise, green, blue, black, depending on the sky and where it is. It can even be red, if there is a lot of sand or silt in the water. The Red Sea often appears red because of red algae that live there. The Black Sea at times can look almost black because of a high concentration of hydrogen sulphide. As for Homer's 'wine-dark sea' some people see in water what they want to see. In fact, inexplicably, the Greeks had no word for 'blue'.

In a glass, water is colourless. In quantity, a lake or a river, for example, it generally appears blue. But is it? I had always assumed that it was blue because it was reflecting the colour of the sky. (Why is that blue anyway?)

The perception of colour is a tricky issue, particularly when it comes to green and blue. I remember an argument with a Swedish woman who thought our eldest daughter's cot was blue. I thought it was green. I also thought she was just being difficult until I discovered that there are people whose languages do not distinguish between blue and green. In the Welsh language, for example, grass is literally 'blue straw', and not green at all. This inability to distinguish between blue and green is most evident among peoples who either live up mountains or near the equator. In ancient Egypt the word for water was *uat*, which also denoted the colour green. The theory is that ultraviolet radiation, which is stronger in these places, causes a progressive yellowing of the eye's lens, making one less sensitive to short wavelengths such as blue and green.

Whether or not water is blue or green may depend on your location or your language – but the question remains, does water have an intrinsic colour?

Water does have an innate blueness. Even though water is generally perceived to be colourless, odourless and tasteless, it is protean. It can be acidic or alkaline. It is probably this undistinguished but ubiquitous nature of water that makes it so hard to understand. It is rather like the murderer in the G. K. Chesterton story who turns out to have committed the crime dressed as a postman. Nobody suspected the postman, nor even remembered seeing him. It is as if he were never there. The appearance of a postman, just like the presence of water, is so commonplace that nobody notices it.

It wasn't until 1993 when Charles L. Braun and Sergei N. Smirnov from the Department of Chemistry at Dartmouth College, Hanover, published a paper, *Why is Water Blue?*, that it became clear that water is both innately blue but also picks up other colours (mainly blue) from reflection. 'Water owes its intrinsic blueness to selective absorption in the red part of its visible spectrum,' write the authors. 'The absorbed photons promote transitions to high overtone and combination states of the nuclear motions of the molecule, i.e. to highly excited vibrations. To our knowledge the intrinsic blueness of water is the only example from nature in which colour originates from vibrational transitions. Other materials owe their colours to the interaction of visible light with the electrons of the substances.'

I didn't find this altogether comprehensible. So I asked Dr Water.

'Is water blue because it's blue or because it gets its blueness from somewhere else?' I said.

'Both,' he replied. 'Spectra [the range of colours in visible light when separated by a prism] can be measured from reflected light, but also from the bulk. They are caused by, and provide information about, molecular vibrations, that is within molecules and between molecules. The spectra of water are particularly complex.'

While I am struggling to understand this latest complex thought – and all from something that I thought was innately simple – Dr Franks is showing me illustrations in a German magazine devoted to water and the environment. He speaks perfect English, but how come he understands German?

'I lived there,' he said.

'So when did you come to England?'

'1939.'

Franks is one of the lucky few, a Jew who not only escaped the Nazis, but also had the good fortune that his parents joined him in London, rather than being sent to a concentration camp. He doesn't say it, but I sense his obvious love of life has been heightened by his exposure to and knowledge of the horrors that could have affected it. We talk briefly of Primo Levi, who not only wrote the superb account of Auschwitz in *Is this a Man?* but also *The Periodic Table*, one of the finest books ever written about science. He tells me Leonardo da Vinci wrote a book on water, published by the Vatican.

Franks, his face growing flushed with excitement, starts telling me other things about water. For example, that if water is absolutely clean, you can cool it down to -40°C.

'Why would you do that?' I ask.

'As a way of storage,' he says. 'But also it develops properties that are absolutely fantastic. And here is something equally strange: life needs water to flourish. But as soon as life is dead, water becomes corrosive. It rots, it rusts things. Why is that, do you think?'

'I have no idea.'

'Nor have I.'

The place is filling up. Dr Water decides that he will go home for lunch, while I plan to look around the library. Perhaps I will find that book by Leonardo da Vinci on water. We shake hands, and walk together to the exit.

'There is nothing remarkable about water,' he says. 'It's everywhere.'

He turns up his collar and walks out of the British Library, into a light London drizzle.

* * *

Mael appears one morning to give us lessons in water divining. He is from Brittany and helps out occasionally in the garden. I have asked him to trace the source of the spring. He is tall, more than six feet, with a mass of brown hair and a wispy beard, and thin as a prophet. In his hands he has four copper rods, which we will use for finding water. He shows us how to hold them: elbows in to our sides, arms horizontal to the ground. The rods sit in short pieces of bamboo, which allow them to rotate if necessary. He tells us that as we are made of seventy per cent water, we are sensitive to water elsewhere. If we tell our minds to find water and walk with the 'baguettes', we will find water. The main thing that we are finding is that it's funny that the copper rods are called 'baguettes'. Then of course you realise that the French word for stick was used for bits of wood and copper before it was applied to bread.

He explains that there are underground water channels that run like veins in your body; if water is detected, the rods will cross. He sets the children off. My eleven-year-old daughter Julia goes in one direction; Hugo, my thirteen-year-old son, goes in the other. Julia seems quite open to the idea, while Hugo clearly thinks it is a bit of a prank and is keen to get back to watching the cricket. First Hugo heads to the spring, where he knows there is water; then I find him down by the swimming pool. 'There's water here,' he cries. I was reminded of one of the *Swallows and Amazons* books, where the Walkers go looking for water. Roger, the youngest, who is also the clown of the family, runs off in a strange direction, much to the amazement of his siblings, and announces: here's some water. He twitches the divining rods over a glass of water that he had hidden in the grass.

I relieve Hugo of the rods and send him back to the cricket. Meanwhile, Julia seems to be having some success. Her rods have crossed and Mael, who is following her with his, confirms the presence of water. I walk over to the spot but nothing happens. No twitching, no movement, nothing. Once you have found the presence of water, you need to establish how deep it is. Mael has two methods for determining this. One is to stamp his foot over the water like an angry child. Each stamp is equivalent to a metre's depth. After he has stamped his feet eight times, the rods cross. Another method is to start walking away from the water and count each step. The first step stands for zero. After nine strides, the rods cross again.

The next stage in our education – even though I have proved useless as a water diviner – is to use wood as a divining rod. Mael cuts two forked pieces, shaped like a Y, from a laurel tree. In France they call it the 'Crown of Caesar'. 'The best woods to use are those that grow by water, such as willow or alder,' says Mael. He instructs Julia to hold the branch by the two forks, with palms up and thumbs out. One's arms are held into the sides, as with the divining rods. Then he and Julia start walking up and down the garden again. The branch appears to twitch in Julia's hands. The end rears up. When Mael appears, the same thing happens to him. I try it. Nothing. They then set out to determine in which direction the current is running. If you follow the current the branch remains horizontal. If you walk against it, the branch rears up. As they both walk up the hill, the branch points upwards.

Julia is visibly tired by this point. I put this down to late nights watching television, but Mael explains that water divining is a tiring business. She is sent indoors to lie down, while Mael and I move on to tracking the course of our spring. This is not going to be easy. In fact, it is most likely to be impossible, because the countryside is rough and impenetrable. It is what they call *garrigue* down here, after the short, spiky holm oak trees that grow everywhere. But there is also rosemary, thyme, laurel, and a variety of sharp, prickly bushes designed to retain their moisture in the long, hot summers as well as deterring anything from eating them. If our spring ran through a grassy field it would be easy to follow. Instead we discover that the line runs straight up the large hill that sits to the south of the property. Dodging between rocks and pine trees, fighting through the scrub, Mael advances with his copper rods. I follow slowly, wondering whether I can drive up the track and meet him at the top. At the top of the hill the water seems to continue in a southerly direction. This is almost 180 degrees away from where I thought it came from. The terrain is worse than ever. We agree to mark the place and return in long trousers and boots.

It is a tantalising prospect. Looking for a source is like a journey back in time. It inspired Victorian explorers, who were desperate to find the source of the Nile. I recall the words of Seneca in *Naturales Quaestiones*: 'When you have come to understand the true origin of rivers, you will realise that you have no further questions.'

The sky is grey, with the threat of snow. Pale smoke is pouring from a chimney. Lined up against a brick wall, in their black and white striped pyjama outfits – ironic that their clothes, although seemingly designed for a bedchamber, afforded them little sleep or rest – the men are cadaver thin, barely alive, hardly able to stand up. The lettering on the building Arbeit Macht Frei *is a terrible lie. They aren't free, they are slaves. The work is killing them. They are suffering from malnutrition, disease, loneliness and dehydration. When the few grey snowflakes fall, they offer a tantalising taste of water, but the flakes they are able to catch in their mouths taste of ashes.*

A young man in his twenties with thick blond hair and eyes the colour of the Mediterranean marches over to the line of workers, and stops in front of an old man who is gasping for breath. With each inhalation he is trying to recall the summers of his youth, in particular the stream near Poznan where he and his brothers used to bathe. They would go down to the river on warm summer evenings. The water was so clear you could drink it. It was there he met Eva, who became his wife. What had happened to her? He thought of her and their child, but mostly he thought of the water.

The tall, blond officer is carrying an object, shaped like a Thermos flask. It is silver, the colour matching the monochrome of the scene. He stands in front of the old man, and opens the flask. The old man looks up into the sea-blue eyes. He hears the sound of running water. The German is letting the fresh water pour onto the ground, splashing the old man's boots and running away across the frozen ground. The old man can hardly speak, his mouth is so dry, but he utters a single word: 'Why?'

He falls to the ground. His body is dragged away to feed the furnaces.

2

Manhattan's Massive Midtown Transfer

I go on loving you like water
'The Tennis Court Oath', John Ashbery

AS YOU WALK DOWN 9th Avenue towards 30th Street you pass ethnic shops, barbers, dry-cleaners and car parks. This is a part of Manhattan that you don't see in the movies. Woody Allen has probably never even driven through here. An evil wind is blowing off the Hudson River, whipping up dust, sending paper bags flying through the air and making you wish you had worn more clothes that morning. The few people you see are wearing hooded tops and camouflage jackets, as if they had just been out hunting deer. There is very little sign of life, apart from a few pigeons sitting on graffiti-covered walls. At the corner of 30th and 11th Avenue there is a construction site, full of cranes, sheds where you can hear the hiss of welding, and a couple of Portakabins. This is the headquarters of one of the most ambitious water projects in the world, one of the largest construction projects in America, which is taking half a century to complete, though when the digging is finished this site will disappear and all you will see is another car park.

'Pretty strange,' says Ted Dowey, executive construction manager of the project. 'Two billion dollars and all you get to see for it is a hatch.' He is a tall man in his fifties with dark hair and a goatee. He looks like a roadie for a heavy metal band. He has been working on the City Tunnel Number Three for more than twenty years, so is a relative newcomer to the project. There are people who spent all their working life on the 'Big Dig', retiring before the work has been finished.

In the 1950s the decision was taken to build an alternative water tunnel to carry water to Manhattan's eight million people. It was the time of the Cold War. The new tunnel is built more solidly than either of the city's other two tunnels, strong enough perhaps even to withstand a nuclear strike, although how that would help all the dead people in the city probably hadn't been considered. There is already City Tunnel Number One, built in 1917, and City Tunnel Number Two, finished in 1937. Both are functioning well, but officials couldn't stop the flow of water to carry out maintenance and were worried that if anything happened to either of them, the city's water supply would run dry.

The action is all taking place underground. On a map in the Portakabin office, Ted explains the basics of this $670 million extension, known as the Manhattan Spur. It has been dug more than sixty storeys down, nearly 600 feet underground. This was partly because the rock, Manhattan schist, is more solid at this depth. It is also to leave at least 200 feet between the new tunnel and the old tunnel.

The water is highly pressurised because it comes via aqueducts from lakes and reservoirs located some 300 feet above sea level on the slopes of the Catskill Mountains, and then travels deep underground. If it were allowed to, it would force itself up to the surface and spray like a fountain over the city. The engineers don't want this, so they have devised a series of shafts that bring water up to a distribution tank, like a reservoir, near the surface, from where it is pumped around

Manhattan. There are nine shafts being built to bring water up from the tunnel.

The digging of the tunnel itself has been finished. All it needs now is to be lined in concrete, allowed to dry, then filled with water. Our plan is to go down one of these shafts. First, Ted explains how the digging was done.

'We used a hard-rock main-beam boring machine,' he says. 'This contained twenty-seven steel cutters, each capable of exerting 70,000 pounds of pressure. The machine is assembled underground, is 100 feet long with a further 700 feet trailing behind. It contains fire equipment, ventilation equipment, computers and even a dining car for the workers. It can dig eighty feet a day, working twenty-four hours, five days a week, with three shifts.'

It is hard to imagine how dark, difficult and unpleasant this work must be. You might suspect that it would be left to the most unfortunate of immigrants to carry out this task. You would be wrong. New York is highly unionised and the city is paying for this work. By tradition, anything that takes place more than fifty feet below the city is the preserve of the Sandhogs, the nickname of the same union that built the Brooklyn Bridge in the 1870s; the digging was mainly through soft earth as they built the bridge's underwater caissons. The real name is the Tunnel Workers Union, Laborers Local 147, although nobody uses it. Most people don't even know it.

'I once challenged the leader of the union to tell me its full name and he couldn't,' says Ted.

These workers earn $35 to $38 an hour. In a good year, with bonuses and overtime they can make between $70,000 and $120,000. This is about the same as a reporter on the *New York Times*. Mind you, the work is considerably more dangerous, if you exclude the risk of cirrhosis that many journalists flirt with. Digging underground can be a life-threatening business. Twenty-four people have died on the Big Dig, a rate of about one death per mile. They die in many ways: rockfalls, being knocked down by the railway trucks that shift the muck, electric shocks, being hit by winches, slipping and falling down one of the shafts, or being blasted by dynamite.

So why do they do it?

'The money. That's what I go down there for,' says Dennis O'Neill, fifty-four, talking to the *Daily Construction News*. O'Neill has been a sandhog since 1970, when work began on the water tunnel. He also worked on subways and other projects. 'It's a different world down there. You start when you're young and dumb . . . and after a while you make a name for yourself, then it's ten years, next it's twenty years, next it's thirty years.'

The digging machine is guided by a laser. Traditionally, and this is how the other tunnels were dug, they used old surveying methods that relied on techniques such as suspending a fifty-gallon drum down the shafts like a plumb line.

'We were only off by nine inches after five miles,' says Ted. 'We discovered at one stage that we were two feet off track but just brought it back into line. It's not as if we are building a rail tunnel which has to be exact.'

Before we venture down the tunnel, Pete is brought in to give us a safety lecture. With his grey hair, sensible glasses and slightly red face, Pete looks every inch a construction worker, a look reinforced by his black sweatshirt reading 'Milwaukee' and blue jeans. Before he arrives Ted tells us that Pete is eighty years old, but perhaps this is a joke. He doesn't look that old – no more than seventy – but sunlight is known to be ageing and Pete has apparently spent most of his life underground, so that should knock a few years off.

When he comes through the door, he is wearing a brown safety hat. He takes it off and we notice that there is a gash in it.

'What's the most dangerous part of the tunnel?' he asks.

We all look at each other. 'No idea.'

'The shaft. The guy who was wearing this hat was hit by a falling rock. It went through the hat and partly through his head. He fractured his skull and needed fifty-two stitches. The rock broke an eye socket, his nose and his sinus cavity. It also took out four of his teeth. So. Pay attention when you are at the bottom of the shaft. Listen to the bottom bell guy. He's the guy who tells you that it's safe to walk below the shaft.'

Pete tells us that the greatest danger in the tunnel is fire. He shows a couple of canisters, rather like a camping gas cylinder. Inside each one is a gas mask. If there is a fire this will give us forty-five minutes of breathing. It looks a pretty basic piece of equipment, but he insists that we pull it out of the canister and over our heads. There is a nose tag that blocks the air to the nose.

'Only breathe through your mouth,' he says. 'And remember, if there is a fire, the shaft, your means of escape, is suddenly turned into a chimney.'

The tunnel is lit, but what do we do if the lights go out, apart from panic? According to Pete, we stay calm. Then we put our hands down into the two inches or so of water flowing beneath our feet. We find out which way the water is flowing, then walk in that direction. Tunnels are purposely built with a slight incline towards the shafts so that ground water can be collected in one place.

'You should also look out for locomotives,' he says. The

tunnels are narrow and there's no room for you to hide if one is coming. And you won't hear, you'll just be turned into a hamburger. So listen out for either a whistle or an air-horn. They don't go very fast, just eight or ten miles an hour, but it's fast enough.'

He also tells us that there is a yellow handle every hundred feet or so containing compressed air. Any problem with smoke and we can just huddle over one of those. It sounds pretty impractical. Even so, Pete's words are getting to me. I am beginning to wonder if I want to go down this tunnel. But there is no turning back. We put on waterproof jackets and walk towards the shaft. I feel like a man heading to a hanging, and what makes it worse is that it is my neck on the line.

So it is a shock to get into a rickety lift and find a young lady at the controls. Her name is Hazel, perhaps because of her lively brown eyes, or maybe her mother's favourite book was *Watership Down*. She has worked for three years on the job, manning perhaps the least glamorous elevator in New York. Why work here when she could be in Saks or Tiffany's? She says she is very happy and enjoys the job. Maybe she likes men in rubber boots and hard hats. Ted must have taken my look of surprise for one of concern.

'Don't worry,' he says. 'There are no women working in the tunnel. There are no female sandhogs.'

The lift makes its way slowly down. Ted is saying something, but I can't hear and I couldn't really care. I am focusing on survival. We get out of the lift and into a shower of water. It is like being at an unfinished Underground station, or at King's Cross after the fire. There are sparks coming from a welder, and in the gloom I can make out a group of men standing around, watching the man with the flame. We move quickly away from the shaft and stand in the rail track. Ted points.

'That way is north,' he says. 'Direct to 60th Street and no stop signs.'

We aren't the first observers down the shaft. New York's billionaire mayor, Michael Bloomberg, has been down some months earlier. Together with Emily Lloyd, commissioner of the Department of Environmental Protection, he put on the same safety gear, got in the lift and went down the 550 feet to the tunnel, operated the boring machine, made the final cut to mark the milestone, and signed their names on the tunnel wall.

'The Third Water Tunnel is the single largest infrastructure project in the city's history,' said Bloomberg. 'The building of Water Tunnels One and Two were essential in New York City's evolution into a world business and cultural centre and the third tunnel will help keep our city thriving through the twenty-first century. We can live without a lot of things; water is not one of them. It would be a very big problem if one of those two tunnels were to collapse in any one portion. It could take up to a year to dig down, repair it, and get it back in service . . . One of the great fears is, if today you turned off one of those valves, you may not be able to get it back on, or maybe the tunnel may collapse if there's no water in it.'

We walk in the opposite direction to 60th Street, following the track south. The tunnel grows smaller. There is water underfoot and fine sand. It is like walking on a beach when the tide has gone out. Except for the noise. Above our heads is a yellow tarpaulin tube, made out of the same material they use for bouncy castles. It is blowing fresh air into the tunnel and making a hell of a racket in the process. We walk past a crusher, used for turning drilled rock into a manageable size, that is then carted to the surface. The rock is hard and rough, the colour of dark copper. In the sunlight schist glistens, but here there is only artificial light. There is also an electric cable running alongside, capable of delivering 13,000 volts.

We turn a corner and stop. This is an intersection, where two tunnels are due to meet. Ted calls us closer to him, so he can talk without shouting. Even so, it's tough to hear what he is saying above the sound of the yellow bouncy castle breathing like an asthmatic.

'We have no complaints with how they built the old tunnel,' he says. 'The problem is, we have no way of shutting off the water in case we want to do maintenance. That is, until we have this new tunnel. Then we are going to get in there and redo it. Here we are building a valve chamber, so that in the future we will be able to stop the flow of water if we need to.'

The expandable valve system has been designed by Malcolm Pirnie, design engineers based in White Plains, New York. This allows future stages of the tunnel to be connected without draining them of water, or taking them out of service. It also means you can carry out maintenance on selected portions of the tunnel, removing the worry about not being able to close the valves once they are open. Three of the huge chambers have already been built, at Van Cortland Park in the Bronx, at Central Park in Manhattan and at Roosevelt Island. Van Cortland Park is the largest chamber, some 620 feet long, 42.5 feet wide and 41 feet high. It contains thirty-four stainless steel valves, which are electronically operated. Each valve chamber has a series of conduits of valves and flow meters to control, direct and measure the flow of water in sections of the tunnel.

To date they have spent more than $1 billion on stage one of the tunnel. They went to the Water Board and asked for more money. 'The Water Board said, "First show us that this one works." Luckily it does. There are over 300 million gallons a day going through, and a leakage of less than two gallons a day.'

David Hockney's version of the American Dream, in which every home has its own swimming pool and a diving board

The Water Board was right to demand to see the tunnel working. The history of water in Manhattan since the days of the Dutch has been one of intrigue, incompetence and deceit and, in the process, saw the creation of one of America's largest banks, Chase Manhattan. Back when Manhattan was known as New Amsterdam – when there were less than 1,000 people living in its southern tip and its governor was a one-legged man called Peter Stuyvesant – the water supply came mainly from waterfalls, rivers and streams on the island. A British naval officer, Captain Richard Nicholls, sailed into the harbour, and claimed the territory for the king. The stone fort did not fire even one of its twenty cannons. Some claim that the inhabitants were happy to succumb to British rule because they were tired of the twenty-year rule of the one-legged despot. Others, including Stuyvesant himself, say the reason Fort Amsterdam gave up without a struggle is that they were running low on water. He had failed to order the digging of a well in the fort and they were down to their last twenty barrels.

As the city grew under British rule, water continued to be a problem. A Swedish visitor, Peter Kalm, who visited in 1748, wrote that 'want of good water lies heavily upon the horses of the strangers that come to this place; for they do not like to drink the water from the wells of the town'. But there was one popular watering hole. It was a freshwater pond known as the Collect, with a nearby spring called the Tea Water Spring. A handle was put on this spring and the place rechristened the Tea Water Pump. Water sellers drew the water and sold it around town in casks, at a price of one cent per gallon. Called 'tea-water men' there were so many of them that the council started regulating them in 1757.

Eventually the pretty pond was overused and degraded. Clothes were washed in it, sewage was poured into it, dead livestock were thrown into it. Near the end of the eighteenth century it was described as a 'common sewer' by a newspaper and filled in and the surrounding land levelled. Demand for clean water had never been higher. Yellow fever, cholera and typhoid epidemics hit the city. Nobody knew the cause of these, but some enlightened citizens realised that better water was essential. 'The health of a city depends more on its water than all the rest of the eatables and drinkables put together,' said Dr Joseph Browne, who suggested that the city should look outside Manhattan for its water supply. The city debated for twenty years or so whether it should have private or public water supply; Dr Browne was in favour of a private provider, the city council wanted it under their control, but they didn't have enough money. Instead, they committed the most grievous blunder, still practised to this day by various city and state governments around the world: they gave a monopoly to a private company. On 30 March, 1799, state lawmakers passed an Act for supplying the City of New York with pure and wholesome water. The company chosen to perform this service was the Manhattan Company. Aided by Aaron Burr, a senator, the company added to its bill of incorporation the right to use surplus capital in any transaction consistent with state law. At that time there was only one bank in New York, set up by Alexander Hamilton in 1784. One company with its own monopoly was about to challenge another monopoly. In its first year the Manhattan Company sank a well, built a 550,000-gallon reservoir and laid six miles of wooden pipes that connected 400 houses. The original logo of the Chase Manhattan Bank supposedly represented old wooden water pipes.

The Manhattan Company was probably the first to see what many financiers have subsequently appreciated: water generates healthy cash flows. However, it also realised that selling water was a bore, and required considerable capital expenditure. It set up a discount and deposit house on Wall Street. This quickly attracted the attention of Alexander Hamilton, who owned the Bank of New York. As well as competing financially, they also fought politically. Hamilton managed to scupper Burr's chance of becoming governor in 1804. As a result Burr accused him of slander and challenged him to a duel. On 11 July, 1804, the two men, together with their seconds, met in Weehawken, New Jersey. Hamilton's son had died in a duel three years earlier. Hamilton met the same fate, killed by a ball from Burr's pistol.

The Manhattan Company continued to show only sporadic interest in supplying water, its customers complaining of poor water quality and, sometimes, no water supply at all. Meanwhile the company invested in engineering projects such as the wooden Cayuga Bridge, which spanned a mile and a half over Cayuga Lake and Montezuma Swamp in western central New York, lending $150,000. Shareholders made money, but the residents went thirsty. Not that water was ever really Manhattan's drink: Peter Kalm complained that even the horses disliked drinking the water. People drank tea, but mainly beer. Moreover, the brewers were focused on trying to keep people drinking beer rather than water.

It was an Asiatic cholera epidemic in 1832 that started to focus minds on the water supply, but also a number of fires. The Great Fire of 1835 began in the evening of 16 December. It was a cold evening, but that didn't stop the blaze. Flames were seen coming from a five-storey building near Wall Street. Soon the chill wind had spread the fire, destroying nearly 700 buildings in the process. It was so cold that when the firemen drew water from the rivers, it froze in their pipes before they could douse the flames. The Merchants Exchange, a three-storey marble building, was gutted, its sixty-foot cupola crashing to the floor, wiping out in the process a statue of Alexander Hamilton. Many people and businesses were bankrupted. Everyone agreed something must be done.

A year earlier the city had approved a plan to bring water from the Croton River by building a series of aqueducts, Manhattan having finally moved off the island to get its water. Most of the workers were Irish. Work was halted for a bit after a brawl, apparently caused by whiskey and 'religious difficulties'. They built 114 stone culverts up to twenty-five feet across, thirty-three circular stone ventilators fourteen feet high, and six waste weirs to allow excess water to escape from the aqueduct. This work was followed by the creation of the Croton Dam. By the winter of 1841 it was nearing completion. A hundred-foot stone dam had been built, together with a 250-foot earth embankment, fifty-five feet wide at its top. It had been an unusually warm winter. Rain started falling on 5 January, melting the eighteen inches of snow on the ground. The snow, combined with the rain, swelled the reservoir to bursting. The weirs were choked and could no longer cope. In the early morning of 8 January the dam's walls gave way, taking out a gap about 200 feet wide. In the deluge some fifty people were thrown into the flood, their possessions and livestock washed away. Two men sought safety in a tree, which was uprooted and carried downstream. They both drowned. Another man, known only as Mr Bailey, was seen wading through waist-high water, carrying his father and a bag of gold. Fortunately all three made it to safety.

The Croton Dam was rebuilt. Other dams and reservoirs were commissioned. It seems that once you start building water storage the work never stops. They built an Egyptian-style reservoir on Murray Hill, complete with columns and obelisks on what is now the Great Lawn in Central Park, which held twenty-four million gallons of water. Yorksville Reservoir stood forty-five feet above street level and covered four acres. On 27 June, 1842 the first water flowed from the dam through the aqueduct to the reservoir on 40th Street. The locals were delighted. On 14 October it was inaugurated with the firing of cannons, the ringing of church bells, and a five-mile procession, complete with balloons and fireworks. Only one person sounded a sour note, and he kept his thoughts to himself. In his diary, the former mayor Philip Hone wrote: 'It is astonishing . . . how cheerfully [citizens] acquiesce in the enormous expense which will burden them and their posterity with taxes to the last generation. Water! Water! is the universal note which sounded into the masses . . .'

He was right. The spending continued, while the abundant water was used recklessly. There were few water meters. The city's population was growing, as were its businesses. Street hydrants were opened and left running – children would play in the water. Usage soared to a daily consumption of sixty gallons per person. Water rates went up, but it hardly stopped the waste. From twelve million gallons a day in 1842, less than ten years later New York was using forty million gallons a day.

So more money was needed to build yet more storage. A second reservoir close to Yorksville Reservoir was designed, with more than one hundred acres purchased in what is now Central Park. Called Lake Manhatta, it took four years to finish, interrupted by financial depression and the start of the Civil War. It opened on 20 August, 1862 and was hailed by the *New York Times* as the largest man-made lake in the world. Crowds gathered to watch the water start to fill it. But it was no great spectator sport. The water took a week to cover the bottom layer and six months to fill.

Less than two years later, the city's water supply was under threat from Confederate soldiers, who plotted either to blow up the aqueduct or poison the water. They concluded that they would need too much poison to affect the water supply, so set fire to a number of hotels instead.

As New York continued to grow so did its demand for water. New reservoirs and aqueducts were built, moving further southwest into Delaware and north up into the Catskill Mountains. The city behaves like an alcoholic, always needing more, creating secret caches in case its supply is suddenly threatened. Today its water comes from eighteen reservoirs and three lakes in seven counties, a watershed of more than 2,000 square miles. And the spending may not be over, even once Tunnel Number Three is finished and the last sandhogs have come up for air. In July 2006 the *New York Times* reported that high levels of turbidity – cloudy water – might mean that the city would have to invest in water filtering plants. For years, ever since the Croton was dammed, New York has prided itself on its clean, clear water, and it is determined to keep it that way.

Much of New York City's early infrastructure has now been replaced or has fallen into disuse. Its oldest bridge, the High Bridge, which linked northern Manhattan with the southern end of the Bronx, has been closed for more than four decades. Its purpose was to bring water from the Croton River to the city. Originally built of brick and granite, and designed with a series of grand stone arches in homage to the Roman aqueducts, a large section of the arches was replaced by a single steel girder, so that ships using the Harlem River could pass under it. Having long ceased to be an aqueduct, the narrow footway along the top was finally closed in the 1960s because of vandalism. In a $60 million restoration programme carried out by the New York Restoration Project the walkway is about to be reopened. Soon you will be able to walk where water flowed.

Back underground, I asked Ted what was the worst thing that could happen to hamper work in the tunnel.

'That's easy,' he said. 'Fire in the shaft. Imagine if the elevator caught fire. So we put sprinklers throughout. However, one weekend the sprinklers went off for no reason and the tunnel was flooded. We lost two weeks' work, had to dismantle the crusher, dry it out, then put it back together.'

'How scared are you of terrorists?' I ask.

'The Department of Environmental Protection has its own police force of 180 officers patrolling 2,000 square miles of country, including the critical infrastructure and the watershed. There has been a full review by the Army Corps of Engineers that started in 1999 and has cost more than $100 million. We've tripled the police department, acquired new capabilities, there is a detective bureau, we have new boats, electronic surveillance and tighter control. But yes, it's a threat.'

'And would that threat be poisoning?'

'The eight million people of New York use some billion gallons of water a day. You'd need a lot of contaminant. We sample the water at one hundred strategic points and we have automated water monitoring. The bigger threat would be if anything happened to one of the other two tunnels before this one is complete. If one of those tunnels goes, this city will be completely shut down. A terrorist bomb in the right place could do that. There would be a fire risk and nothing to drink. It would be much worse than September 11. There would be no water getting into New York City.'

Water experts say that even though the old tunnels are holding up well, if anything were to go wrong, it would go all at once, like a building collapsing. City Tunnel Number One, the oldest tunnel, which carries water to lower Manhattan, downtown Brooklyn and parts of the Bronx, is thought to be the most vulnerable. But if one of the aqueducts went, that would cut off the entire city's supply. It wouldn't take a day or two to reconnect the water; it could take years.

When the flood came there was no warning. It had been a dark and wet autumn. Eventually the rains turned into snow. There was ice and for a while they skated on the lake. The children liked to skate. They felt free, away from the restraining hand of a governess or a bossy parent. When they fell it hurt, but as the weeks went on they learnt new techniques. One of the girls skated in arabesques and was beginning to learn how to jump and land without falling. But one afternoon after school the big farm lad skated too far from the shore and the ice began to crack under his weight. That was the end of the skating. The following day it rained. And all through the next evening. There was a stillness in the air and an unusual warmth. When the dam burst it did so silently, as if it didn't want to alarm anyone or draw attention to itself. Houses downstream suddenly filled up with black water. Trees and cattle and people began to move in slow motion. It was difficult to protest. The only sound that was heard that night was when the female skater, famous for her arabesques and stately jumps, was hit on the side of her head by her skates. She followed her screams downriver.

3

What Did The Romans Do For You?

> He sat down, then got up to drink some water which he
> found on a side table. 'Only water is really good,' he
> thought like a true Sicilian; and did not dry the drops left
> on his lips.
>
> *The Leopard*, Giuseppe Tomasi di Lampedusa

IMAGINE THAT WE ARE all wiped out tomorrow by a disaster
such as a nuclear war, a colliding asteroid or from eating too
many hamburgers. Vegetation would begin to cover the cities.
Soon Tower Bridge in London would be a convenient way for
monkeys to cross the River Thames, swinging hand over hand
from lianas; the Eiffel Tower would be a trestle of vines,
swarming with bees and butterflies; while the Empire State
Building would be no more than a canopy covered in cran-
berries. As the years roll by, most of man's great monuments
would disappear. Milton Keynes would waste away, the
Périphérique of Paris would crumble, and the wooden temples
of Kyoto would be chewed by ants and collapse at the first
earthquake tremor.

Some time later, a visiting spaceman, pausing on his Grand
Tour of the solar system, would hover over the remains of
some of these buildings, and maybe mutter the lines he could
remember from his schooldays of Percy Bysshe Shelley's
'Ozymandias':

And on the pedestal these words appear:
'My name is Ozymandias, king of kings:
Look on my works, ye Mighty, and despair!'
Nothing beside remains. Round the decay
Of that colossal wreck, boundless and bare
The lone and level sands stretch far away.

On his tour around the world the spaceman would note amid the debris a large number of constructions with no discernible purpose. If he narrowed his green eyes and looked closer, he would see that they all had one thing in common: they were used either to carry or to store water. He would scratch his green head and conclude that something curious had been going on. What was this precious substance that earth's inhabitants had made such an effort to move? Why was it so popular? Did it sparkle like diamonds? Did it make tomato plants grow or was it used to tell the time? Was it used for fighting, religion or lovemaking?

The answer is yes to all of those. But the most enthusiastic builders of aqueducts and dams used the water for a different purpose altogether: self-aggrandisement. Along with their rule of the Mediterranean, nothing made the Romans prouder than to consider their aquatic achievements. They weren't the first to devote time and effort to such matters. As with all things at that time, innovation came from the East. There were early aqueducts in Urartu (modern Armenia) and Assyria. Assyrian King Sennacherib built a canal to link the Atrush and Kohsr rivers around seven hundred years before the birth of Christ. In Judea, Hezekiah brought water from the spring of Siloah to the city of Jerusalem by means of an underground conduit more than 500 metres long. The Greeks adapted from China the inverted siphon, which is a means of getting water to run uphill (think of how water in a straw is a higher level than the water in the glass). They built aqueducts in Ephesus, Methymna, Philadelphia, Antioch on the Meander, Antioch in Pisidia, Laodicea and in Pergamon. Most of their famous battles took place near legendary springs, partly, one supposes, because before it can fight, an army needs to drink.

The most impressive of all is the Madradag aqueduct at Pergamon. A series of lead pipes took water up and down the city, with a hydraulic gradient of 1.3 per cent, four times steeper than the best-known Roman siphon at Beaunant on the Gier aqueduct in Lyon. I visited Pergamon as an undergraduate, but was so taken by the remains of the theatre, cut out of a steep hill like a piece of sculpture, and the watermelon sellers in the nearby town, that I failed to investigate the water system.

A Roman would have been appalled by my indifference. Waterworks were the very pinnacle of public works. As Frontinus, along with Pliny the main Latin writer who dealt extensively with the topic, said in *De Aquaeductu Urbis Romae*: 'Just compare the vast monuments of this vital aqueduct network to those useless pyramids, or the good-for-nothing tourist attractions of the Greeks.'

As well as noting the dismissive sideswipe at the Greeks, perceived even 2,000 years ago as no better than gigolos or tour guides living on their looks and past glory, it is worth remarking how essential water was to Roman life. It is hard nowadays to imagine a city celebrating the construction of a new water treatment plant. Brussels, political centre of Europe, until the last years of the twentieth century did not even have a waste-water treatment plant, but nobody rejoiced when it finally built one. Even dams, which once excited the crowds, have been much disparaged by the Green lobby, and seem to have lost both their lustre and ability to awe.

But for a Roman city, having an aqueduct was the best thing imaginable, comparable to an American city having its own giant sports stadium with a sliding roof, or a modern French city its own ice skating rink and tram network – or even a city winning the right to host the Olympic Games. Just as with the modern Olympic Games, some cities even went bust in the process of building their aqueduct. Pliny writes of Nicomedia running into serious aqueduct financing problems, an early warning to cities such as Montreal which is destined to keep paying for its Olympic glory for many years to come, or even London, busy calculating the sums for its Olympic victory to host the 2012 Games and realising that they don't add up. At least they might get the logo finished before the flame is lit.

In all cases it was the city that came first, not the aqueduct. Rome, for example, which by AD 400 was home to some nineteen aqueducts, managed to survive for more than 400 years without a single arched stone structure carrying a drop of water. And even though most of the great cities – Rome, London, Paris, Istanbul, New York – all grew up on riverbanks, most did not take their water supply from the river. This is because water is heavy and difficult to transport without the aid of mechanical pumps. (Later, once steam power had been invented, London drew its water from the Thames.) River water could be used in times of shortage, but it was mainly useful as a means of transportation – for both cargo and human waste – and occasionally for Rome, as a means of defence.

Before Rome grew too large, the Tiber acted as a moat. At a pinch you could defend or destroy the bridges and the water would act as a barrier. The first bridge across the Tiber was called the Pons Sublicus, the 'wooden bridge', which was built around 625 BC. One morning in 509 BC the Romans woke up to find Etruscan forces on the other side of the river. A young soldier named Horatius Cocles – literally Horatius the one-eyed – persuaded two noblemen to stay with him to repel invaders, while people behind them worked to destroy the bridge. Horatius and his two companions resisted the Etruscan charge, then he sent the two men back across the bridge, moments before it collapsed. He fell wounded into the river, but returned to his side. The story first appeared in Livy's *History of Rome*, though there was already an air of myth about it then. The tale was used many years later to encourage the defence of the North Bridge in Concord, Massachusetts, against British forces during the American War of Independence. When the Pons Sublicus was rebuilt, it was done using just wood and wedges, and without nails, rather like a wooden Russian church. The idea being that a bridge without nails could be dismantled more quickly in times of trouble.

Drinking water, even for cities, generally came either from springs or from wells. Near rivers there are always underground watercourses and these can be easily tapped. So why did cities go to the trouble and expense of building massive stone constructions, many of which are still visible and likely to remain so until a Martian visits?

Because they could. But also for the baths, which needed more water than the usual sources could supply. Public baths developed into the favourite social activity of the Roman Empire. Just as the British have pubs and the French have markets and demonstrations, the Romans had baths. They were a democratic institution. Every Roman citizen had the right to a free bath. Even the soldiers, posted to the bleakest outpost of the Empire on Hadrian's Wall, forced to watch for Scots coming out of the mist, were able to enjoy baths because the forts were positioned wherever there was a suitable water supply. It was a place to mingle, to gossip, even to impress your neighbours. The loucher the emperor, the more extravagant the baths. A resident of Antioch, once the most important city in the East, had the pick of no fewer than eighteen establishments for his daily ablutions.

In decadent Rome, bathing was an essential part of Trimalchio's banquet, as Petronius describes in his *Satyricon*. Culture, gossip and sex combined in one democratic institution. No matter how rich or well born you are, this counts for little when you are sitting around naked in a steam bath. The character Eumolpus outlines some of the activities: 'You know, I was almost beaten up even while I was taking my bath, just because I tried to recite a poem to the people sitting around my tub. After I'd been thrown out of the bath, I began going round every nook and cranny and calling out "Encolpius" in a loud voice. And somewhere else a naked young man, who had lost his clothes, was demanding someone called Giton with equally indignant shouts. And while the boys just ridiculed me for a lunatic with the most impudent imitations, a huge crowd surrounded him with applause and the most awestruck admiration. You see, he had such enormous sexual organs that you would think that the man was just an attachment to his penis. What

The tomb diver in Paestum is a rare example of Greek painting. Is he diving into the Underworld or just a cool pond?

a man for the job!' The man with the impressive organs gets taken home by a Roman knight, and Eumolpus, apparently less well endowed, has to fight to get his clothes back from the attendants.

Bathing was an essential part of everyday life. And as the public baths grew more popular, they consumed greater and greater quantities of water. 'The normal reason an aqueduct was built was to supply the baths,' writes Trevor Hodge in *Roman Aqueducts and Water Supply*. Hodge's is the definitive work on the subject. 'Of course the water was also used for other purposes, ranging from domestic supplies to garden irrigation, aquatic shows, flour mills, decorative fountains and what Frontinus calls with a shudder "uses too foul to mention" (presumably public toilets); but the voracious appetite of the Roman baths for constant and vast supplies of water made them a prime consumer.'

One of the aqueduct's key features was its wastefulness. It is likely that as much as half the water that started down any aqueduct failed to reach the city. And even once the water got there, it continued to flow without stopping. There might be water storage tanks before the water was dispersed throughout the city, but these were mainly to build up pressure so that the fountains soared high into the air. Once the aqueduct had been built and the pipes connected to the source, the water flow did not stop. Nowadays one always thinks of Mediterranean people being thoughtful and careful with their water. Sometimes excess is best.

As Trevor Hodge says: 'The particular feature of the aqueduct water that should be celebrated above all others was its profusion; hence the emphasis on cascades and fountain jets. Water not carried in jars, not hauled up, pot by pot, out of wells, but endlessly tumbling, night and day, out of a great spout in the city centre – that was the true magic of the aqueduct.'

And imagine Rome, in AD 400, with nineteen aqueducts

carrying fresh spring water to 926 public baths and 1,212 fountains. The scale, even the sound of the water and its presence in the air must have been terrific. Even Pliny was impressed. 'It must be admitted that this is the greatest wonder the world has ever seen,' he said. By 410, however, the Visigoths had looted the city, an experience repeated in 455 by the Ostrogoths. By the end of the century most of the population had fled to Constantinople or the new capital at Ravenna. The aqueducts were empty, the fountains silent. Maybe the Romans were being punished for their profligacy? As Henry David Thoreau wrote in *Walden*, published in 1854: 'Water is the earth's eye, looking into which the beholder measures the depth of his own nature.' The moral decay and political corruption of the late Roman Empire can be measured by the flow of water per minute. The bigger the flow, the greater the waste.

How much water actually flowed through Rome's aqueducts? Hodge estimates a flow of between 3.5 and 5.5 kilometres per hour. Some of the aqueducts were more than thirty kilometres long, so it could take up to ten hours for the water to reach the city. Then the water kept flowing, into the baths, spilling over into the fountains, through the vegetable gardens, and back into the rivers and down into the sea.

They may at times have wasted it, but the Romans certainly knew how to use it. At Bulla Regia, a Roman city in Tunisia, they even came up with what is probably the closest thing to our idea of air conditioning. The buildings were buried in the ground because of the heat, with water piped through the roof to cool the air.

One thing the Romans appreciated about water was how essential it is to keep it moving. The Roman Screw was not a sexual technique practised after a long banquet but a ribbed piping, rather like the barrel of a rifle, which made the water inside rotate. This oxygenated the water and kept it fresh. For all their engineering ingenuity, the Romans may have started an unwelcome trend that persists in many places to this day: the idea that water is something to be given away for free. In the Roman Empire you did not pay for water. There was a charge if you wanted it brought to your door, but this was based on the diameter of the pipe, not the consumption.

Hodge's magisterial study of aqueducts is comprehensive and well written, but there is one Roman aqueduct that escapes his eye. We are all familiar with the Pont du Gard, the aqueduct that was built to bring water to Nîmes from a spring near Uzès. Even by Roman standards the aqueduct was a feat of engineering, made entirely of cut stone without mortar, three storeys high with large arches. When the Roman Empire fell, the aqueduct was abandoned. The locals eventually started using the stone for their own projects. It was rebuilt on the orders of Napoleon III in the nineteenth century, and is now the second most visited tourist site in France. Drive an hour and a half to the west and you reach Béziers, which was established by the Romans. The Languedoc was their first colony outside Italy, with Narbonne as its capital. Between AD 50 and AD 80 they built an aqueduct from the source at Gabian, some thirty kilometres from its destination in Béziers. Very little is known about the aqueduct, few traces of it remain, and to the best of my knowledge, no more than five people a year pay any interest in it. But I happen to know the world authority on it. He agreed to take me to its source. We drove up to a plateau above Gabian, a small village of around 700 people, with a post office, an infants' school, a bakery, a general store, a tabac, a chemist, a bar and not much more. It is the nearest village to our house.

Jean-Pierre, our guide, directed us up a road by the cemetery, one that I had never taken before. There was nothing there but wind and vineyards, and a small hut surrounded by a wire fence sitting in a grey field. The field was grey because of the centuries of limescale that had come from the spring, explained Jean-Pierre. He is a man of Gabian, more than seventy years old, who has only left France once, to fight in the war in Algeria. He has never been to Paris.

The journalist Frank Johnson came with me. With his mop of grey hair and wearing a lightweight suit, he cut a raffish figure. Frank had been one of London's finest journalists, a former editor of the *Spectator*. He still wrote a weekly column in the *Daily Telegraph*. This was fated to be his last summer in the Languedoc: already ill with cancer for more than five years, he would die in December 2006. A man with an obsessive interest in French history, he could recite the names of all the prime ministers of the Third Republic, indeed any republic. An admirer of both General de Gaulle and Marshal Pétain, he showed little interest in Jean-Pierre's diggings. Practical history was not his thing at all. He was dismissive of the work of historians such as Fernand Braudel and his Annales School of History, who looked at history not just through events on the battlefield, but also in the kitchen and bathroom. Frank's view was that everyday life was mundane; what counted was what happened at court and who was in power.

'There are traces of habitation here dating back more than 7,000 years,' said Jean-Pierre. He showed us a large hole he had dug near the spring, going down layer by layer as if in a time machine. Jean-Pierre had found a ring here dating from around 200 BC, depicting Menelaus and Machaon. I saw Frank stifle a yawn.

'There would have been a temple built here to commemorate the source,' said Jean-Pierre. The temple has gone; now the entrance to the spring is guarded by a small hut. The Romans built steps down into the spring. Jean-Pierre showed us pictures of the steps, but we couldn't go down them: the entrance is now locked on the orders of the mayor. Ever since 9/11 the French state is taking no chances. It's hard to imagine that the water supply for a small French village near the foothills of the Espinouse Mountains is high on Osama Bin Laden's hit list, but it's better to be safe than sorry.

There are few traces left of the aqueduct now, but Jean-Pierre drove us to a hill outside Magalas, another small village about five miles away. Just before reaching it we went up a narrow track and parked. Pushing through clumps of cannisses – a wild bamboo-like shrub native to the Midi – we saw the remains of a metre-tall pipe made of Roman concrete, through which the water would once have flowed. There would have been men working all along the aqueduct's route, charged with keeping limescale deposits from forming inside the tubing, but also ensuring that nobody was tapping into the water supply. Water has always been a valuable commodity in the south of France.

Eventually the aqueduct fell into disrepair and was abandoned, probably towards the end of the Roman Empire some time around AD 400. Stones were taken; the pipes clogged up. But still the spring kept flowing. The limestone plateau north of Gabian soaks up the winter rains like a giant sponge and releases the water through a number of springs. In W. H. Auden's poem 'In Praise of Limestone', he describes a Mediterranean landscape, its butterflies and lizards, where the main rock is limestone:

From weathered outcrop
To hill-top temple, from appearing waters to
Conspicuous fountains, from a wild to a formal vineyard . . .

He could be describing this landscape that we are looking at now. It is a long and ambiguous poem; some critics read it as an allegory of Mediterranean civilisation, of religion, or even of the human body. Auden said in a recording that he had 'always had a thing about limestone; this poem is about Florence'. Limestone was used in the building of the pyramids in Egypt; it was also used extensively in Manhattan. One of Auden's brothers was a geologist, so an interest in rocks clearly ran in the family.

The poem starts by insisting that limestone is particularly attractive because of its relationship with water. There are other rocks, clays and gravels, which are fine to those who wish to move the world. But limestone, for the narrator, belongs to an older, more ambiguous time. The focus shifts. The poet now addresses one person, referred to only as 'dear'. He accepts that this landscape is not as sweet as it looks, but it was the place where everything started, 'Where something was settled once and for all'. He is not specific as to what that something might be; maybe Christianity?

The poem ends:

Dear, I know nothing of
Either, but when I try to imagine a faultless love
Or the life to come, what I hear is the murmur
Of underground streams, what I see is a limestone landscape.

In the 'murmur of underground streams' there is an echo of T. S. Eliot's phrase 'murmur of maternal lamentation' near the end of *The Waste Land*. Women and water, not for the first time, are closely linked as the source of life.

It wasn't until the twelfth century that anybody thought again about capturing the underground streams near Gabian. The bishops of Béziers took over control of the spring, created a reservoir and used the water to mill corn. By the end of the nineteenth century this had developed into a complex of five separate watermills, built descending the hill in a horseshoe shape, all sharing the same water. It was then delivered to the people of Gabian, with any excess used for watering gardens. Access to this water became the focus of a prolonged court case that started in 1895. The mayor said that the village should have first call on the water; the mill owner wanted to maintain the status quo.

After a number of years of disputes and legal opinions, the case was decided in favour of the people of Gabian. So the mills are now empty, abandoned and in the process of falling down. According to Jean-Pierre, there are still large parts of the mill nearest the spring still standing, its stone exterior resisting the wind and rain that given enough time will reduce it to little more than a pile of rubble. 'Come,' he said. 'I'll show it to you.'

Jean-Pierre took us first to see the reservoir built by the bishops of Béziers. It is an unusual expanse of water, about twenty metres long by five metres wide, in a landscape that, in the summer at least, is devoid of water. Most of the rivers run dry. The only plants that grow here are those that are able to withstand the drought and the fierce north wind that dries washing in minutes: holm oak trees, olives, rosemary, thyme, lavender and oleander.

Then he took us to see the workings of the mill. You can see where the water would run, and observe how over the years it has marked the stone it flowed over: billions of gallons left their trace. To get the wheel moving at the right speed, neither too fast nor too slow, required a flow of 451 litres per second, according to Jean-Pierre. Each mill possessed a well about fifteen metres deep. When the first well was full – filled by the water from the reservoir – the miller released a valve that directed a jet of water onto the millstone, generating the power to grind the corn. When the water from the first mill had been used, it was sent down an underground pipe to the next mill, and the same action was repeated. This went on until all five mills had used their fifteen metres of water, and then the water was directed to the village of Gabian, when it was briefly filtered then used for washing, gardening and even drinking, and then the well was filled again, and the process was repeated. But most of that knowledge is now lost.

I wondered how many other water-powered mills, gardens and fountains were now redundant, either because the water had dried up or the knowledge had died. I was reminded of the description of the waterworks at Boot Magna Hall at the beginning of Evelyn Waugh's *Scoop*:

> The lake was moved by strange tides. Sometimes, as at the present moment, it sank to a single, opaque pool in a wilderness of mud and rushes; sometimes it rose and inundated five acres of pasture. There had once been an old man in one of the lodges who understood the workings of the water system; there were sluice gates hidden among the reeds, and manholes, dotted about in places known only to him, furnished with taps and cocks; that man had been able to control an ornamental cascade and draw a lofty jet of water from the mouth of the dolphin on the south terrace. But he had been in his grave fifteen years and the secret had died with him.

While I was clambering over the mills, I heard Frank on his mobile phone, busy trying to find a table for lunch. Jean-Pierre was explaining that the spring's water is still a matter of dispute more than a hundred years on. The new mayor, a man from Magalas, is trying to force through the building of a housing estate. The locals are worried that there won't be enough water to go around. It is the kind of case that is very hard to settle: the developers will call in paid experts to make all sorts of claims; the locals will question these claims, but ultimately the housing estate will get built, because there is money to be had for just about everyone concerned. I don't know if it has happened in this instance, but I know mayors in the region who have been offered new houses in Spain or Morocco as gifts in return for granting planning permission in France.

Frank and I drove to the neighbouring town of Pézenas for lunch. We sat in the shade of a plane tree and listened to a fountain and ordered a carafe of water, but drank mainly wine.

On his next visit to our house Mael brings a pendulum, not divining rods. He reminds me of Professor Calculus, the dotty scientist from the Tintin books. The professor would run around with a pendulum trying to prove all sorts of things, most of which turned out to be false.

Mael's pendulum is called an Egyptian pendulum, for it is the same shape as those found in Egyptian archaeological sites. Those were made of clay; Mael's is made of wood. It is about five centimetres long, the size of a fountain-pen lid, but curved at the end like a torpedo. There is a string tied through the loop at the top. I am allowed to hold the pendulum, but not to use it. 'A pendulum is very personal,' says Mael. 'You cannot lend them. The weight and balance are very important.'

He plans to measure the energy levels – measured in thousands of Bovis – of various glasses of water. The Bovis Scale, which was developed by a French physicist – or all-round crank, depending on your point of view – named Antoine Bovis, measures both what he called 'natural earth energy' and whether a substance has a positive or negative charge. Bovis formulated this theory while carrying out research on the pyramids in Egypt during the 1930s. For living organisms, 6,500 Bovis Energy Units is neutral. From 0 to 6,500, the charge is in the negative range, while above the 6,500 point the energy gradually becomes more positive, or life-enhancing. The desired minimum energy level for humans is between 8,000 and 10,000 Bovis Energy Units, or slightly positive. The earth itself creates energies between 7,000 and 18,000 Bovis. Different energy levels are caused by under-ground streams, magnetic sources, even geological faults. But for all I know, it's a lot of mumbo-jumbo.

Mael has brought a bottle of his own tap water. I have a glass of water from our tap, which comes from the source. I also fill up a glass of water directly from the source. Mael holds the pendulum over the source water. 'I shall ask for the vibration of the water,' he says. The pendulum starts to move. In his other hand he holds a piece of cardboard on which he has marked out what looks like a protractor. Professor Calculus indeed. The pendulum swings until it moves rhythmically alongside the 10,500 Bovis. Then we try the water from our tap. This comes out at 8,500 Bovis. The decline in energy, Mael explains, is because our water is lightly filtered by a salt system to remove some of the limescale, and also that it sits in a holding tank before being pumped into the house.

Then Mael holds the pendulum next to the tap water from his village. No more than 6,000 Bovis. 'There is less energy in the water,' announces Mael. Hugo has joined me for this experiment. He looks on with a cynical air but comes to life when Mael tells us that he can measure our energy levels. Somewhere between

8,000 and 10,000 is good. Hugo first. He measures out at 7,000 Bovis. Then me. I am tired that morning, a combination of early morning bike rides in preparation for a journey from Montpellier to Notting Hill Gate that I will do in a month's time, and late nights. No more than 6,000 Bovis.

'You've got as much energy as that glass of water,' says Hugo. He goes off for a swim, but Mael and I continue our experiments. He explains that you can recharge the energy levels in a glass of water with the pendulum. He takes the glass from his village, holds the pendulum over it, and it begins to rotate. 'It will stop when the water is charged,' he says. Sure enough, the pendulum stops. Then he measures the energy level of the glass again. Up to 10,000 Bovis. I ask him if he can recharge my energy levels in the same manner, but he thinks not.

The next step is bordering on witchcraft. Mael has explained to me that he likes water divining because it combines the practical with the magical. He was happy to pass on the knowledge to Julia, seeing it almost as a spiritual duty, as a religious elder might pass on the practice of the Eucharist to a supplicant. He refused any money for his time. 'Because water is free, one should not charge for passing on the knowledge of how to find it,' he said.

But what we are going to do next is not rational. Mael claims that every cell has a memory. Moreover, water can respond to questions. This is what happens when you look for water with a divining rod. Now he is making an even greater claim: that water understands. 'Water reacts to sound,' he says. 'Certain words modify the shape of the cells. Which shows how important words are to people. Again, because we are made up of seventy per cent water, when we are insulted, or made love to, not only do we hear it but our bodies react to it.'

To test this barely credible hypothesis, Mael takes the glass full of water from our tap and says '*guerre*' or war into it. The pendulum registers a Bovis level of just 2,500, down from its earlier level of 8,500. Then he says '*paix*' or peace into it. The energy level returns to normal. Then he says '*amour*' or love. Like a lover that has been stroked, the glass of water fairly buzzes with energy, up to 13,000 Bovis.

'It's the power of love,' says Mael.

How, I ask, does he explain that water can understand? And how do we know that water speaks French, not English? He looks at me patiently, like a person trying to explain how it is one can ride a bike.

'Man invented language,' he says. 'But where did that language come from? Think of the first lines of Saint John's Gospel: "In the beginning was the word, and the word was God."' I thought of the words of Helen Keller, the American writer who went deaf and blind at the age of nineteen months. She had a moment of epiphany as water from a pump was being poured over her hands in the garden. 'The mystery of language was revealed to me. I knew then that "w-a-t-e-r" meant the wonderful cool something that was flowing over my hand. That living word awakened my soul, gave it light, joy, set it free,' she writes in *The Story of My Life*.

Mael tells me that tests have been done on bottles of water. The molecules are sensitive to what is written on the bottle. For example, if 'peace' is written on the label, the energy level will be positive; if 'pain' or 'hate' is written on the label, the energy level will be negative. This hypothesis is similar to the theory behind homeopathy, which works on the principle that water has a 'cell memory'. Homeopathic doctors believe that you can dilute a substance to an almost infinitesimal degree. In 1988, Professor

Jacques Benveniste claimed that water could 'remember' an anti-body long after it had been washed out, a claim that not surprisingly has been dismissed as pseudoscience or just plain nonsense. More recently in an issue of *Homeopathy*, other scientists claimed to have found evidence that water has a memory. The act of dilution, they said, imparts something to the water. What this is remains unclear, and certainly not proven nor, to my way of thinking, particularly believable. The *Lancet*, a medical journal, said in 2005 that homeopathy's only benefits are due to the placebo effect, but this has had no effect whatsoever on stopping people from believing in its benefits.

The American magician, James Randi, has put up a $1 million prize for anyone who can show the existence of the paranormal. This would include showing that water has a memory, or that you can detect homeopathic dilution. The prize is significant enough to encourage research but to date, nobody has come forward to claim the prize.

It was the 1950s, his first trip to London. Oil wealth had made the visit possible. He was lucky enough to be the son of a sheikh. The Americans were investing millions into the region, and his father was the man they had to bribe to get what they wanted. 'You must go abroad,' said his father. 'Learn the ways of the West.' Though he liked riding his camels in the desert and hunting with his falcons, he did as his father told him. He took an aeroplane for the first time. He didn't believe that it would be able to take off; it was nothing like as streamlined as his favourite bird. Everybody was very nice to him on the flight. The air stewardess praised his costume and offered him some wine to drink with dinner. He only ever drank water, so he politely refused. The travel agent had booked him into Claridge's. 'Only the best for the son of the sheikh,' he had said. That first night he did not go down to dinner, but sat in the bathtub, running the water endlessly, marvelling that a country could be so rich that the water never stopped running out of the taps.

4

Waters both Lovely and Deadly

'Mr Bond.' Goldfinger's eyes had a faraway, withdrawn look. 'I will tell you the truth because you will have no opportunity of passing it on. From now on, Oddjob will not be more than a yard from your side and his orders will be strict and exact. So I can tell you that the entire population of Fort Knox will be dead or incapacitated by midnight on D-1. The substance that will be inserted into the water supply, outside the filter plant, will be a highly concentrated form of GB.'

'You're mad! You don't really mean you're going to kill 60,000 people!'

'Why not? American motorists do it every two years.'

Goldfinger, Ian Fleming

WATER IS GENERALLY PERCEIVED as benign, beneficial and life-giving. It sparkles. Seeing an expanse of water raises the spirits, however long and tiring the journey. Nowadays people will travel miles just to sit by it, sunbathe, and even swim in it. A house on a lake or by the seashore is always more expensive than one inland, just as the hotel room with a view over the water commands a higher rate than the one overlooking the car park. Nearly 2,500 years ago the Greek general Xenophon wrote a book called *The Anabasis*. *Anabasis* means a journey into the interior, and in the book he recounts the tale of an expedition into Persian territory. His prose style is straightforward, the Greek clear and unadorned. Although the Greeks won the battle of Cunaxa in Babylon in 401 BC, their leader Clearchus was killed. The Greek soldiers, known as the Ten Thousand, were stranded in unfamiliar territory and had to find their way home. After many adventures and a long march from Babylon to the Black Sea, they finally caught sight of the water, and let out what has become a famous cry: '*Thalatta, thalatta,*' or 'Water, water.' They didn't just react in this way because they thought the sea could take them home to their families in Greece. They were gladdened to see water after marching around a dry and dusty Asia Minor.

The sound of water is pleasing. On the beach, the rhythm of the waves can be like the sound of somebody you love breathing while asleep, or it can be fierce and savage, landing on the pebbles like an angry army, or pouring over a waterfall. Either way, its energy is invigorating. A river makes a happy gurgling, like a favourite child's laugh; and a fountain, tinkling in the afternoon heat, makes the air seem fresher just from the sound. Luis Barragan, the Mexican architect, said: 'Architecture, besides being spatial, is also musical. The music is played with water. The importance of walls is that they isolate one from the street's exterior space. The street is aggressive, even hostile; walls create silence. From that silence you can play with water as music. Afterwards, that music surrounds us.'

In Botswana, they take it even further. The national currency is called *pula*, the same word for rain, so valuable is it and so welcome when it falls your way. Listening to the sound of rain in a dry country is like hearing money pour into your bank account. And calling your currency the same word that you use for water is in turn reminiscent of F. Scott Fitzgerald's book *The Great Gatsby*. The eponymous hero is a young man who has made millions thanks to his gangster connections, dealing in bootleg liquor and gambling, with the sole motive of making money. But

Gatsby also has a soul. He is in love with Daisy Buchanan, whom he loved years earlier before they lost touch. She has since married somebody else, but he has rented a house opposite hers in Long Island Sound in the hope that she might drop by one evening. When they finally re-encounter each other, it is a momentous event. The only way he can think to describe her voice is to say that it sounds like 'money'. It is the most valuable and attractive thing he can think of; I suppose there could also be a certain metallic quality to it, a harshness like coins. If Gatsby had been Botswanan, or had grown up in a place where water was scarce, he would have said that her voice reminded him of 'water'.

When I was a child, we lived in Crowborough, a town on the edge of Ashdown Forest in Sussex in the south of England. There was never any shortage of water. My brother and I had two rooms in the attic. As the house stood on the top of a hill, it was my father's proud boast that we slept in the highest rooms in Sussex. For much of the year the house was wreathed in fog. When I read the Sherlock Holmes stories – Conan Doyle, incidentally, ended up living and dying in Crowborough and was reputed to be buried in a Turkish rug in his garden – the foggy haunts of Holmes and Watson were immediately familiar. Crowborough was a gloomy and dank place. My father was reluctant to spend money on heating the large house, so the best way to get warm after a walk or a bike ride or a rugby match was to run one of the large Victorian baths with piping hot water and dare oneself to get in adding hardly any cold. The bathroom would be as foggy as the world outside. The mirrors would be sweating with perspiration and cloudy. It was like having a bath in a steam engine. When the water had gone cold, I would get out, wrap myself in towels and brush my teeth, leaving the tap running at full blast.

The narrator of Geoffrey Household's *Rogue Male* spends

Soviet babies enjoying a hot bath with their friends just after the fall of Berlin

most of his time in a ditch or a den of his own design. On the one occasion that he takes a hot bath, he revels in it: 'Their water, thank God, was hot! I had the most pleasurable bath that I can ever remember. I have spent a large part of my life out of reach of hot baths; yet, when I enjoy a tub at leisure, I wonder why any man voluntarily deprives himself of so cheap and satisfying a delight.'

The sensual pleasure of bathing or swimming should not be overlooked. Apart from the gruesome murder of Jennifer Leigh's character in the shower in *Psycho* – so gruesome because it is so unexpected, shot so explicitly with the screeching music and the screams, but also because we are always naked and vulnerable in the shower – films normally depict bathing as something pleasurable. Who can forget Julia Roberts in the giant bubble bath in *Pretty Woman* listening to Prince on her headphones? Or Greta Scacchi in *White Mischief*? Or the sirens, washing clothes in the stream in *O Brother, Where Art Thou?* Tabloid newspapers in England were terribly excited when actress Sienna Miller described the 'very erotic' bath scenes with Keira Knightley in the film *The Edge of Love*, based on the life of Dylan Thomas.

As well as actresses, children especially seem to love bath time. There is no nicer end to the day than to bathe the children, wash their hair, and make them sit quietly by the fire while you read them a book. The water, while initially it may excite them, eventually calms them. They are clean and fresh and ready for bed. They will sleep well.

Water is also the biggest killer of children in the world. According to the United Nations, 6,000 children die every day from water-related infections. The world was shocked and America was traumatised on 11 September, 2001, when those two planes flew into the World Trade Center. But consider this: every day it is as if 6,000 children are loaded into twelve jumbo jets. They take off. Some of the children are fiddling with their seat belts, chatting to their neighbours, they might even be playing in the aisles. Some might be screaming. But soon they will all be screaming, for once the pilot gets to 30,000 feet, he gets out of the plane and opens his parachute. Goldfinger could have answered Bond by saying that every ten days 60,000 people are killed by water – maybe not in Kentucky on the day he planned to rob Fort Knox, which is why he had to add poison to the water supply. But 6,000 deaths a day from dirty water is two million deaths a year. Most are under five years old. But you probably won't know any of them, for they all live – and die – in the developing world.

There are many ways that water can kill you or your toddler. The World Health Organisation lists these hazards: anaemia, arsenicosis, ascariasis, campylobacteriosis, cholera, cyanobacterial toxins, dengue fever, diarrhoea, fluorisis, Guinea worm, hepatitis, Japanese encephalitis, lead poisoning, leptospirosis, malaria, malnutrition, methaemoglobinaemia, onchocerciasis, ringworm, scabies, schistosomiasis, spinal injury, trachoma, typhoid and paratyphoid enteric fevers. Oh, and let's not forget drowning.

Around thirty years ago, health organisations working in the Indian subcontinent determined that much of Bangladesh's ill health stemmed from drinking groundwater. If they could only build wells, the people would be much better off. Funds were raised – remember George Harrison's concert for Bangladesh? – boreholes were dug. Suddenly every village had its own pump. Water was fresh, abundant and clean. For a while, everything seemed fine.

Then people started appearing at health centres complaining of bloody diarrhoea, vomiting and abdominal pain. As the years passed, they came back with skin pigmentations and hyper-keratosis, and some time later, with cancer of the skin, lungs, bladder and kidney. It gradually became clear that the rural population of Bangladesh was being slowly poisoned. Arsenic is naturally present in some part of the earth's crust. It dissolves into the water, is odourless and hard to detect, until it explodes like a dirty time bomb. According to World Health Organisation estimates, arsenic poisoning will kill some 250,000 people a year in Bangladesh. It is safe to use the water for washing and cleaning; but drinking it is deadly. It's a slow death, lasting up to twenty years for an adult, although it's a quicker, but still painful, death for a child.

Why didn't the well-intentioned fundraisers spot the danger? Arsenic is hard to detect, but the reality is that they probably didn't do enough testing. They were convinced they were doing the right thing, and once enough people believe something, it becomes a self-fulfilling prophecy. Everyone agrees this is the right thing to do, so it must be right.

In London there is a Soho pub in Broadwick Street called the John Snow. It is rather a pleasant surprise to have an excuse to visit a pub while researching a book on water. It is a typical London pub, one that hasn't yet been sold to a chain or a City type who wants to turn it into a gastropub serving veal chops, broad beans and beer from microbreweries. The night I visited it was full of antipodeans drinking cheap beer out of plastic glasses. The pub's name does not commemorate the career of John Snow, the Sussex and England fast bowler (and occasional poet), but that of another John Snow, an earnest, lugubrious doctor who proved what some had suspected for years: drinking water can be bad for your health, even fatal. This is news that most regulars in a pub would readily endorse. Upstairs in the John Snow is a small account of his achievements, stuck on the wall in one corner, hiding the rather expansive flock wallpaper. In a frame is a photo of him taken when he was forty-three: with his mutton chops, thick eyebrows, large forehead and receding brow, his legs crossed with one hand in his lap and the other on a table, wearing a frock coat, a stiff collar and bow tie, he looks distinctly odd, as if he has had too much ether or is in need of a stiff drink. If he were sensible, he would not have touched water. In those days to drink it in London was to flirt with death at every sip.

Snow was born in York on 16 March, 1813, the eldest of nine children. His father was a labourer who worked his way up from cart driver to farmer to landlord, buying and renting land and housing. At fourteen, the bright Snow was taken out of school where he excelled at sums, and was packed off to Newcastle to be a pupil to William Hardcastle, one of the city's brightest medical men. However, it was still a dangerous thing to tangle with doctors. As Keats wrote in a letter: 'In disease medical men guess; if they cannot ascertain an illness, they call it nervous.' My Yorkshire grandmother, who died in 2001 aged ninety-seven, was of the same opinion, despite all the medical advances of the twentieth century. After suffering a fall in her nineties, she was reluctantly encouraged to visit a doctor. 'Ah yes,' he said, looking at his records. 'You haven't visited me since 1963. How have you been for the last thirty years?' She had a point: it was MRSA that finally did for her in a hospital in Shoreham-by-Sea.

In Snow's time there weren't many things a doctor could do for a patient, but most of the things they did do were lethal. This included bleeding, often with the help of leeches; prescribing opium; and encouraging a large intake of alcohol. During the nineteenth century cholera epidemic, death rates at the London Homeopathic Hospital were three times lower than at the Middlesex Hospital. This was not because homeopathy was a miracle cure, but because doing nothing was more effective than regular medical treatment.

Snow was a diligent pupil. He also sounds a bit of a bore, at least not the sort of person you would hunt down for a good night out. His favourite pursuits were long country walks and swimming, neither of which is objectionable. But he also became a staunch advocate of temperance, a vogue that was sweeping the country in the 1820s, and took it one step further, taking the pledge of abstinence. He fell under the spell of John Frank Newton, who insisted that fruit and vegetables were the best food for man, and that meat-eating was the cause of many illnesses. The poet Percy Bysshe Shelley became one of his most famous disciples.

Snow was eighteen when cholera hit Newcastle at the end of November 1831. There had been numerous recent cholera epidemics in both Asia and Continental Europe, originating from the Sunderbund swamps of the Ganges Delta in India in 1817, although the disease had probably been killing people locally for thousands of years. Its name comes from the Greek words for 'bile' and 'flow', from the nasty brown fluid that sufferers secrete. If you catch it you start vomiting and having diarrhoea. The transformation is rapid: a healthy person can turn into a shrivelled corpse-like object within a couple of hours. In Sandra Hempel's history of cholera *The Strange Case of the Broad Street Pump*, she quotes the British doctor Ashbel Smith's encounter with the disease: 'The sufferer takes on "that frightful choleric decomposition of the features of which language can convey no adequate idea . . . voice nearly extinct or heard only in a feeble whisper; extremities cold, shrunk, livid or marbled; the skin of the hands, forearms and feet . . . wrinkled like a washerwoman's . . . scrotum livid and contracted . . . thirsty torturing . . . from a vein opened, the blood flows not at all or with great difficulty, is a of a deep, dark colour, and at the end of some hours resembles a feebly coagulated vegetable jelly."'

The suffering is an accelerated version of the dehydration that the American explorer from the prologue encountered in the desert. Cholera is a bacterium; but what people often die from is dehydration. You can actually survive a cholera attack if you are given enough water to drink, but nineteenth-century doctors didn't hit on that as a cure. They preferred other tricks to try to keep their patients alive, including bleeding, administering laudanum – a heady mixture of opium and brandy – covering the feet in boiling water, hot poultices on the stomach, enemas, and weird potions containing among other things pepper, spices, ammonia, turpentine, sulphuric acid, creosote and bismuth, a metal whose salts were also used, in vain, to try to cure syphilis.

The cholera outbreak of 1817 swept through India into Nepal and Afghanistan. It went south to Oman and East Africa, and east to Burma, Thailand, Mauritius, Indonesia, Borneo, the Philippines, Japan and China. There was a lull, and then it appeared in Persia and the Ottoman Empire. In north-west Syria, at the port of Latakia, cholera looked across the Mediterranean towards Europe, and paused. Then it reappeared in Egypt in 1826, and this time made it across the Atlantic, pitching up first in Canada, then causing havoc in New York, and spreading to Detroit, Philadelphia, Baltimore, Washington DC and New Orleans. In 1827 it was in Russia. Europe would be next.

Faster than Napoleon, it closed on Moscow. Then swept through the rest of the country, finally reaching the imperial city of St Petersburg. Then it went south to Hamburg, Berlin, Paris, Vienna. The British government set up a Board of Health. As they took minutes and made recommendations, cholera landed in Sunderland, a town in the north-east of England, between Durham and Newcastle, on the banks of the Wear. It didn't take long to reach Newcastle, where the young Snow was waiting. He was posted to the Killingworth Colliery, where he recalled watching fit miners being struck down by the epidemic and being carried vomiting to the surface. Little is known of how he treated his patients. Some 235 died that year in the parish, more than double the average. Then, in the autumn of the following year, cholera disappeared. Most people moved on too, but Snow would never forget the experience.

He moved down to London, to the Westminster Hospital, to learn surgery with doctors such as Sir Anthony Carlisle, who had studied art under Joshua Reynolds before turning to medicine. Carlisle counted Samuel Coleridge and Charles Lamb among his friends. Snow qualified as a doctor in 1838 and set up in practice in Frith Street, where you can now find Bar Italia, the finest coffee shop in London.

Snow became a successful doctor. He was an expert in anaesthesia, especially the use of ether, which allowed doctors to operate on unconscious patients. Before that, it had been a case of holding them down and sawing fast. The highlight of his career was administering chloroform to Queen Victoria on the occasion of the birth of her eighth child, Prince Arthur. But still nobody knew what caused cholera, nor how to treat it. By 1848, when cholera was once again threatening British shores, the government convened another Board of Health, this time led by the diligent Edwin Chadwick, a lawyer-turned-social reformer. Chadwick's central thesis was that bad health was caused by bad smells: disease was transmitted through the air. This became known as miasma theory, from the Greek word for pollution. It became almost universally accepted, and in a sense, it was right. Bad smells often led to diseases. However, the smell did not transmit those diseases. In the case of cholera, the disease was spread by the *Vibrio cholerae* virus entering the water supply. Sewage plus water meant death. And the water did smell pretty foul; many people were saved by refusing to drink nasty-smelling water.

How did Snow set about proving his suspicion that water, not air, was the carrier of the disease? There were two main lines of inquiry that he followed when the cholera reappeared in 1854. In those days – as indeed it is now – London's water was supplied by the private sector. However, from an economic purist's point of view it was a better solution then because there was at least competition between the companies, rather than it being handed over to a private monopoly. In parts of south London you could choose between the Lambeth Water Company and the Southwark and Vauxhall companies. Originally both sold water straight out of the polluted Thames, but in 1852 the Lambeth Water Company moved its supply westward to Thames Ditton, away from the shit and the movement of the tide. When people started dying in 1854, Snow was able to show that you were less likely to succumb if you were drinking water that had not been tainted by pollution.

But before he knew it, he had an epidemic on his doorstep. At the end of August 1854, people began dying in and around Broad Street, and quickly. Within ten days, 500 people were dead. The cholera was indiscriminate, taking babies, mothers, fathers and old people alike. It was happening just around the corner from his practice in Frith Street. Those that could fled. Those that couldn't prayed, and many died. Then, within the month, the epidemic was over. It soon became clear that everybody who had died had been living within 250 metres of Broad Street. It seemed to point to Chadwick's theory of miasma. Snow set about recording the deaths on a map, a technique that later became famous and a vital tool in epidemiology, the study of how diseases spread. Each short, black line stood for a death, like coffins stacked up by the door.

As Snow went from door to door, scratching lines on his map, there appeared to be no pattern to the deaths. But as he looked further, certain facts emerged. Fifteen lines here; only two next door. There was a workhouse in Poland Street, where very few people died. He learnt that they had their own well. Nobody who worked at the Lion Brewery became ill, because they were allowed – and preferred – to drink beer instead of water. Then there were a couple of reported deaths, well outside Soho, that puzzled Snow for they seemed to have no connection with Broad

Street. Susannah Eley, the widow of the owner of Eley cartridges, whose family business was in Broad Street, had moved to Hampstead. Her sons ran the business, employing some 200 people. However, she retained a fondness for the water from the Broad Street pump and every day her sons sent her a bottle of water. A niece who lived in Islington had been staying with her. She managed to make it back home, but died soon afterwards.

Snow became convinced that the Broad Street pump was responsible for the deaths. Somehow, the cholera bacterium was contaminating the water supply and killing anyone who drank it. He lobbied a meeting of the board of governors of St James Parish, explained his findings, and told them that the only way to prevent further deaths was to stop people drinking the water. The board didn't necessarily agree with Snow, but what did they have to lose? They ordered the removal of the handle of the Broad Street pump. The deaths continued for a week or so, and then stopped. Dr John Snow had proved the link between contaminated water and cholera and disproved the notion of miasma, even though it took some years for this to be widely accepted. But taking away the handle didn't eradicate the cholera, which just went elsewhere, to South America, Africa, even back to Asia. Or it lay dormant, waiting to strike again.

In Gabriel García Márquez's *Love in the Time of Cholera*, Dr Juvenal Urbino is a celebrated doctor. 'He was aware of the mortal threat of the drinking water. The mere idea of building an aqueduct seemed fantastic, since those who might have supported it had underground cisterns at their disposal, where water rained down over the years was collected under a thick layer of scum.' His father, also a doctor, does his best work fighting to contain an outbreak of cholera, until the disease claims him as its most notable victim. In typical magic-realist fashion, when he becomes aware that cholera has him in its grip, he hides away in a utility room in Misericordia Hospital and pens a twenty-page letter to his wife and children in which 'the progress of the disease could be observed in the deteriorating script'. If only some of Snow's patients had had the opportunity of dying in such a lyrical manner. Cholera's only other appearance in the book is at the end, as a device to allow the lovers, Urbino's wife and the suitor of her youth, Florentino Ariza, to cruise up the river without stopping for cargo, passengers or mail. 'The only thing that would allow them to bypass all that was a case of cholera on board.' They hoist the yellow flag and begin their cruise, in the hope that their isolation will last forever.

Cholera still strikes today, in places such as Angola, Burundi, Kenya, Mali and Mozambique. Just ten years ago, according to figures from the World Health Organisation, a total of 118,349 cholera cases and 5,853 deaths were reported in Africa. A dramatic epidemic affected the countries in the Horn of Africa, where a large number of deaths occurred. Most outbreaks followed heavy rainfalls and flooding. All were caused by ingestion of the bacterium *Vibrio cholerae* from the excreta of an infected person. Poor infrastructure may be the cause, but greed and neglect are probably to blame. It is possible to build and run a water supply network that delivers clean and safe water. But if you skimp on the chemicals and the treatment, people will die.

Water can kill, but first it can drive you mad. Nobody knows the name of the man who invented the water torture, but it is generally assumed that he was Chinese. Drip. The Chinese are very good with water. They were probably the first to make water go uphill, using bamboo pipes that suck it up. There is no evidence that the Chinese did in fact torture people by putting their heads under a dripping tap until they went mad, but it is possible. Drip. In the sixteenth century an Italian called Hippolytus de Marsiliis – the Italians are another race with an affinity for water – having observed water's ability, given enough time, to cut through stone, used to torture people by having cold water dripped slowly on the body, preferably the forehead. If you can make the drips random, that will apparently send the victim mad more quickly. Drip, drip.

Drop. Human rights organisations accuse the present Chinese government of using a different water torture. The detainee is immersed in a pool of filthy water for weeks at a time. When the victim is pulled out the body will be covered in sores and he will be unable to move for weeks. But the Chinese don't hold a monopoly: the United States government has been condemned for using 'waterboarding' to extract confessions from detainees in the War on Terror. The technique is as follows: the victim is strapped to a large board, and hands and feet secured; the board is tipped so that the feet are higher than the head; the head is covered by either a cloth or a plastic film. Then water is poured over the face. While no water may actually get into the mouth or nose, the brain thinks it is being drowned and panics. CIA personnel who have tried it on themselves have lasted an average of fourteen seconds before breaking down. Victims say they are scarred for life; they are scared of taking showers, even of the rain. In a radio interview with Scott Hennen of WDAY, Vice President Dick Cheney apparently condoned the use of water torture:

> Hennen: Would you agree a dunk in water is a no-brainer if it can save lives?
>
> Cheney: Well, it's a no-brainer for me, but for a while there I was criticised as being the vice president for torture. We don't torture.

The White House later cleared up any confusion by saying that US officials don't discuss interrogation techniques because they are 'classified'. White House press secretary Tony Snow added that Cheney was not referring to waterboarding, but only to 'a dunk in the water'. One reporter commented: 'So dunk in the water means, what, we have a pool now at Guantanamo and they go swimming?'

An earlier use of this method of torture was dreamt up by agents of the Dutch East India Company during the Amboyna Massacre in 1623. Cloth was wrapped around the prisoner's head, and then water poured gently over the cloth so that only water, not air, could be sucked in. This process was repeated a number of times. One unfortunate's face swelled up like a watermelon; his cheeks were said to be like great bladders and his eyes popped out beyond his forehead.

One advantage of water as a form of torture – with the possible exception of the last incident – is that while it scars, perhaps permanently, it leaves no visible trace. Other regimes have forced pressure hoses into captives' orifices, forcing them down their mouths or up their anuses. Unpleasant, but to the naked eye at least, untraceable.

Ever since the first woman on earth celebrated her thirtieth birthday, the search has been on for the fountain of eternal youth. Spanish explorers claimed that the aquifers under what is now called Florida contained magic powers to rejuvenate the body and skin. It was probably just a marketing ploy. But many claims are made for the rejuvenating powers of water. The French, for example, are great believers in salt water. They have thalassotherapy spas around the coast. Every summer the woman who looks after my children goes to Brittany for a month to treat her aching back. Dirty water can kill you; purified water can heal you. It can also rejuvenate you.

Different cultures, though, have varying definitions of what constitutes cleanliness. Napoleon wrote to Joséphine de Beauharnais: 'I will return in five days. Stop washing.' For fastidious Americans, Japanese, even the British and most French people these days, such an instruction would be unthinkable. The pungent scent of a woman who hasn't washed is no longer erotic; it's disgusting. Even musk, once considered the ultimate in aphrodisial scent, is shunned, with modern women preferring lighter smells such as orange blossom and jasmine. The Greeks pioneered bathing, even though the Egyptians were shocked by their habit of sitting in stagnant water. The Spartans, meanwhile, believed that washing with warm water was the first sign of moral laxity. Cold water would suffice. This may be acceptable in the Peloponnese, but generations of public school boys, particularly in austere institutions such as Gordonstoun, which recommended a cold shower before breakfast, have cursed their Spartan habits. (The Victorians thought that a cold bath or shower would curb the sexual instinct, a view that may be misguided; more recent tests show it to be a stimulant.) The Romans, as we have seen, were also enthusiastic bathers. Washing was one of the benefits of Empire. When the Christian Church split between the Catholic and the Orthodox churches, you could almost argue it was divided into those who washed and those who didn't. Constantinople took the bathers, and the practice continued in the famous Turkish bathhouses. The Catholics, on the whole, preferred to avoid bathing. Monks wore hair shirts, fertile breeding grounds for lice and other insects, as if following Saint Jerome's instruction: 'Who bathes in Christ does not need a second bath'. Eventually the Black Death helped close Europe's bathhouses – they were wrongly perceived to be circulating the disease – and even the rulers preferred not to bathe. Elizabeth I quipped, 'I bathe once a month, whether I need to or not.' Her successor, James I, was reputed only to wash his fingertips. It was a widespread view that disease entered the body through the pores of the skin. Wash them, and you could allow in any number of foul contagions.

Washing came back into vogue in the eighteenth century, when it became clear that while unclean water could transmit disease, clean water was a positive benefit. Fresh cold water, especially salt water, was celebrated for its rejuvenating powers. As the Victorians started building clean water supplies and sewerage, they started producing propaganda. Charles Kingsley's *Water Babies* is the account of a young chimney sweep, saved by prayer and cold baths.

Americans in turn took to bathing with puritanical zeal, almost forcing immigrants from smelly Old Europe to adopt new washing habits. Some took this to extremes. Howard Hughes, playboy and billionaire, became obsessed with germs and disease, and finished his years washing compulsively. No American home or hotel is complete without washrooms, power showers and that ultimate middle-class status symbol, a hot tub in the garden.

The Asians have always appreciated the pleasures and rituals of washing. The Japanese bathhouses in Kyoto are a fine place to linger. My favourite is Minami-Funaoka-cho where there is a cypress-wood tub, which lends an amazing fragrance to the water. There are also some magnificent carved wooden panels in the changing rooms, made during the Japanese invasion of Manchuria.

In parts of Africa, there is less emphasis on bodily odours. It's okay to smell. Napoleon would be happy there. It's strange and slightly disconcerting when you catch the natural scent of an attractive woman. The smell is feral and quite unsettling. This is how it must have been for nearly every generation before the twentieth century. It wasn't because of the body odour but returning from a trip to Lagos, Nigeria, I stopped in London and visited the Mandarin Oriental Hotel in Hyde Park in an effort to experience the recuperative powers of water. I had planned to have a massage, but they like you to spend half an hour or so beforehand in their water treatment facilities. They call it a 'Heat and Water Oasis'. There is a Turkish bath, a sauna, kept at a lower temperature than normal, and a plunge pool. Or as they call it, an 'Amethyst Crystal Steam Room', which blends heat and water through delicately lit semi-precious stone; a 'Sanarium' – a sauna without the heat turned up; and the 'Vitality Pool', where, according to the brochure, you lie 'in hot mineral water on a suspended cushion of air whilst being gently massaged by hydrotherapy body jets'. The flight from Lagos had been long. For reasons known only to British Airways, they announced as we were boarding the flight that there was no jet fuel in Lagos, so we would be making an unscheduled stop in Parma, Majorca. This happened at 3.30 in the morning. It's not the ideal time to be told to put your seats in an 'upright position'. We arrived at Heathrow airport three and a half hours late. I was ready to plunge in the plunge pool. I enjoyed the Turkish bath, although I am not sure I got much out of the crystals; I didn't go in the Sanarium; I prefer saunas to be hot, so the sweat runs down your cheeks. A lukewarm sauna is like a tepid cup of tea. I did go into the Vitality Pool, and the water was soft and warm. Unfortunately, the nice Australian girl who took my shoes and showed me to the changing room omitted to tell me that I had to turn a switch to make the Vitality Pool vital. If only I had known that there were hydrotherapy body jets, I could have been massaged as well.

When I was taken upstairs to the treatment room, I was put in the hands of a fine-looking young Italian girl called Elena. The first thing she did was to invite me to sit down in a chair. Then she produced a bowl of warm water and washed my feet. I don't recall ever having had my feet washed before. It felt rather biblical or Homeric. I liked it very much.

I returned to London a few months later, this time to the Elemis Spa at the Intercontinental Hotel in Park Lane. I was given a spell on what is called a 'dry flotation bed' and a treatment called an 'Exotic Frangipani Body Nourish Float'. First a comely girl called Lisa covered me in frangipani oil as I lay on a bed. The brochure that they had given me to read while I waited was lyrical, almost poetic. 'Warmed Monoi oil – a blend of frangipani flower extract and coconut oil – is drizzled over the body in this decadent treatment. Drenching the skin with moisture, this exotic wrap polishes and scents the skin. For added relaxation try having this therapy on the dry flotation bed.' I would. Once I had been drizzled, a couple of arms of plastic were wrapped around me, rather like a wet macintosh. The arms and the base of the bed were then inflated with water. I was on a waterbed. A blindfold was placed over my eyes and Lisa massaged my feet. After half an hour it was time to come down. The bed was deflated and my body suddenly felt heavy again, each vertebra hitting the bed seemingly with a bump. It was a pleasant enough experience, but it was Monday morning and I had a lunch to get to, so perhaps I wasn't in the right mood.

The strangest of all these water therapy experiences occurred in the spa at the El-Minzah Hotel in Tangier. My wife and I were taken into a steam room, where there was running water and ledges to lie on. We were instructed to take off our clothes. The air was tepid, moist, almost dank, the sort of place in which an eccentric American millionaire would house his collection of orchids. Once we had started sweating, a large woman came through the door and proceeded to cover us in thick, slimy mud. She seemed oblivious to our nakedness. The mud was then washed off by frequent jugs of water poured over us. The muddy water disappeared down the drain; we were clean and glowing. The large woman left us.

But how does one know whether water is healthy or polluted? How can you be sure it is going to do you some good? Sometimes it is impossible to tell just by looking. So I decide to take the water from our spring in for testing. There is a laboratory in Béziers where they will test it for €70. I am instructed to fill two vials with water and bring them in. There is a wait of about a week, and then I receive a letter. As I open it I wonder: what if it is bad news? What if the water is undrinkable – or tainted with arsenic? Will we start going blind?

My eye goes straight to the conclusion and the news is good: the water is potable. Above is a more detailed description. Visually, it says it is 'limpid'; this is good, apparently. Then the pH. This is 8.1. It should be between 6.5 and 9, so it is okay, but is quite alkaline. Pure water is supposed to have a pH of 7. Nature has its very own litmus paper: the hydrangea plant gives blue flowers when the soil is acid; pink when it is alkaline. In our garden, the flowers would be pink. The limestone that has slowly filtered the water will have imparted its chalky taste and feel. The water contains less than 0.1 milligrams per litre of nitrites and less than 10 milligrams per litre of nitrates, both of which are acceptable. There are also fewer than 0.10 milligrams per litre of ammonia and 45 milligrams of sulphates, both of which are well within limits.

So how does this compare with other waters? In Avène, a

spa town less than an hour away from us, a mini industry has sprung up catering for people with skin diseases and sensitive skins. The Avène cosmetic range includes some of Europe's best-selling beauty products. According to their promotional literature its water 'takes a forty year slow journey underground through the Cévennes Mountains and is enriched with precious minerals and trace elements. Of constant composition, Avène Thermal Spring Water has a low mineral content (207 mg/l) and therefore respects the natural balance and the sensitivity of the skin without causing dehydration or irritation like other high mineral content thermal waters. It is bacteriologically pure, with a neutral pH (7.5) and rich in silica (14 mg/l) which soothes sensitive skin.'

God knows how they work out that it takes forty years for a drop to travel from the mountain to the source.

The concert is about to begin. It will be the first major concert in Red Square since the fall of Communism. Everybody wants it to succeed, but the weather forecast is bad. The television cameras are in place, the crowd is swelling, even the band is awake and sober, but the sky is black and blue like a bruise. Then, on a sign from the Kremlin, an order is despatched. The air is suddenly full of the sound of aeroplanes, although you cannot see anything from under the cloud cover. Within an hour the sky is blue, the band is ready to play. Nobody doubts that the planes sprinkled silver iodide on the clouds, encouraging them to disperse and drop their water elsewhere.

5

The Exquisite Taste of Water

'I can't tell you how he amuses me, he doesn't drink anything but water,' said Mme Verdurin.

À la recherche du temps perdu, Marcel Proust

IT IS MIDDAY ON a spring Saturday on the rue Saint-Honoré and already Colette's is packed. It is one of the flashiest shops in Paris, selling mainly useless items such as watches, clothes, underwear, stationery and manga comics, most of which you can buy much cheaper elsewhere – but here they carry the epithet 'designer'. The people shopping all seem to have been designed too. The men have sheared hairstyles and serious glasses. The women are thin. Next to me a tall woman, well over six feet, dressed in a leopard-skin fur coat and wearing sunglasses, is buying a DVD made by Helmut Newton. There is a photograph of a woman in bondage on the cover. I wonder how she plans to spend the afternoon.

And the music. It is mellow lounge music, the sort of thing they play at the Buddha Bar. Once unusual, it is now as ubiquitous and irritating as elevator music. But we are not interested in comics or black underwear. We are off down the metal staircase to the bar in the basement. The room is quite small, with pine wooden tables and benches. Stark white lights hang over tables, like striplights at a workplace. What shall we drink? A Bloody Mary, perhaps? A glass of champagne?

No such luck. Here the choice is limited to water. If you like your water without bubbles, you can choose from: 420, a volcanic spring water from New Zealand, 1 Litre, a Canadian number, Antipodes, no need to guess where that comes from, Aqua Luna, from Germany, Apollinaris Silence, also from Germany, Bling from Tennessee, Blue Keld from Yorkshire 'naturally balanced', Cape Karoo from the eastern cape of South Africa, Chantlemerle from the Ardèche in France, Cloud Juice '9750 drops of rainwater from Tasmania', EA from Germany, Elsenham 'from Elsenham's pure, confined aquifer' in England, Evian, Fine from Mount Fuji in Japan, Gerolsteiner Stille from Germany, Gleneagles 'beneath the rainbow' in Scotland, Glenlivet Speyside also from Scotland, Heartsease from England 'a water that mends broken hearts', Hildon from Hampshire in England, Kiren from Senegal, Lauquen from Patagonia, Lauretana 'very slightly mineral, among the lightest in Europe', Llanllyr – the list says from England but this name sounds suspiciously Welsh to me, Malmberg 'pure for 5,000 years' (no mention of what it was like before then), Ogo from Switzerland, the 'next generation of oxygen water', Pineo from Catalonia, Quarzia from Italy, Saint-Georges, spring water from Corsica, Sei from the Catskill Mountains in New York State, Sunshine from Austria, rich in lithium and bicarbonate of soda, Surgiva, lightly mineralised water from Italy, Tau from Wales, Tynant Or and Tynant Rouge, also from Wales, recognisable by their distinctive bottles, Vilas del Turbon from the Spanish Pyrenees, Villers, natural mineral water, Voss, artesian water from Norway, Water from der Supermarket from Germany, 'buy it and it's yours', Wattwiller from the Vosges Mountains, Wildalp from the Austrian Alps, Wild Water from New Zealand 'the country's premium mineral water' and Zilia, a spring water from Corsica.

Prefer bubbles? Then chose from Apollinaris, Badoit, Blue Keld, Chateldon 'first mineral water bottled in France in 1650', Elsenham, Ferrarelle from Italy with a subtle taste, Gerolsteiner from Germany, Gleneagles, Glenlivet Speyside, Hildon, Iskilde discovered in 2002 near Lake Mosso in Denmark, Lauchstadter from Germany 'since 1710', Lauretana, Llanllyr, Montes Gaz from Austria 'rich in mineral elements', Ogo, Pedras Salgadas from Portugal 'lightly sparkling, good for the digestion', Perrier, Pineo, Quarzia from Italy, Ramlosa from Sweden, 'since 1707 the water of the Swedish royal family', Saint Geron, San Pellegrino, Spa Verte/Spa Rouge from Belgium, St Gero from Germany, 'naturliches Heilwasser', Surgiva, Tau, Tynant Rouge, Vals, Ventadour, Voss, Wattwiller Jouvence, and Zagori from Greece, 'renowned for its superior quality'.

And you thought water just came out of a tap. Italians are the biggest drinkers of bottled water in the world, quenching their thirsts with some fifty gallons each a year, with the French not far behind. The Americans drink around eighteen gallons, with the Brits, less thirsty or perhaps less picky, languishing on less than ten. Desperate to get my average up, I chose the bar's best-selling number, a bottle of Saint-Georges spring water from Corsica. I asked the barman, a thin, tall, good-looking man, why it was the best-selling water.

'It is the cheapest,' he said. 'And the bottle has been designed by Philippe Starck.'

I have to say the bottle's not much to look at. No strange shapes. No cunning lid. I have to think that Starck was having an off day when he came up with this design. And the taste:

without any bubbles, the water was as flat as Paris tap water. It didn't taste much different either.

I was joined at the bar by two English men in their thirties. One ordered the same bottle as me; the other was keen on a red bottle of Badoit. What's that like, he asked? I was able to tell him. By now I knew all about the taste of water.

I had spent an evening at Galeries Lafayette, a department store, also in a basement. In the kitchen section there is a small glass cube, where you can learn to cook sushi, bouillabaisse, cassoulet, possibly even boiled eggs. There is a stove and a sink. We were there to learn all about the taste of water, under the watchful eye of Dominique Laporte, crowned best sommelier in the world in 2004. He would teach us to use some of the same techniques you might use in wine tasting – assessing the nose, the attack and the finish – and apply them to water. We would determine the quality of the bubbles. Would they be crackling, frothy or fleeting? But what sort of person chooses to spend Friday night drinking water anyway? I accosted the first couple that came in. They were in their late twenties, a good-looking pair. Shouldn't they be in a bar somewhere listening to lounge music?

'I work for the company that organises this event,' explained the girl. 'He is my boyfriend.'

Next in was a journalist from *Le Parisien*. Finally there was Rebecca. She was there, she said, because she liked water. There was no time to enquire further, because the best sommelier in the world in 2004, a wiry, dark-haired man – a man with suspiciously white teeth for somebody who spends his life slurping tannic substances and one who looked disturbingly young to know so much about wine – was pouring water into plastic glasses. The labels had been obscured, so there was to be no cheating. This was a shame. I have always found a sly peek at the label a huge help during blind wine tastings. We wouldn't be able to smell the water, he said, partly because water has very little odour, but also because the plastic would mask it. He didn't really explain why we were not using proper glasses, but I suspect he thought it wouldn't make any difference, and he didn't want to do the washing-up.

'Only a very experienced sommelier can detect any difference in smell,' he said. The subtext being that us clowns would detect nothing. 'Now I want you to taste the first glass.'

I did. It was slightly bubbly, slightly salty. Tasted just like water. The same was true for the second glass. The third was a bit more bubbly.

'It has bigger bubbles,' agreed Dominique. 'But it is very short in the mouth.'

Number four tasted like the first two, but with more bubbles. I glanced over at the publicity sheet from Badoit. 'Not all sparkling waters taste the same,' it said. No. Some have more bubbles. Number five was another disappointment for Dominique.

'Too bubbly,' was his verdict.

He explained the difference. Some mineral waters, such as Badoit and Chateldon, are naturally gassy. As the drops of water percolate through the rocks, they pick up carbon dioxide. These waters are naturally sparkling. Others, such as Perrier and San Pellegrino, are still waters charged with a dosage of carbon dioxide during the bottling to give them a bit of fizz. This makes them less authentic. The marriage of water and gas is not so natural.

However, there is a catch. The French government decrees that for the nation's well-being all bottled water must be filtered for iron. This removes the bubbles as well, even from the naturally sparkling waters. The best of the sparkling waters then put the same natural carbon dioxide back into the water it has just been removed from. For Dominique at least, this explains why the bubbles were better integrated in the Badoit (green) and the Badoit (red).

Badoit red label is a new concept. Listen to the marketing people and you would think they had found the Holy Grail, whereas all they have done is inject more bubbles into the water once it is in the bottle, probably to compete with the popularity of the extremely fizzy Perrier and San Pellegrino.

This being France, we couldn't drink without eating something. A chef, Sullivan Alvarez from the Café de la Paix, was on hand to show us how to make chicken kebabs and a tuna carpaccio. This, I felt, would have been the ideal opportunity to open a good Chablis. But Dominique, best sommelier in the world in 2004, had other ideas.

'I want you to taste each dish with both the green- and the red-label Badoits,' he said. We did as we were told. We could all tell that one was fizzier than the other. Rebecca, the woman who liked water, seemed particularly excited by this.

'The green-label Badoit goes better with the fish,' said Dominique. 'It is more the equivalent of a white wine. However, I think you will agree that the red label goes better with the chicken. Its powerful bubbles rinse out the palate.'

Everyone agreed. We had been at this for an hour now, and I sensed everyone wanted to get out and have a drink. I know I did.

'Do people really take water this seriously?' I asked.

'They should. People should look to drink mineral water. And not just drink water, but drink a water.'

'And tap water?'

'Paris tap is surprisingly good,' said Dominique. 'Or Château Chirac as a lot of people call it, because Jacques Chirac used to be mayor of Paris.'

So back in Colette's water bar I was able to explain to my two new English friends why they should try Badoit red label, preferably with a piece of chicken on a skewer. But I was shocked to discover that the designer crowd was choosing spring water over mineral water. Conventional wisdom, particularly among London's top chefs, is that you should drink mineral water over spring water. Both are collected more or less in the same way. Spring water – such as the best-selling Saint-Georges from Corsica – comes straight out of the ground. Mineral water, which can spend years filtering through rocks and picking up some of their minerality on the way, including touches of magnesium and sodium, is supposed to be collected underground. In reality, there is very little difference in taste or composition. What separates them is the amount of testing and time it takes to have a water declared 'mineral'. And once that has been done, you are not allowed to treat it or alter its composition. Spring water can change with the seasons.

In *The Anatomy of Melancholy* Robert Burton recommends rainwater as the 'purest' drink. Rainwater is hard to capture – particularly in the Mediterranean. But after a particularly wild storm I managed to get hold of a cupful containing a couple of inches. It's true it contains few impurities, because it has been filtered by the earth's natural system. It tastes almost soft, void of any distinguishing features, like cotton or fresh air. In contrast Lord Byron preferred soda water to rainwater. He thought it was the best cure for a hangover.

'Let us have wine and women, mirth and laughter,' said Byron's Don Juan. 'Sermons and soda water the day after.'

I was momentarily tempted by a bottle of Bling water. At €50 a pop, this comes all the way from America, in a bottle decorated in rhinestones. My daughters would love the bottle. If it were a person, it would be Elton John. I had a cup of coffee instead, and walked out through the Tuileries gardens. I reflected on the work of the German-based Water Liberation Movement, a shady, secretive organisation. It had calculated that some one per cent of Europe's water was locked up in bottles, so at the turn of the millennium they invaded a number of supermarkets and small shops and 'liberated' the water by throwing it down the nearest drain. The hope was that it would revive the aquifers and re-enter the water cycle. Across the busy road was the Seine; its water was the colour of camouflage.

But can one really differentiate between the taste of various waters? And even if you think you can, why would you bother? People expect to pay for bottled water, another of those curious characteristics of water, for it is the commodity that everybody wants for free. But put it in a bottle and it seems man-made, no longer a gift from God. At the Four Seasons Hotel in New York, a bottle of Evian from the minibar costs $10. For this you could fill your bath in Manhattan with tap water for a month. Why are people happy to pay for bottled water? What other commodity do you buy where the differentials in price are so huge? Of course you know in a restaurant that you are paying two, three, some-times even four times as much for a bottle of wine as you would pay in an off-licence. But you accept that as part of the deal. The restaurant has had to choose it, store it and serve it. They will have to wash the glasses, print the wine list and pay the sommelier. But would you buy it if it were 1,000 times more expensive than at home? I don't think so. Yet you never hear anyone in a restaurant declaring water to be a universal human right. Most decent restaurants will happily bring you a carafe of tap water, although they would, of course, prefer you to buy a litre of Badoit or San Pellegrino. At the 1,000 per cent mark-up. And in America, things are even odder: one of the most popular bottled waters, Aquafina, is filled directly from a tap. It used to be marked discreetly with the letters PWS. Now PepsiCo has been forced to spell it out: Public Water Supply. There is also pressure on Coca-Cola to follow suit and come clean by admitting that Dasani, America's best-selling bottled water, comes from the same source, that is, a tap. Not so, according to a spokeswoman for Coca-Cola: 'We don't believe that consumers are confused about the source of Dasani water,' she said. 'The label clearly states that it is purified water.'

American consumers may be less demanding or just more gullible than others. Coca-Cola tried to introduce bottled water into the British market, but as soon as it was pointed out that the contents were tap water, there was a press outcry, and the bottles were withdrawn from the shops. Yet sales of bottled water have been booming. According to *The Economist*, Americans spent around $11 billion buying 8.25 billion gallons in 2006, an increase in volume of 9.5 per cent on a year earlier. The average American drank 27.6 gallons of bottled water last year, up from 16.7 gallons in 2000. In Britain, sales of bottled water have jumped from 218 million gallons in 1998 to 502 million gallons in 2006 – worth $3.3 billion and accounting for fifteen per cent of the total soft-drinks market. Its share is forecast to rise to twenty-one per cent next year.

But what of its taste? If anything, water is famous for its lack of taste, except in a few remote villages in Greece, where the old boys sitting in the shade will praise the taste of their own village's water supply above all others. Water is a universal solvent, a mixer. You wouldn't dilute drinks with it if you thought the taste would change, would you? (I am not including here Russian robber barons or Chinese tycoons, known to pour Coca-Cola into the finest of clarets.) But most of those drinks that children love – lemonade, grenadine, even Coca-Cola – are at least ninety per cent water. Adults use water as a mixer too. Whisky drinkers hold that the best malt should be freshened with an equal amount of cool loch water. The best beers are those that are made from the finest waters. Take Harvey's in Sussex, brewed using water drawn from the Ouse, or Brakspear's, made from Thames water. In Sarajevo, during the four-year siege and a water shortage in the city, the local brewery continued making beer, called *Sarajevsko pivo* by the locals, using water from its own well. So miraculous was its appearance in a city under siege that eventually the beer was widely assumed to have magic powers.

For Michael Mascha, an Austrian who went to live in California nearly sixteen years ago, bottled water has become a passion. 'It started out as a hobby, now it has become a mission,' he says. The catalyst was his doctor, who warned him to stop drinking wine because of a serious heart condition. 'I had 500 bottles of wine in my cellar, most of which I gave away to friends. The rest I kept just in case I get a terminal disease,' he says. Once he started drinking nothing but water, he began to realise that not all water tastes the same. He believes that people do not pay enough attention to the water they are drinking, particularly in the United States. 'It is not easy,' he says. 'Americans in general like processed food. Processed means safe, it means science.' He has replaced his wine cellar with a water cellar. He likes to think of himself as the Robert Parker of water, and has written a book called *Fine Waters: A Connoisseur's Guide to the World's Most Distinctive Bottled Waters*. Whether he will get such a slavish following as Robert Parker, the American who turned wine-tasting into a numbers game, is doubtful, but at least his approach is not so didactic.

Mascha doesn't have a favourite water, but he likes waters that are high in mineral content, with a distinct taste, and that are naturally carbonated. There aren't that many waters that fall into this category – Vichy Catalan is perhaps the most obvious example. He likes to hold dinner parties and serve a different water with each course – matching low mineral content waters with foods that you would normally serve with white wine, reserving more mineral-rich waters for food that would go well with red wine. Mascha does admit that water does not have the range of taste of wine – the difference in taste is very subtle, with bubble size being the biggest distinction – but he thinks the market is only going to get bigger. And he dismisses the criticism that bottled water is environmentally unfriendly as the complaint of those who view water only as a commodity. 'I agree that bottling tap water makes no sense,' he says. 'It tastes no different and you have to go to the supermarket and pick it up in plastic bottles. People would be better off buying a simple water filter. However, if you accept that waters have different tastes, just as wines taste different, why shouldn't you bottle and ship them?' Critics might counter that an appreciation of water takes a Proustian sensibility – and to sip and slurp water when many children are dying for lack of it also shows a certain lack of sensibility. Nobody ever died for lack of a bottle of Pichon-Longueville, although there have been times when I might have been willing to kill for one.

Drink this water and one day you'll have a beard like mine

Like many European habits, the custom of buying and consuming bottled water originated in France. In the seventeenth century, they started drinking it for their health. Doctors peddled the theory that certain waters, high in salts and minerals such as Vichy water, were good for the liver. Vichy water certainly tastes bad enough to make you think it may be doing you some good. Now it is declared bad for you because it is so salty. Equally, tap or well water during that period probably wasn't safe to drink. When I first ventured to France more than thirty years ago, I was warned by earnest parents not to drink the water. French sanitation needed no explanation: the typical whiff of a French toilet was warning enough not to linger any longer than strictly necessary, particularly if it was one of those with just a hole in the ground, as if somebody had made off with the toilet in the middle of the night.

However, even though French tap water has become potable, even pleasant, the custom of drinking bottles of the stuff at mealtimes, particularly in restaurants, has become strong enough for it to persist. Now, when I am in France, I see English people call for a *carafe d'eau* but rarely French people. They claim it is not just a matter of health; it's also a matter of taste. But is it? After all, water that comes from a spring, however pure, is then piped, bottled, given a nip of gas, stored, shipped, sold, delivered, chilled, then opened with a hiss at your table. I suspect the reason many people prefer slightly fizzy water is that the bubbles make the water come alive. From still water it's only a short step to stagnant water. But the water you would get from the tap – if then served with ice cubes and a slice of lemon – would taste as good as anything you would get from a bottle. Or would it?

The worst-tasting drinking water I have encountered is in the United States. It is worse than the tap water in Barcelona that comes from the Ter Llobregat groundwater system, which is so heavy in minerals, mainly gypsum, that you can taste them even after filtering. The municipality is spending a fortune building new dams and filtering plants. No doubt the untreated mineral water will continue to be bottled and sold at a premium. The water in Washington DC is so laced with chlorine that it tastes as if it has been drawn straight from the local swimming baths. This reminds me of the French Vigipirate Plan, which is designed to stop terrorists striking at France's water supply. One of the ways to safeguard the water supply is to lace it artificially with chlorine. The effect is the same: the water is undrinkable. You cannot blame anyone in Washington DC for buying bottled water to drink, although locals tell me that if you leave tap water in the glass for a while the taste of chlorine clears. And in Starbucks, at least, they encourage you to buy bottled water with the lure that your purchase will help bring drinking water to people unlucky enough not to have a Starbucks within strolling distance.

Ethos Water, retailing at around $1.80 a bottle, was set up by two friends and so-called 'Green entrepreneurs', Jonathan Greenblatt and Peter Thum. Greenblatt grew up in a small town in New England, and ended up working in the public service, mainly at Bill Clinton's White House. During that time he travelled to many developing countries, including Haiti and the Gaza Strip. 'It was quite a shock for someone who had lived a comfortable life in New England to see people struggling in those conditions, without paved roads, without electricity and without running water,' he says. 'Those impressions always stayed with me.'

He left the White House to do a graduate degree, then started working for a software company. In 2002 he received a call from Thum, his business school classmate, who had been working at McKinsey in South Africa and had a background in the soft-drinks industry. Thum had done some research and believed there was a business opportunity to create a bottled water that would help people in need of clean water. 'Based on my experience, I also knew that the lack of clean drinking water is one of the biggest challenges facing mankind,' says Greenblatt. 'Ethos seemed like a novel approach to change the world through the simple step of changing consumer behaviour.' The two partners spent some time researching and brainstorming, as graduate students are fond of doing. They discovered the size and scale of the American bottled water business, one that is focused mainly on price and convenience. 'Taste is not a factor for most consumers,' says Greenblatt. 'And we knew it would not be a key success factor for Ethos. We wanted to sell a spring water, but more importantly, a water with a mission.' But can bottled water – plastic bottles that is – ever be green? According to the Earth Policy Institute, an American environmental organisation, ten million barrels of oil are used every year just to make the plastic bottles for the American market. 'It's not an unreasonable question to ask,' says Greenblatt. 'It's unclear whether someone could enjoy the same success with a similar bottled water product today. When we launched the business, concern for climate change was neither as mainstream nor the criticism of bottled water as pervasive. Regardless, we were not aiming simply to create a new brand of bottled water. We wanted to do some good and change the way that people think about water.'

If you were thinking of setting up such a business today, you would probably try to persuade coffee shops and restaurants to sell tap water and give the proceeds to water projects in the developing world. But in 2002, full of noble intentions but with little cash flow, the partners worked from Jonathan's son's bedroom, running up their credit cards and relying on friends for 'lunch money'. They launched the product in 2003. The water was supplied by local springs in order to minimise their carbon footprint. For example, they initially used water from Baxter Springs in the Sierra Nevada Mountains to serve the southern California market. For the East Coast they used water from a natural source called Tomhicken Springs in the Pocono Valley. 'The idea of shipping water from Fiji to New York is ghastly on many levels,' says Greenblatt. 'You consume massive amounts of fossil fuels to move the product across the planet. You are stripping the locals of their most precious resource. Plus the economics of the freight are upside-down. We discovered that the right thing to do environmentally is often the right thing to do economically.'

They had a bottle and they had water, but they needed economies of scale. The breakthrough came at a technology conference in 2004, where they met Pierre Omidyar, the founder of eBay, who agreed to invest in Ethos to ramp the business and its social mission. His investment helped get the product into Whole Foods Market, the leading natural food retailer in the United States. a chain of mainly organic produce shops. The next step was even more important. After a meeting with Starbucks' Chairman Howard Schultz to discuss the coffee retailer acting as a distributor, the response was better than either of the partners could have expected.

'They told us they wanted to acquire the company,' says Greenblatt. 'It gave us a chance to achieve what we had set out to do.' Ethos' initial goal and aspiration was to donate fifty per cent of its profits to bringing clean water to people in developing countries. But they weren't making any profits. Starbucks agreed to pay a nickel for every bottle they sold – now and forever. In addition, the company agreed to give $10 million to the cause. 'From the start of our relationship with Starbucks we suddenly would give a hundred times more than our commitment to that point,' says Greenblatt. In 2006 Starbucks and Pepsico negotiated an agreement to distribute Ethos Water beyond Starbuck stores to an additional 10,000 outlets.

But isn't five cents a bottle peanuts when a bottle sells for between $1.80 and $2 in Manhattan? 'Of course it would be marvellous if Starbucks could give more, but it's a step in the right direction. It's about starting a conversation about how to end the world water problem.'

Greenblatt won't say how much he and Thum pocketed from the sale of Ethos to Starbucks, but reports suggest it is in the region of several million dollars. They at least have solved their own financial problems and Jonathan's son has his bedroom back. Greenblatt no longer works with the company, but is now teaching at the business school at UCLA and advising various companies and non-profit organisations.

Critics say that Starbucks' acquisition of Ethos Water was an attempt to give it instant Green 'street credibility'. Yet it is curious that you have to search the Starbucks website carefully before you find any mention of it. Shouldn't it be flagged on the front page, like the different coffees and free songs that you can download from your favourite coffee shop? And given the scale of the world water problem, isn't $10 million small beer? Greenblatt agrees, but says that money is not the issue.

'Water Aid, the London-based charity, suggests that for $25, you could give someone water and sanitation for life. There are some 2.5 billion people without sanitation in the world. Do the math. That's something like $60 billion. Even if Starbucks gave ten cents a bottle, rather than five, or a dollar a bottle, it wouldn't come close to solving the problem. But Starbucks has some 9,000 stores. That's 30–35 million people a week to whom we can get the message out. We want to create a social movement to solve this problem – and Starbucks uniquely can make this happen. I am optimistic that we can tackle this. Think about it: a hundred years ago in America, people were dying of cholera, African Americans were second-class citizens, and women didn't have the vote. That's all changed. In fact, this year, it looks like we might even have a female president.'

Ethos and Starbucks have been busy organising water walks in America, publicising the issues of unclean water and the lack of sanitation in the world. The first was in Washington DC in 2004, with just a hundred people. In 2007 more than 10,000 people around America walked in cities such as Seattle, Chicago and

Atlanta. Starbucks also created a virtual walk online for those unable to pound the streets. 'In Africa, women walk up to six miles a day to get water,' says Greenblatt. 'We wanted to raise awareness of the issue. This is how you start a movement.'

Movements are all very well, but in my experience there is no substitute for hard cash. I think poverty is directly related to water issues. Diseases caused by dirty water stop people working; women walk miles and queue for water when they could be doing something more productive. In America they solved some of the poverty in the deep south by improving the water supply. Couldn't they do the same elsewhere?

'What about all the money you Americans are spending on the Iraq war?' I asked. 'Wouldn't some of that help?'

The line goes quiet. 'America is spending some $25 billion a month in Iraq. You bet it would help.' The Nobel Prize-winning economist Joseph Stiglitz suggests that the total bill for the war in Iraq is $3 trillion. That could pay for a lot of dams, pipes, and water treatment plants.

It was also a matter of ethics that persuaded Katie Alcott to set up a bottled water company that would use its profits to bring clean water to villages in the developing world. It began with first-hand experience of the horrors of unclean water. Katie, then eighteen, was staying in a village in Kashmir, teaching in a community school. One day she was invited to lunch by the parents of one of her pupils. She forgot to take a bottle of water, but the parents insisted that she drink their water. 'It's fine, it's clean,' they said. 'We drink it all the time.'

That afternoon when she returned to her lodgings, she was already feeling unwell. By the evening, she was lying on the bed, vomiting and suffering from diarrhoea. On her return to

England, she was subjected to many tests by different doctors. Their best diagnosis was that she had caught some kind of amoebic dysentery. 'It returned once a month for about a week for a couple of years,' she says. 'It was like a period, only worse.' It will probably never leave her system.

Once she had recovered she continued travelling, to Africa, South America and to Asia. Everywhere she noticed that water was a constant problem. When she wasn't travelling, she was studying Fine Arts at Bristol University. After university she had a spell as a photojournalist in South America, then returned home, penniless, to live with her parents. She took a job for a small local consultancy firm doing 'social network analysis'. It wasn't what she wanted to do. She confided to her then boss that she wanted to work in the developing world. He suggested that she should do something using her experience in business, but be based in England. His interest wasn't just professional; they are now married. But not before Katie had gone off to Mali for a month.

'It was while I was in Mali that I had the idea of setting up a brand of bottled water, the profits of which could be used to finance projects in the developing world,' she says.

In September 2004 she assembled a core team of five people, all volunteers. In April 2005 the first bottles of Frank Water started appearing in shops and bars in the west of England. Why 'Frank'?

'We went through hundreds of different names,' she says. 'Good Water. Angelic, loads of others. They were all too soft. We decided we wanted a hard-hitting brand that would create awareness as well as supplying a solution.'

The water in the bottles comes from a family-run business that used to be a dairy farm. There is a spring in the grounds and now water bottling has become its main activity. What about the taste? Katie says that it's good-tasting water, but at less than seven degrees, the temperature most people like to drink it, all water tastes the same because the tongue's taste buds are chilled. It is a bit like drinking chilled white wine. It can be hard to detect the taste, which is just as well because most white wine would be undrinkable at room temperature. Her view was upheld in a tasting carried out by *Decanter* magazine at the end of 2007. A group of sommeliers and wine critics solemnly sipped twenty-two different bottled waters, a glass of Thames tap, and a sample from the dispenser at the magazine's offices. The most expensive was a New Zealand water, 420 Volcanic, which you can buy at Gordon Ramsay's restaurant in Claridge's for £50 a litre – a full glass will set you back £12.50. It was not very popular with the tasters; one described it as having 'little nose, slightly disjointed texture and a touch rough. Possibly tap water?' Indeed not. The real tap water, supplied at a cost of less than a penny a litre to every Londoner, came third in the tasting, with critics calling it 'clear, with a pure appearance and similarly pure nose. Clean taste, and soft texture. Attractive.'

Katie is aware that bottled water is not the most ecologically sound business – Greens would rather that you drank tap water – but the bottled water market in the United Kingdom is worth £2 billion a year and growing.

'What's the point of trying to stop people from doing something they want to do?' she says. 'Our water is mainly for people on the move. We also wanted to ensure that there was a real commitment to giving away the profits,' she says. 'We did not want this to be tokenism, some kind of greenwash as the supermarkets do.'

Frank Water is committed to supplying 200 litres of purified water in a developing country for every one litre of water it sells in England. In practice this means giving away at least ten pence for every litre sold. Frank Water is priced as a premium product, sold for the same amount as Evian water. You can pick up a 750 ml bottle for around eighty pence; or closer to four quid if you are in Bordeaux Quay, a smart restaurant in Bristol known for its support of local suppliers and recycling just about everything.

'I'd just like to encourage other companies such as Danone and Nestlé to do more,' says Katie. 'If they only gave a penny a bottle, it would be something.'

To see how the money is spent you have to travel to Uttar Pradesh. Here just £7,000 – and they try to encourage the locals to contribute to the cost so there is a collective sense of ownership rather just another aid handout – can provide a purification plant with sand filters, carbon filters and UVC filters, guaranteed to take out 99.999 per cent of impurities and bacteria. According to Ashok Gadgil, Frank Water's local partner in India, it is this degree of purity that is crucial, for it ensures the elimination of cryptosporidium that causes diarrhoea in children.

'At the moment we are just working in India,' says Katie. 'But we have plans to start a project in Ghana.'

It was another of those evenings that start early and don't get going until late. The Irish writer was happy to be in Paris, away from the jealousy and hypocrisy and constraints of Dublin. There was food in the restaurants, pretty women in the bars, the hotels were cheap if not particularly salubrious, and there was much drink to be had. Well beyond midnight, there was a plan afoot to go to another bar. Where were the other people who had been with him earlier? he wondered. The girl – what was her name? – proposed a bottle of Vichy water. Then they could go dancing. 'Nonsense,' he said. 'If God had meant us to drink water, he wouldn't have put salt in most of it.'

6

Poetry In Motion

COUNTESS: Should I throw myself in the river? Which is colder,
the water or her heart?

Lulu, Alban Berg

EVER SINCE EARLY MAN sat in his cave and heard the first drop of water, he has been trying to depict it – the sound, the sight of a large body of water, how it moves in the wind, how it looks when the sun shines on it and where it comes from. This summer, sitting on a rock on the eastern tip of Ile de Porquerolles, one of the Golden Isles just off the southern coast of France, I looked at the sea and the sun's reflection in it. At times it looked like somebody had emptied a bucket of diamonds over the surface; at others, as if the water were full of paparazzi, whose camera bulbs would flash every so often like a hundred stars. Approximately one thousand and three hundred years earlier, Tu Fu, possibly China's best poet, who lived during the Tang dynasty, sat beside the Yangtse River one night and watched the stars playing on the water in a similar fashion. His short poem, 'Stars and Moon on the Yangtse', contains these lines:

> The Yangtse's shallows limpid since just now.
> Reflections, pearls from a snapped string:
> High in the sky one mirror rises.

I love that image of pearls scattered over the still waves: there is an air of glamour, even decadence, as if the evening has ended in violent dancing or love-making.

Poets love water, particularly its slipperiness, its elusiveness, and its transitory nature. They remember Heraclitus, the Presocratic philosopher, who said: 'You can never bathe in the same river twice.' For T. S. Eliot, the River Thames in his poem *The Waste Land* is the narrative link between City workers crossing London Bridge, Mr Eugenides, Elizabeth and Leicester, and a seduction in a narrow canoe near Richmond. There is another leitmotif that runs through the poem, which is a lack of water. There are cicadas, but no water; a hermit-thrush who sings like water, but there is no water. And the prophecy: 'Fear death by water.'

Homer was the Western world's first major poet. Being Greek, water was important to him. In the *Odyssey* he describes two fountains, one for the populace, the other for the king:

> Two plenteous Fountains the whole Prospect crown'd
> This through the Garden leads its Streams around,
> Visits each Plant, and waters all the Ground:
> Whilst that in Pipes beneath the Palace flows,
> And thence a current on the town bestows:
> To various use the various Streams they bring;
> The People one, and one Supplies the King.

The presence of water immediately alerts us to the fact that this is a fine place. These fountains have a good supply and water the flowers and the people. And one of the streams supplies the king. It is like a benediction. People used to living in a dry land would immediately recognise that this is a place truly blessed.

Pindar's 'Olympion I', written to celebrate Hieron of Syracuse's victory in a horse race, begins: 'Water is best'.

Ovid, the Roman writer who was exiled to the Black Sea coast for an unknown crime, dwelt on one of the more puzzling aspects of water in his *Ars Amatoria*:

> What is softer than water,
> What harder than stone? Yet the soft
> Water-drip hollows hard rock.

Was he thinking of the hard-hearted emperor who refused to allow him to return to his beloved Rome?

One of the best-loved lyrics in Latin is Horace's 'Fons Bandusiae'. This ode inspired not just Joyce but generations of poets before him, including William Wordsworth, Hartley Coleridge (Samuel's son) and William Gladstone. As everybody seems to have translated this poem, here is my version:

> O Bandusian Spring, glittering like glass
> Worthy of sweet wine and flowers
> Tomorrow you will receive a young goat
> Whose swelling horns predict both
> Love and War
> In vain: for your cold waters
> Will run red with the blood
> Of the favourite son of the herd.
>
> The raging heat of the dog days
> Cannot reach you, your fresh waters
> Refresh the weary ploughing oxen
> And cool the wandering herds.

> You will become a famous fountain
> When I sing of the water,
> Murmuring, through rocks
> Under a shaded oak tree.

It is worth nothing that Horace describes the water from the spring as being like 'glass'. Clear glass wasn't produced in Rome until the first century AD, some years after Horace's death in 8 BC, so he is implying that the water is tinted either blue or green, but brighter. Little is known about the Bandusian Spring itself, or why Horace wrote about it – although this has not stopped the speculation. The poem may have been written to coincide with the festival of springs known as the Fontanalia, which took place on 13 October. The spring he describes could be on Horace's farm in the Sabine Hills, whose water he describes in his epistles as being good for 'headaches and the stomach'. Horace holds the spring in such veneration that he is willing to sacrifice a young goat to it, and allow the clear waters to run red with blood.

At the beginning of the 1900s Norman Douglas, the travel writer, set out to locate the famous spring. In *Old Calabria* he journeys to Venosa, but instead of one spring, he finds two. Both are flowing copiously. But neither fits the description; perhaps the fountain has moved since Horace's day? There might have been earthquakes or landslides. Instead of oxen cooling themselves in its waters, there are laundry women squabbling. He concludes that the way to see the fountain is to close an eye and use one's imagination. 'The ever alert, the conscientiously wakeful – how many fine things they fail to see! Horace knew the wisdom of being genially unwise; of closing betimes an eye, or an ear; or both. *Desipere in loco . . .*'

If the Greeks and Romans celebrated water in poetry because of its scarcity, the Chinese and Japanese wrote about it because it was so plentiful. The master of haiku poetry was Basho. He was born in 1644 and died in 1694. Haiku, the three-sentence, seventeen-syllable poems, can be said to have begun and ended with Basho, although there were other notable proponents, including Issa and Buson. They are curious things, at best almost dreamlike, celebrating the transitory, the ephemeral, the ambiguity of life. There is much of the natural world: trees, clouds, the sky, moonlight, wind all feature heavily. As you would expect, there are a number on water. Here is one by Chiyo:

> Since morning glories
> hold my well-bucket hostage,
> I beg for water

Morning glories are funnel-shaped flowers that unfurl and come to life in the morning, hence the name – and the slang meaning. They are known as *asagao* in Japanese and were very popular in Japan as ornaments. The sentiment of the poem implies that the speaker prefers ornament to anything else, even water. He could dig up the flowers, and drink the water, but he is too much of a dandy to do so. And this from Basho:

> At the ancient pond
> a frog plunges into
> the sound of water

This image is timeless, but also strange. It is not the water that makes the noise, but the movement of the frog plunging into it. By transferring the epithet, the haiku shows the link between life and water, between the frog and the pond.

The importance of water and life is celebrated in Rudyard

Kipling's poem 'Gunga Din'. It tells the story of a regiment's *bhisti* or water carrier. It begins with the memorable lines:

> You may talk o' gin and beer
> When you're quartered safe out 'ere,
> An' you're sent to penny-fights an' Aldershot it;
> But when it comes to slaughter
> You will do your work on water,
> An' you'll lick the bloomin' boots of 'im that's got it.

The poem's narrator, a soldier in India, spends most of his time berating Gunga Din, although he describes him as 'the finest man I knew'. Like Velazquez's water seller, he is poorly dressed in rags and his only field equipment is a goatskin. His job is to go round offering refreshment to the troops, dodging the bullets. Even though he is part of the 'blackfaced crew', his courage under fire leads to him being described as 'white, clear white, inside'. One night the soldier is hit by a bullet. Mad with thirst, he is spotted by Gunga Din, who comes and gives him some water:

> 'E lifted up my 'ead,
> An' he plugged me where I bled,
> An' 'e guv me 'arf-a-pint o' water-green:
> It was crawlin' and it stunk,
> But of all the drinks I've drunk,
> I'm gratefullest to one from Gunga Din.

Gunga Din carries the injured soldier to safety, but is shot in the process. '"I 'ope you liked your drink," sez Gunga Din', then dies. Kipling has in recent years been denounced as a racist, and his description of Gunga Din as 'blackfaced' but 'white inside' is distasteful. But the overriding sentiment of this poem is one of respect and appreciation for the man who saved his life:

> You Lazarushian-leather Gunga Din!
> Tho' I've belted you an' flayed you,
> By the livin' Gawd that made you,
> You're a better man than I am, Gunga Din!

Lazarushian leather seems to be an invention of Kipling's, referring to Gunga Din's leathery skin, the goatskin and also to Lazarus, the beggar in the Bible who goes to heaven, while the rich man who denied him a sip of water is sent to hell. Water carriers also appear in song. Huddie Ledbetter, nicknamed Leadbelly, was an American blues singer. He spent a number of years in Harrison County Prison. One of his most famous songs is a call for water:

> Bring me little water, Silvy,
> Bring me little water, now,
> Bring me little water, Silvy,
> Every little once in a while.

The song tells the story of a husband and wife who are harvesting in the fields. The husband is thirsty and keeps calling his wife to bring him water. She answers:

> Don't you see me coming
> Don't you see me now
> Don't you see me coming
> Every little once in awhile.

He says, 'I can't see you, the corn's too tall.'

The song has been covered by many singers, including Woody Guthrie and Pete Seeger, but for me it is Leadbelly's voice that expresses the anger of the oppressed, the thirst of a worker that cannot be slaked.

Ted Hughes captured the relentless nature of water in his

poem 'How Water Began to Play': 'Water wanted to live / It went to the sun it came weeping back / Water wanted to live / It went to the trees they burned it came weeping back / They rotted it came weeping back / Water wanted to live /'.

The poet describes water visiting flowers and returning; going to the womb; going through a stone door, searching through time and space but 'It came weeping back it wanted to die / Till it had no weeping left / It lay at the bottom of things / Utterly worn out / utterly clear'.

It is a sad, bleak poem, portraying water as a Flying Dutchman figure, condemned to circulate forever, eternally rejected.

I have always found Hughes rather gloomy. And I think he is wrong. Water is not 'utterly worn out' but continually refreshed, as if it has discovered the elixir of eternal youth. I prefer this anonymous quote from the British Museum:

> Here is a glass of water from my well,
> It tastes of rock and moss and earth and rain,
> It is the best I have, my only spell,
> And it is cold, and better than champagne.

Or the ending of Hilaire Belloc's poem 'Tarentella':

> No sound:
> But the boom
> Of the far Waterfall like Doom.

But not all poets thought of water as lovely and lyrical. For the anonymous author of 'Clementine', the story of a gold-miner's daughter, water is something terrible, that takes his love away from him:

Light she was and like a fairy, and her shoes were number nine,
Herring boxes without topses, sandals were for Clementine.

Drove her ducklings to the water, every morning just at nine,
Hit her foot against a splinter, fell into the foaming brine.

Ruby lips above the water, blowing bubbles soft and fine,
Alas for me! I was no swimmer, so I lost my Clementine.

Nor would it appear that Clementine was much of a swimmer, which is a surprise given her size nine feet. But the last word on poets and water should probably go to Horace. He wrote in his *Epistles*: '*Prisco si credis, Maecenas docte, Cratino, nulla placere diu nec vivere carmina possunt quae scribuntur aquae potoribus.*' Loosely translated, this reads: 'If you believe Cratinus from days of old, Maecenas, as you must know, no verse can give pleasure for long, nor last, that is written by drinkers of water.'

While poets throughout the ages have been captivated by water's slippery charms, some prose writers treated water merely as an agricultural commodity. Coronarius' *Agriculture* is full of advice on how to find it and how to move it so as to best water crops. There is an extract in Stephen Switzer's *A Universal System of Water and Waterworks, Philosophical and Practical, in Four Books, faithfully digested from the most-approv'd writers on this subject*, published in London in 1734, in which Coronarius suggests the following means to find water: 'Wherever you are desirous of finding it with certainty, there must a ditch be made of three foot deep, and taking a leaden vessel, or earthen pot, made in the form of a semicircle, at sunset rub it over with oil; then prepare a piece of wool, half a foot long, and washing it very carefully, and drying it afterwards, you are to bind on a small stone in the middle of it, and fix it in the middle of the pot or vessel with wax: then turn the mouth of the pot downwards in the trench you have thus caus'd to be dug, taking a particular care, that after it is so turn'd the wool may hang down in the middle of the vessel; which done, you must cover your vessel with earth a foot thick, and keeping it so all night. Uncover it in the morning, before the sun rises; and if there be water in the place, you will perceive the pot to have small dewy drops hanging on its bottom, and the wool to be wet.

'If the wool be very full of water, and the drops hanging on the pot be very large, you may conclude you are not very far from the spring; but if it be only moist, though there be a spring in that place, yet it lies very low, and not to be come at without a great expense, and much difficulty; but if none of these symptoms appear, you must make the experiments in another place . . .'

It is funny to think of readers in the eighteenth century, book in one hand and earthen pot in the other, rubbing it with oil and preparing bundles of wool, all in the hope of finding a spring. In the city there were other ways to procure water. Before there was bottled water in every Starbucks, you could buy it from water sellers. Norman Lewis in his book *Naples '44* describes the scene in Sicily:

Last Sunday was so hot that the first of the water sellers even came on the scene. These picturesque figures and the equipment they carry are hardly changed from representations of them in the frescoes of Pompeii. The water seller sells acqua ferrata, which is powerfully flavoured with iron and drawn from a single hole in the ground somewhere in Santa Lucia. The water is contained as illustrated at Pompeii in rounded earthenware vessels (*mmommere*) shaped like a woman's breast – an excellent example of marketing ingenuity on the part of the ancients – and *a cup of it costs three or four times the equivalent price of wine*. The water seller also sells lemon squash made on the spot with fresh lemons and a great display of dexterity with his enormous iron lemon-squeezers. A teaspoonful of bicarbonate soda goes into the glass, causing a violent eruption of spume. Many of our soldiers – who regard all things foreign with suspicion – have found this an excellent remedy for hangovers.

Writers have often been drawn to water. Flaubert's study at Croisset faced the River Seine; when writing became difficult he would put down his pen and watch the river like television. Water for him was invariably linked to sensuality. He described swimming in the river like having 'a thousand liquid nipples travelling over the body'; on his trip to Egypt he explored the baths in Cairo and the River Nile with pleasure. In Madame Bovary the river was a place for seduction. Emma and Léon enjoy three carefree days at the Hotel de Boulogne, 'a real honeymoon' if there is such a thing with a lover. The lovers go boating, land on an island where they picnic and make love. It is an idyllic scene; they enjoy the sound of the water rushing past as if hearing it for the first time.

If water can convey a mood, it can also suggest a sensation. Henry James in *Portrait of a Lady* has this lovely image: 'To cease utterly, to give it all up and not know anything more – this idea was as sweet as the vision of a cool bath in a marble tank, in a darkened chamber, in a hot land.' Nowhere more refreshing can be imagined. John Cheever's short story 'Artemis, The Honest Well Digger', opens with the attraction of water: 'Artemis loved the healing sound of rain – the sound of all running water – brooks, gutters, spouts, falls, and taps . . . Men sought water as water sought its level. The pursuit of water accounted for epochal migrations. Man was largely water. Water was man. Water was love. Water was water.'

Rivers can be symbolic, as in William Faulkner's *As I Lay*

Dying, where the family of Addie Bundren have to work together to get her body across the river; or act almost as a character, as the Mississippi does in Mark Twain's *Huckleberry Finn*; or just be a convenient prop. In A.A. Milne's *The House at Pooh Corner* how could Winnie-the-Pooh and Christopher Robin have played poohsticks without the river?

There are a thousand other examples of writing on water, but for me there is one example from James Joyce's *Ulysses* that is the most outstanding. It is just one sentence, but positively Proustian in length. He mixes the mundane with the magical, which seems to me the very essence of water. This sentence occurs late in the book, the penultimate episode, sometimes referred to as Ithaca, when Leopold Bloom returns home after his evening's drinking session with Stephen Dedalus. Dedalus has left him: he is a hydrophobe – his last bath was in October of the previous year – he even dislikes 'the aqueous substances of glass and crystal' and distrusts 'aquacities of thought and language'. Bloom is a lover of water. As he fills the kettle, he considers the city's water supply in Roundwood reservoir in County Wicklow and the surveyors who created the infrastructure. Then he asks himself: what do I, waterlover, drawer of water, watercarrier, admire about water?

Its universality: its democratic equality and constancy to its nature in seeking its own level: its vastness in the ocean of Mercator's projection: its unplumbed profundity in the Sundam trench of the Pacific exceeding 8000 fathoms: the restlessness of its waves and surface particles visiting in turn all points of its seaboard: the independence of its units: the variability of states of sea: its hydrostatic quiescence in calm: its hydro-kinetic turgidity in neap and spring tides: its subsidence after devastation: its sterility in the circumpolar icecaps, arctic and antarctic: its climatic and commercial significance:

Joyce, the almost blind, bookish writer, forced to give language lessons to supplement his income, is alive to water's climatic and commercial importance, seemingly years before anybody else twigged. But there is more. Like a mountain stream, the sentence is gathering pace:

> its preponderance of 3 to 1 over the dry land of the globe: its indisputable hegemony extending in square leagues over all the region below the subequatorial tropic of Capricorn: the multisecular stability of its primeval basin: its luteofulvous bed: its capacity to dissolve and hold in solution all soluble substances including millions of tons of the most precious metals: its slow erosions of peninsulas and islands, its persistent formation of homothetic islands, peninsulas and downward-tending promontories: its alluvial deposits: its weight and volume and density: its imperturbability in lagoons and highland tarns: its gradation of colours in the torrid and temperate and frigid zones: its vehicular ramifications in continental lakecontained streams and confluent oceanflowing rivers with their tributaries and transoceanic currents, gulfstream, north and south equatorial courses: its violence in seaquakes, waterspouts, Artesian wells, eruptions, torrents, eddies, freshets, spates, groundswells, watersheds, waterpartings, geysers, cataracts, whirlpools, maelstroms, inundations, deluges, cloudbursts: its vast circumterrestrial ahorizontal curve: its secrecy in springs and latent humidity, revealed by rhabdomantic or hygrometric instruments and exemplified by the well by the hole in the wall at Ashtown gate, saturation of air, distillation of dew: the simplicity of its composition, two constituent parts of hydrogen with one constituent part of oxygen: its healing virtues: its buoyancy in the waters of the Dead Sea: its persevering penetrativeness in runnels, gullies, inadequate dams, leaks on shipboard:

We should pause and note the amusing alliterative 'persevering penetrativeness'; a runnel is a small stream or rivulet, but there is no time, for the sentence is flowing on, it is as if this is Heraclitus's river and we can't read it twice:

> its properties for cleansing, quenching thirst and fire, nourishing vegetation: its infallibility as paradigm and paragon: its metamorphoses as vapour, mist, cloud, rain, sleet, snow, hail: its strength in rigid hydrants: its variety of forms in loughs and bays and gulfs and bights and guts and lagoons and atolls and archipelagos and sounds and fjords and minches and tidal estuaries and arms of sea: its solidity in glaciers, icebergs, iccfloes: its docility in working hydraulic millwheels, turbines, dynamos, electric power stations, bleachworks, tanneries, scutchmills: its utility in canals, rivers, if navigable, floating and graving docks: its potentiality derivable from harnessed tides or watercourses falling from level to level: its submarine fauna and flora (anacoustic, photophobe), numerically, if not literally, the inhabitants of the globe: its ubiquity as constituting 90% of the human body: the noxiousness of its effluvia in lacustrine marshes, pestilential fens, faded flowerwater, stagnant pools in the waning moon.

What a sentence! At its end it meanders like a river coming to a delta, finishing in marshes and stagnant pools. This is classic Joyce, combining everyday objects and observation with elaborate detail and using long, unfamiliar words such as scutchmills, anacoustic, minches and lacustrine. Lacustrine is one of my favourite water-related words, even if the meaning is prosaic: it means lake-like, or anything pertaining to lakes. If there can be any criticism, it could be to point out that scientists calculate the amount of water in the human as more like 70 per cent, depending on body size, and rarely 90 per cent. Otherwise it is perfect: there are whole books written on water that are less informative and certainly less interesting than this one sentence.

My three favourite books that deal with water, particularly our personal and intimate relationship with it, are John Cheever's 'The Swimmer', Charles Sprawson's *Haunts of the Black Masseur* and Roger Deakin's *Waterlog*. They are all from the twentieth century; perhaps we needed to view water with a sense of loss before we could fully celebrate and appreciate it. Cheever's is just a short story, but he says as much in a few pages as others manage in 200. Cheever's hero is Neddy Merrill, a sporty, slender man who decides one morning that he will swim the eight miles to his home in Bullet Park, criss-crossing the suburbs, splashing through the pools of his friends and neighbours. You know you are in the suburbs from the first sentence: 'It was one of those midsummer Sundays when everyone sits around saying, "I *drank* too much last night."' It's an affluent place where there is little to do but seduce your neighbour's wife and drink heavily. Ned dives into the first pool – he has an 'inexplicable contempt' for men who get into a pool any other way – swims a choppy crawl across it, gets out, hitches up his trunks and sets off on his journey. He would prefer to swim without trunks, but that is not feasible. He decides to name the journey after his wife, and call it the Lucinda River. 'The day was lovely, and that he lived in a world so gener-ously supplied with water seemed like a clemency, a beneficence.'

He slips into the next pool, and meets the wife, who offers him a drink. He manages to get away as two carloads of friends show up, and sneaks into a couple more pools without being noticed. At the Bunkers' there is a party. He is greeted by the hostess, says hello to a number of friends and acquaintances, and accepts a gin and tonic from the barman. At the Levys' the house is empty, but he swims the pool and helps himself to a drink. He shelters from a storm. It is not just the weather, but the mood of the day is changing. The Lindleys have not cut their grass, the Welchers have drained their pool. His next stretch of water is the public pool at the edge of the village of Lancaster. He doesn't like the look of the water; it smells of chlorine. 'Neddy remembered the sapphire water at the Bunkers' with longing and thought that he might contaminate himself – damage his own prosperousness and charm – by swimming in this murk, but he reminded himself that he was an explorer, a pilgrim, and that this was merely a stagnant bend in the Lucinda River.' He swims across it without pleasure, and is chased out by the lifeguards because he isn't wearing an identification tag.

He swims in a couple of other pools and encounters neighbours, even a former girlfriend. It becomes clear that something is not quite right with Ned, that his life is falling apart. The swimming is a metaphor for his dislocation, for his desire to escape. Everyone else uses swimming pools as either a status symbol or the setting for a party. Only Ned swims. He no longer has the energy to dive into the final pool, but walks down the steps. Instead of a crawl, he performs a 'hobbled sidestroke'. When he gets out, he struggles up the drive of his own house. There is nobody there. Where is the maid, he wonders? Where are the children? The place is boarded up. He looks in the windows. The place is empty.

This is the American dream turned sour, with the swimming pool a metaphor for success. If you are affluent your pool is sapphire blue; if you are poor you are condemned to the chlorine-choking public pool. Poor Neddy, so confident, fit and athletic at the beginning of the day, is now a quivering man, rebuffed by a barman and a former mistress, who now cries for the first time since he can remember.

Haunts of the Black Masseur: The Swimmer as Hero by Charles Sprawson is a cult book: when I meet someone who knows it I find it hard not to like them. I don't recall why I bought the book in the first place; I stumbled across it in a bookshop in Lewes, the way you find a flower in a forest. I was intrigued by the subtitle *The Swimmer as Hero* and also by its look and feel. My copy is a first edition published in 1992 – I'm not sure if there was a second edition, although there was a paperback – and I bought it the year it came out. The cover is one of Leni Riefenstahl's divers, arms out wide, back arched, legs together – her politics were distasteful but she took good photographs – while the back cover is a moody shot of a swimming baths, complete with mosaic tiles and Roman columns. It is one of the few books that I don't lend even my best friends; the library staff at the International Swimming Hall of Fame in Fort Lauderdale Florida say that it is the only book that has ever been stolen, and I don't want to risk losing my copy.

In the first few pages Sprawson introduces us to a glimpse of an exotic past. The opening line of the book is romantic and intriguing: 'I learnt to swim in India, in a pool donated to the school by the Edwardian cricketer Ranjitsinhji.' We learn enough about Sprawson to want to hear more, but not so much that he bores us. He is the antithesis of the writer who wracks his brains to persuade a publisher to give him a hefty advance, then goes off on a harebrained scheme, such as lugging a fridge around a country or crossing the Antarctic with a camel, just so he can write a book about his adventures. He is not a professional writer, but deals in eighteenth- and nineteenth-century Continental paintings. He is reluctant to write another book, although various publishers have spent hours trying to persuade him to change his mind.

Sprawson's subject is swimming, a pursuit that I had always enjoyed but never really appreciated, both the curious psychology of the swimmer and his 'feel for water'. He charts the beginning of the cult of swimming by the Greeks and Romans: 'Swimming was so popular that the inability of the Emperor Caligula to swim caused comment,' he writes. With the coming of Christianity, swimming was seen as the pursuit of the devil and discouraged. It took the Romantics, Byron, Shelley and Pushkin to break the taboo. Byron was a famous swimmer, specialising in long swims partly because his club foot was not adept at walking; Algernon Charles Swinburne enjoyed being beaten by pebbles churned up by a rough sea. By the nineteenth century young Englishmen, mainly public school boys, took to swimming in wild places, communing with nature. Then came the Americans, and the great Australians. The Japanese saw swimming as an expression of nationalism and samurai pride. Zelda Fitzgerald, Scott's wife, was unable to keep out of water, jumping naked into a fountain in Union Square and, later, fully clothed into the Pulitzer fountain in New York on their honeymoon.

Thomas Eakins' Swimming has more than a hint of homo-eroticism. Eakins is in the water bottom right, gazing at the boys.

Among the history and the literature, Sprawson adds pithy accounts of his own adventures. He meets a boyhood hero, the Australian Olympic swimmer Marcus Rose, and challenges him to a race (Rose wins comfortably); swims the Hellespont, the channel near Istanbul that separates Europe from Asia then, on discovering that Byron found his crossing of the Tagus in Portugal more hazardous, resolves to follow in his wake. The water is dirty; where once there were orange groves and vineyards, there are now oil refineries. Sprawson gets halfway across and is picked up by a patrol boat and interrogated. Nobody is allowed to cross without a safety boat and a permit. There is a sense that the golden days of swimming are over, but Sprawson does not labour the point. The writing is as elegant and unhurried as the Japanese Crawl. The title pays homage to Tennessee Williams' short story, 'Desire and the Black Masseur', in which a man called Anthony Burns receives a strong massage from an African American. They engage in a sadomasochistic relationship, which finishes when Burns, with his consent, is tortured and eaten by the masseur, and his bones put in a bag and tossed into a lake. Sprawson visited the same swimming baths that Williams frequented – and had a massage from Jackson, the same black masseur who worked on Williams. When I phoned Sprawson to ask him a couple of questions about the book, including whether the title wasn't a bit gloomy, he said that he thought that there is something inherently sinister about water. 'But *Haunts of the Black Masseur* is also a metaphor for the soothing effect of water,' he said. I was delighted to learn that he went to Tonbridge School in Kent. Like me, he loathed it. In this magnificent biography of swimming – laced with references to art, architecture, film, literature, musicals and Olympic history – the story is told so well that you cannot imagine that anyone else could add anything to the subject.

Roger Deakin's *Waterlog: A Swimmer's Journey Through Britain* picks up where Sprawson ends. Deakin is not as susceptible to the erotic nature of nude swimming in dark waters – he orders a wetsuit so that he can venture into chilly water, which to my mind is a bit of a cheat, particularly when you consider that people swim in the Serpentine on Christmas Day – but he is alive to the freedom of swimming, and wants to encourage other people to participate in this activity. *Waterlog* is a deliberately subversive attempt to swim in parts of England that are considered by the authorities to be out of bounds. If there is to be a right to roam, should there not also be a right to float? Deakin, like a throwback to the schoolboys of the nineteenth century, is a wild swimmer. Not for him suburban swimming pools; although he says that he was much influenced by John Cheever's 'The Swimmer', he wants to experience something elemental: 'When you swim, you feel your body for what it mostly is – water – and it begins to move with the water around it. No wonder we feel such sympathy for beached whales; we are beached at birth ourselves. To swim is to experience how it was before you were born.'

Deakin encounters surly keepers on the River Test, dragonflies in his moat in Suffolk, and penguins at London Zoo. He is one of the great nature writers of our times, with great powers of observation, knowledge and description. How lovely it would be to go for a swim with him. Alas, he died suddenly in 2006.

These three great swimmers, Neddy Merrill, Charles Sprawson and Roger Deakin, see water as a metaphor for life, although at times you feel that their relationship with it is even stronger than that. It is life. Without water, you feel they would die.

*   *   *

While some sat in caves and thought about how to describe the sound of water, others thought about how to depict it. As well as bison and hunting scenes, water and the act of collecting it feature frequently in cave paintings. It was also a fundamental ingredient of the art itself, being used to dilute and mix the clays that were then daubed on the walls. It remains an intrinsic component in art today – nowhere more so than in watercolours, where the type of water can affect the look or texture of a painting. A hard water, for example, will give a cloudy effect with certain colours, especially blues. Water rich in iron will affect certain pigments; one high in salts can give a granular texture to the painting. 'Watercolour is really just playing with coloured water,' says Simon Fletcher, an artist who works mainly in this medium. 'It's like the puddles you see in a car park, when the oil mixes with the water to create different colours.'

Along with Simon Fletcher, who is widely regarded as the most gifted living English watercolour painter, a good twentieth-century exponent of the art is the Austrian Gottfried Salzmann. He has three main subjects: New York, trees and water. In his water pictures he plays with the way that paint – and water – dries at different times on the same piece of paper. In other words, he is using water to depict water. In a painting such as *Der Himmel aus Wassers – Sky out of Water* – Salzmann shows an expanse of water with just a tiny detail of the bank at the top of the picture. The colours are autumnal, yellows and gold, probably the reflection of the leaves of the trees, but here and there is a glimpse of the sky. The artist has either re-wet and reworked the page after the first application, or added a line of bleach that traces a pattern across the paper. The final effect is something that shimmers with light and movement. Another painting, *Wasser durch Wasser – Water through Water* – is more subtle. Again, at the top of the painting is a thin strip of something recognisable that stops the work being entirely abstract, in this case hulls of a couple of fishing boats as they leave the harbour at Dieppe. Below this, through the bulk of the painting, the colours turn slowly from a cold blue to a warmer green, but applied in such a way you might think they had been sprayed on.

Joseph Mallord William Turner, though, remains the master of watercolour painting. How he worked is shrouded in secrecy. He did not like his techniques being observed. However, a few people managed to penetrate his studio and some anecdotes survive to suggest his methods. It is known, for example, that he would have handles on his painting boards, which he would grip as he dunked the paintings in a bath of water. Then he would hang the paper up to dry – his studio was full of lines of drying paper, rather like a Chinese laundry – then rework the page at a later date. One visitor brought him a painting seeking the master's approval and was rather horrified to receive the curt response: 'Throw it in a bath of water.' The aspiring artist was shocked, even hurt. But what Turner meant was that wetting the page could improve the painting by softening its tones.

Another technique used by watercolourists is to work wet into wet. They start by wetting the paper then use a wet brush covered in paint. How you apply the paint determines how it behaves. Dab the paint and it will flow out, like putting a drop of coloured dye into a glass of water. But if you apply the paint with a firm stroke and make a bold line, you will get a clear edge. Then you can keep adding colour, if necessary drying areas with a sponge.

'It is like painting on the top of a pond,' says Simon Fletcher. 'But you can use water to do everything. It transforms harsh colours into harmonious ones. You can flood a part of the paper to get one kind of effect, or use it to create a barrier round an object and hold it in place. Most people's experience of water-colour is that they stop painting and declare themselves happy with what they have done. Half an hour later, when the page is dry, they go back and discover that most of the colour has disappeared. The trick, if there is such a thing, is to be more bold in the first place.'

There is one technique used for painting water whose audacity can make amateur painters gasp. First you fill in your landmarks, such as a headland or pier. Then you pick your horizon, and colour that in with a blue line. Then you put down tonal degradations, softening and lightening the blue as it approaches the shallows. Finally, using a flat (a large brush with a flat edge), and not dipping it either in water or paint, you make three or four quick strokes across the paper. The action of the dry brush on the rough paper gives you the sparkle that you notice on the crests of waves.

Perhaps the most unusual approach of all was that of Edward Burra, the English watercolourist who died in 1976. His tech-nique was to paint with a glass of water for his brush and a glass of Booth's gin beside it for him in case he got thirsty. Sometimes he would mix the glasses up, but it didn't seem to affect the quality of his work, although it does perhaps explain some of its more louche aspects.

Of course, using water is not the only way to paint it. John Constable, who used mainly oils, declared that it wasn't just the sight of water that inspired him, but its sound. In a letter to John Fisher, an archdeacon who was his first major collector, he wrote: 'The sound of water escaping from mill-dams etc., willows, old rotten planks, slimy posts and brickwork, I love such things . . . As long as I do paint, I shall never cease to paint such places.'

Japanese artists are fascinated by water – partly because they are surrounded by it – but their preferred medium in which to depict it was more often than not in woodcuts. A woodcut does not allow the blurry, vague shapes and arabesques that water-colourists rely on. A high degree of design is necessary, so the water is often shown in a very stylised manner, using rows of waves like seagulls in the sky or swirls to depict a river's flow. Utagawa Hiroshige, the great nineteenth-century artist, part-time fireman and samurai, in his *A View of the Whirlpool in Awa*, creates a sense of movement from a series of whorls and white waves. The Japanese were influenced by the Chinese, as the technique of making woodcuts was brought from the mainland by Buddhist monks, mainly as a way of making books. Some of the best Chinese paintings of water can be found in the New York Metropolitan Museum's collection of Sung and Yuan paintings. They were painted using ink and watercolour on silk, with ink washes that allow for subtle gradings, which can make the water more complex but also unified. The ink tones range from black to grey, and were all applied at the same time so that they run together to create a wet and almost moving body of water. For example, in Sheng Chu's *Angling in the Autumn River*, the small differences in tone and horizontal brushstrokes make the water move like a tidal current.

Just as the Japanese were influenced by the Chinese, so they in turn influenced a later generation of painters including Vincent Van Gogh and Whistler. Van Gogh did not make many pictures that included water, but he did make copies of Japanese prints, such as Hiroshige's *A Sudden Shower Over Ohashi and Atake*. In Van Gogh's version *The Bridge in The Rain (after Hiroshige)* the water in the background is choppy, almost too visible. In the original, the water is present in the sky as well as the river and the rain, as if the world itself, apart from the bridge and the people hiding under umbrellas, is entirely composed of water.

Hiroshige's rain is relentless; the bridge appears to float on the water

Some paintings don't depict water, but activities associated with it. In one of Velazquez's most celebrated paintings, *The Water Seller of Seville*, which hangs in Apsley House in London, the water seller is a dark, tragic figure, with holes in his brown smock. His face is lined. Standing on sunlit corners selling glasses of water is clearly tough on the skin. His hair is cropped. There are two large green earthenware pots filled with water. The water seller, nicknamed the Corsican of Seville according to seventeenth-century reports, is looking down, having just poured a glass of water for a boy standing next to him. He has sweetened the water with a fig. The boy is young and handsome, with curly dark hair, and looks more like a Renaissance prince or a young saint. In the shadows another man is drinking, yet the water seller seems oblivious to both of them. He is alone in his sorrow, as timeless as water. His poverty is acute, but he can bear it: selling water has not always been the lucrative business now undertaken by Nestlé and Danone.

This water seller represents all the water sellers in history. It is a trade that has largely dried up, although leafing through a book of photographs about a journey along India's Grand Trunk Road by Raghuibir Singh, I was startled to see a photo of a water seller in Delhi, taken some time in the 1980s. Unfortunately Singh has cropped off half the water seller's face, but in the nose and set of the mouth, the grey beard, the hunched shoulders and the bony arms holding out a silver cup of water, you get a powerful sense of the same despair in the job that Velazquez so accurately captured.

Leonardo da Vinci was not interested in water sellers, but water itself. He was obsessed with water. Throughout his life he observed water's behaviour, how clouds work, how rivers move, how powerful and gentle it is. 'Water is the driver of nature,' he wrote. 'It is never at rest until it unites with the sea, where, when undisturbed by the winds, it establishes itself and remains with its surface equidistant from the centre of the world. It readily raises itself by heat in thin vapour through the air. Cold causes it to freeze; stagnation makes it foul. This heat sets it in motion, immobility corrupts it. It is the expansion and humour of all vital bodies. Without it nothing retains its form. By its inflow it unites and augments bodies. It assumes every odour, colour and flavour and of itself has nothing.'

In 1502 Leonardo visited the court of Cesare Borgia, Duke of Romagna. There he met Machiavelli, whom Leonardo much admired. Together they developed a plan to link Florence to the sea, bypassing Pisa. Leonardo designed wonderful cranes, pumps and machines to dig the canal. In August 1504, work got underway. If successful, it would divert the Arno away from Pisa, leaving them without water or access to the Adriatic. But the Pisans got wind of this scheme and attacked the workshops. Equipment was damaged, costs soared. In October of that year work was postponed, then abandoned forever.

Codex Leicester – his notebooks, written in reverse in Italian – was bequeathed in Leonardo's will to his pupil Francesco Melzi, then to Milanese sculptor Guglielmo della Porta, before being acquired by Giuseppe Ghezzi in 1690. Ghezzi sold it in 1717 to Thomas Coke, an English aristocrat who later became the Earl of Leicester, and his family kept it until 1980 when it was bought by Armand Hammer, who renamed it *Codex Hammer*. Bill Gates bought it in 1994, and restored the name *Codex Leicester*.

It begins with a bang. 'I recall how, in the first place, I must show the distance between the Sun and Earth, and find its true measure passing one of the beams through a skylight to a dark place; and also to find the size of the earth by means of a water sphere,' he writes. No lack of ambition there. In an earlier work, known as *Manuscript A*, written around 1490–2, Leonardo had also referred to a desire to write a treatise on water, combining his practical and theoretical ideas. He had studied the motion of water, designed water-moving machines and ways to drain the mosquito swamps around Milan. He designed a water staircase at the farm of the Duke of Milan, which is still in use today.

In the Windsor drawings, the so-called 'Deluge series', Leonardo observes that the movement of water is comparable to that of human hair: 'Observe the motion of the surface of water, how it resembles that of hair, which has two motions, of which one depends on the weight of the hair, the other on the direction of the curls; thus the water forms eddying whirlpools, one part of which is due to the impetus of the principal current and the other to the incidental motion and return flow.' About a third of the *Codex Leicester* is made up of drawings of water – flowing, swirling, even sitting on a plant: 'The centre of a particular sphere of water is that which occurs in the tiniest particles of dew, which are seen in perfect roundness clustering upon the leaves of the plants on which it falls; it is of such lightness that it does not flatten itself upon the spot on which it rests, and it is almost supported by the atmosphere that surrounds it, so that it does not itself exert any pressure or form any foundation.'

He is interested in whether water circulates through the earth; how it moves and climbs to the tops of mountains; whether the seas were once higher than the mountains – as Pliny the Elder believed; siphoning, tides, whether there is more water or earth on the planet; and he is fascinated by rivers. He thought 'the body of the earth, like the bodies of animals, is interwoven with a network of veins which are all joined together and are formed for the nutrition and vivification of the earth and its creatures; and they originate in the depths of the sea, and there after many revolutions they have to return through the rivers formed by the high bursting of these veins.' He speculated on whether or not there is water on the moon (he thought there was), on wave motion, the different speeds of river currents, and a sweet drawing of a drop of water hitting a flat surface and exploding in a crown, reminiscent of Harold Edgerton's famous photograph, taken four and a half centuries later. Leonardo discusses what would happen if the Mediterranean were to rise above its shores – prescient perhaps of the threat of global warming – and analyses geo-metrically what would happen to water volumes if there were a universal flood. He studies what happens to a riverbank and a bridge when they are hit by a wall of water. He discusses a later treatise that he plans to write devoted to water: 'First, you will make a book that deals with the places occupied by the fresh waters; the second, by the salt waters, and the third, on how, due to removal of them, these our parts become lighter and therefore recede more from the centre of the world.'

But like many books planned on water, it remained unwritten. However, his musings on the subject, incomplete as they are, constitute the most thoughtful and ingenious – and well illustrated – record that we have of water. Leonardo's notes are worth a thousand finished manuscripts. They were collected by an Italian count called Francesco Arconati, the work called *Leonardo da Vinci, Del moto e misura dell'acqua*, although it doesn't contain anything from the *Codex Leicester*.

For some artists, inspiration came from the source of water itself, a subject often combined with a female nude, for both women and water are perceived to be the source of life. In 1856 the French neoclassical painter Jean Auguste Dominique Ingres completed the painting of a naked young girl, *La Source* or *The Spring*. A young, nubile girl, with a pleasant body but blank expression, balances a large clay pot on her left shoulder. A thin trickle of water is pouring out. There is no mystery here or ambiguity: the girl is the source of the water. The viewer is invited to admire the girl's classical proportions, the full breasts, the thin waist and flat stomach. Her feet are in water too.

On display at the Musée d'Orsay is the *Valpincon Bather*, named after the first owner of a large nude by Ingres. The woman is sitting on a divan. She has a turban on her head and her back to us, her face obscured. There is a large green curtain framing the left side of the painting, and visible bottom left, water is flowing into a foot basin. Elsewhere in the museum there is another painting, also called *La Source*. Courbet's effort owes more to the *Valpincon Bather* than Ingres' *La Source*. His naked woman also sits with her back to the viewer, face turned away so you can only make out her brown hair; she sits on a mossy rock with one hand holding onto the branch of a tree and the other playing with, almost caressing, the water from a small spring. The scene is dark, sylvan. You can hear the water and sense the coolness. In the background a small waterfall descends by some rocks and the river runs by her feet, covering her ankles. Her enormous bottom dominates the painting. It is more like the rump of a horse, bigger than her back, each buttock a massive maturing cheese. If you can draw your eyes away and look closely at the water falling from the spring, you see it has a light, evanescent quality, more like dust than paint, or rather like a cobweb. Close up, it is as if he has not bothered to paint the water at all. But as you get further away you get a feel of the lightness and mystery of the water, falling through her hands like diamonds. There is no sign of her clothes. Perhaps the artist did not have room to include them. Is the girl the source of the water or the water the source of the girl? The painter does not tell us.

A cursory glance at some of the other paintings in the collection proves how difficult it is to paint water well. The Impressionists were the great painters of water; the technique of using just dabs of paint gave them a freedom to suggest the interaction of light playing with water. In a nearby room, Edouard Manet's *Le Déjeuner sur l'Herbe*: the naked girl looks directly out of the painting, the two men, fully dressed, are discussing something, probably literary theory or art, while the fourth member of the picnic is wading in the water, wearing her petticoat. But the water is grey, drab. It is as dull as the Cherwell in Oxford.

Upstairs there is a Claude Monet called *La Seine à Port-Villez*. It shows the Seine rushing past a pink island. The water is bright, pale blue, with flecks of pink in it. It is an example of how too much exuberance when painting water can be inadvisable. It looks like it has been painted by Barbie.

In the Stockholm Museum of Modern Art, there is yet another version of *La Source*, this time by Picasso, painted in 1921. The painting was stolen in 1993, but subsequently found and returned. It depicts the same subject, a woman and a jug, although Picasso's woman is clothed, with the water jug across her thighs. The model was his new wife, Olga Koklova, who had recently given birth to his son, Paolo. One of her breasts is exposed, she has thick, almost Catalan peasant legs, rather like one of Aristide Maillol's sculptures. Situating the jug between her thighs celebrates water – but also woman and water as the twin sources of life.

Of all the senses, water has an immediate appeal to the ear. The tinkling of a fountain, the splash of a stone into a river or the sound of a diver falling into a swimming pool. There is the drumming of rain on a roof, the screech of windscreen wipers, the tumult of a raging river, the soft but steady sound of snowfall, the crack of ice on a lake. The British Library's Sound Archive lists many thousands of different water-related sounds, from water dripping in subterranean limestone caverns in the Dordogne, to a river plunging over a waterfall, to a gondolier shouting a warning before a *vaporetto* hits a landing stage, to a mountain stream trickling over rocks, to a village pond on a summer's evening, to a tropical lake where frogs croak, to heavy rainfall on leaves and in puddles in Peru, to the Bob Dylan song 'High Water (for Charlie Patton)' on his *Love and Theft* album.

It comes as no surprise that water has often featured in music, from Schubert's *Trout Quintet* to Handel's *Water Music*. The D major movement in 3/2 metre subtitled 'Alla Hornpipe' was used in television commercials for the privatisation of some of the British water companies in the 1980s. In Maurice Ravel's *Jeux d'eau* the melody and rhythm of the piano seek to imitate the sound of running water, and even manage to suggest the way that the light plays on it. Or in John Cage's *Water Walk* in which he uses ice cubes, a pressure cooker, a bath, a vase of flowers, a watering can, a siphon, a grand piano, a mechanical fish, an electric grinder, goose whistles, five radios and a rubber duck to produce the music. But it is in opera where it is most prevalent. The opera director Stephen Medcalf goes as far as saying that water is central to opera: 'Fountains are employed to represent youth and purity. Lakes become emblematic of female sexuality. It is not just the practical value to the plot or the symbolic value of water that inspires the composer, it is above all the sound and the movement of water that they love to depict in music, such as crashing waves, gentle swells, gurgling brooks, gushing fountains. The composer can transport the spectator to any water location far more effectively than the scenic designer.'

Water can play a vital role in the setting, the plotting and even in the psychology of an opera. A popular figure in central and east European mythology is that of the Rusalka, by tradition the spirit of a young woman who has drowned herself in a lake or a waterway, usually after being jilted by her lover or having fallen pregnant by the wrong man. Her revenge is to start a career luring unsuspecting young men to their deaths, a kind of enchantment particularly attractive to composers. Water nymphs appear in Lortzing's *Undine* and Rimsky-Korsakov's *May Night*, but most notably in Dvořák's *Rusalka*. In this version of the legend, which owes something to Hans Christian Andersen's tale *The Little Mermaid*, Rusalka falls in love with the prince who swims in her lake. A witch helps her cast a spell that will restore her to human form, but on one condition. If the prince is unfaithful to her they will be both be damned forever. They marry. But soon afterwards, as princes do, he falls in love with a foreign princess and abandons Rusalka. Some time later, he realises his mistake and returns to the lake and begs Rusalka to give him the kiss of death, which reunites them in eternity.

In *May Night* the hero Levko, a young Cossack, is also seduced by a water nymph. His fate is to be dragged to the bottom of the lake where he accompanies the songs and dancers of the Rusalkii on his bandura, a curious sixty-stringed Ukrainian instrument, sounding somewhere between a lute and a harp. For him this night is a rite of passage, which marks his journey from a young tearaway to a man ready for marriage. 'At the heart of this genre of opera lie the themes of sexual repression and awakening,' says Medcalf. 'While composers enjoy playing with watery colours, shapes and textures in the orchestra, directors often cannot resist exploring the Freudian implications.'

Women are inherently sensual when either immersed in or near water – and this is more than just the wet T-shirt effect, or the fact they are wearing few clothes or figure-hugging bikinis. In film we think of Ursula Andress in her bikini in *Dr No*, or Halle Berry reprising the scene years later. For those who prefer the male body, Daniel Craig, the latest James Bond, made an appearance in *Casino Royale* in a pair of swimming trunks that excited some viewers. And Wagner's *Das Rheingold* features some of the sexiest sirens in theatre. Three Rhinemaidens guard the Rhinegold; they cavort in the waves, accompanied by the musical motif of the Rhine, and exchange playful cries like sea lions. When Alberich the dwarf arrives to steal the gold, he is smitten by their looks and demands to have sex with them. Revolted that such a short, disgusting creature should imagine they would deign to pleasure him, they resolve to teach him a lesson. They swim towards him, singing seductively, but dart away at the last moment when he tries to seize them. However, it's a prick tease that backfires because when they are out of range Alberich steals the gold and makes off with it. The first episode of the saga ends with them mourning the loss of their gold and the orchestra sounding the inevitable march of the Rhine.

Water plays a leading role in many other operas, including *The Lady of the Lake*, *The Water Carrier*, *The Pearl Fishers* and *The Magic Fountain*, but perhaps the most interesting is Debussy's only completed opera, *Pelléas and Mélisande*. Based on the play by the Belgian dramatist Maurice Maeterlinck, the text is simple, although rather mysterious, with hidden, opaque meanings. Composed in 1895, the music is impressionistic, with snatches of melody, blends of colour and texture. 'There are occasional startling moments of clarity in this opera,' says Medcalf. 'They are the aural equivalent of specks of light shimmering in the darkness. Flowing through both libretto and score is a continuous stream of water imagery.'

Golaud is hunting in the forest when he stumbles upon the heroine Mélisande who lies weeping by a well. A crown sparkles beneath the surface of the water. She explains that it was given to her by a man, that it fell off when she was crying and she never wants it back. She reveals nothing more about her past life: it is as if the well and her tears wash all memories away. Golaud makes her his wife and takes her back to his castle, where she remains morose, always bursting into tears and sobbing like a child. It is only when she meets Golaud's half-brother, Pelléas, whose sensitivity contrasts with Golaud's more earthy instincts, that she perks up. They soon develop a very close relationship, which brings her evident happiness.

One day Pelléas takes her to a fountain with healing properties in the castle grounds, reputed to be as deep as the sea. As she perches precariously on the edge of the well and reaches her hand down to caress the surface, her long tresses cascade down into the water. The scene is enchanting and tender, but pulses with a sense of suppressed eroticism heightened by the presence of the water. Eventually Mélisande, released from her inhibitions, begins to play with the ring Golaud gave her, recklessly throwing it up and catching it above the surface of the water. As the ring drops into the well and a harp describes it disappearing into the depths, we realise that as the crown falling in the water signified the end of her previous relationship, this is the beginning of the end for Golaud. His jealous suspicions are soon aroused, and Mélisande's joy is short-lived. In the face of Golaud's bullying it is back to floods of tears. All the youthful characters in the opera are prone to sudden bouts of copious weeping. Pelléas himself, Golaud's son Yniold and even the sheep are described as crying. On the one hand it is as if they are weeping for their lost innocence; on the other it is as if the very act of shedding tears is a purification that seems in a strange way to preserve it.

The exact nature of the relationship between Mélisande and Pelléas, like so many other things in the opera, is kept deliberately ambiguous, but the repeated association of Mélisande with images of water suggests that it remains in essence an innocent one. They meet for a second time by the well, this time in secret, and Mélisande admits her love for him. Pelléas is moved to exclaim: 'Your voice! Your voice! It is fresher and purer than water. It is like pure water on my lips . . . like pure water in my hands!' One senses this may be the moment of consummation, but the couple become aware that Golaud is spying on them from behind a tree. They have lost the will to conceal their passion and kiss each other openly and defiantly, as if in a suicide pact, deliberately inviting the wrath of the brutal Golaud. He doesn't disappoint them: he cuts down Pelléas with his sword but Mélisande loses her nerve and runs away, leaving Pelléas to die ignominiously by the healing fountain.

Some months later Mélisande gives birth to a child, but is dying. The cycle of tears is complete when first the child begins to cry, then Mélisande passes away and finally even the hard-hearted Golaud breaks down and weeps. It is as if he earns some measure of redemption through the cleansing power of his tears. The cycle of water imagery is complete.

Passengers fleeing through London Gatwick's North Terminal for the last twenty years have been granted a moment of calm and serenity before they board the plane and are told to buckle up and shut up. At opposite ends of the terminal there are two large water sculptures, *Slipstream* and *Jetstream*, both cones made of polished stainless steel, over which water runs in a wave. The superstitious can throw a coin into the water for good luck. They are the work of William Pye, probably the world's foremost sculptor in water, a curious thing to choose to sculpt perhaps. By nature it is hard to contain, breaks apart when moved, but can also be reflective, intriguing, transparent, and consoling.

Pye grew up in London, but his family had a country house near the Hog's Back in Surrey. There he became fascinated with water, swimming in the lakes and building a waterfall in the garden that still runs. 'There is a spring that flows from the Hog's Back, goes through four ponds, a tarn, Cuttmill Pond, through some common land, through our garden, then on to the River Wey,' he says. 'I have always loved water. I was immersed in it from an early age.' He studied sculpture at Wimbledon School of Art and later at the Royal College of Art, from where he graduated in 1965. While he was at Wimbledon he made a fountain of a young boy blowing, like a kiss, a jet of water. 'I sold it for fifty quid,' he says. 'This was considered very commercial, but it helped supplement my grant.'

He spent the next twenty years making sculptures of polished steel, what he calls 'chromed reflective things, much influenced by the sculptor Eduardo Paolozzi', then started using stainless steel cables. But finally he came back to water. 'All my work is prompted by the possibilities of hydrostatic pressure,' he says. 'It affords wonderful opportunities.'

William Pye's first fountain, blowing a kiss of water for more than half a century

Hydrostatic pressure is the technique that garden designers have used since Roman times to force jets of water up in the air. It does not rely on pumps or volume of water, but is determined solely by the head, which is the distance from the main body of water to the outlet. Assuming you have enough water – and you can do this by allowing for a slight overflow – you can create a constant jet of water that will hold in the same position for centuries. 'I was intrigued by a jet of water that came out of a hole in a wall and into a frog's mouth,' says Pye. 'So I set out to find how it was done and to emulate it.' *Aston Triangle*, made in 1984, exemplifies this technique: two stainless steel poles make up two sides of a triangle, which is planted in a pond. Water shoots out at regular intervals from each pole, creating a trellis effect. Another technique he uses is the roll-wave. He discovered this in Wales. 'Every summer we would go to the Black Mountains and it would rain every day. As we walked I noticed the waves of water pouring down the roads. The smoother the surface, the better the wave effect. Polished stainless steel is the best for patterning. It can also be used on a vertical surface.' It is this discovery that is used in *Slipstream* and *Jetstream* at Gatwick Airport.

Another possibility is to create a vortex or a spiral of water. This is achieved by putting a spin on the water before it leaves the outlet, rather like a bowler putting spin on a cricket ball. Perhaps Pye's most peculiar effect is shown in a work such as *Tarantella*. Here the water has been treated before the outlet to get the molecules to run in parallel so that the jets stay together, rather than breaking up. The spray looks surreal, like pieces of rope. 'People don't believe it's water until they touch it and get wet,' laughs Pye.

Pye believes that we haven't learnt much more about water

than the ancients already knew, and indeed that water's potential is ultimately quite limited. However, he thinks it is all about refinement. 'To be honest, I am bored by huge fountain displays, with lights and sound. I am more interested in precision, almost minimalism, using controlled nozzles. I like the simplicity and stillness of water. I like the range of different sounds. Water captures your imagination.'

Recently he came across his first fountain, the statue of the boy blowing the water into the pond. The grandson of the man he sold it to – a family friend – got in touch. It was in need of restoration, so Pye mended the work and took the opportunity of casting himself a bronze copy. At his studio in south London he is preparing an exhibition for the Royal British Society of Sculptors and a bid for some work in the Millennium Park in Chicago. But what most excites him is a commission he has just received from Salisbury Cathedral to build a new font. At sixty-nine he has no plans to retire. 'This isn't work,' he says. 'It's play.'

The climber paused, swaying slightly. He breathed heavily, steadily, even though he knew that breathing like a hunting dog was not the best thing to do. At altitude you must sip the air, like a wine taster sipping wine. Once you start panting, the effort itself uses up precious oxygen. He had reached the summit, but now he had to get down. And getting down is always the hardest part. If I just stop here for a moment, I'll get my breath back, he thought. He was thirsty too, but he had nothing to drink. There was snow all around him, but it doesn't help climbers. It takes as much energy to absorb the water in snow as it does to melt it. Surrounded by snow, the climber was as marooned as the ancient mariner, who lamented 'Water, water, everywhere, Nor any drop to drink.'

What did he know of snowflakes? That every one is different. But that each part of each individual flake is made from the same repeating patterns. In other words, they are fractals. The term 'fractal' was the invention of Benoit Mandelbrot, a mathematician. Any part of the flake can be multiplied to create the flake itself. Down below, through the swirling snowflakes, he could make out the town in the valley. He had set out from there two days ago, with enough food and water to last him forty-eight hours. This storm was inconvenient. Down there was a roaring log fire, a fondue and a bottle of wine. Here there was nothing but wind and rocks and snowflakes. But most importantly there was nothing to drink.

'If I just rest here for a moment, I'll be all right,' he said to himself.

7

The Angel of the River

Bull-roarers cannot keep up the annual rain,
The water-table of a once green champaign
Sinks, will keep on sinking; but why complain? Against odds,
Methods of dry-farming shall still produce grain.

W. H. Auden

BARRA IS AN UNLIKELY place to launch a revolution, even an environmental one. It is an unremarkable town in the interior of Brazil, a country where ninety per cent of the population prefers to live within scuttling distance of the sea. Few have heard of the place, and fewer have been there. The only notable feature in Barra is the thick brown river that winds round the back of the town.

This is not the Amazon but the São Francisco River. It is shaped like a crooked finger that starts in Minas Gerais, then heads towards the dry lands in the north-east, before turning abruptly south to the Atlantic. The first European eyes to see it were those of Amerigo Vespucci on St Francis' Day in 1501, hence its name. By Brazilian standards it is not especially impressive: at 2,800 kilometres, it is the same length as the Danube. Sir Richard Burton canoed down it in 1855, and wrote a dry account of his journey. Otherwise it has led a rather uncelebrated existence.

But that peaceful life is suddenly under threat. In 2005, Brazil's President Lula signed a decree that would inaugurate a vast irrigation project, drawing water from the river and pumping it through a series of canals to the dry *sertão* of the north-east. According to the government this would benefit ten million people. To its critics the scheme is ill-conceived, helping only a few rich farmers who will waste water on irrigating crops. And it would mean the death of the river.

As the bulldozers moved in, one man was preparing to fight. Father Luiz Cappio, the Bishop of Barra, installed himself in a whitewashed church in Cabrobo, and sent an open letter to President Lula. 'Either you rescind the decision, or I will starve to death in protest,' he wrote. 'I will exchange my life for the life of the river.'

For eleven days the Bishop of Barra lay in the church, with nothing passing his lips except the occasional glass of São Francisco River water. For eleven days the president of Brazil watched and waited. As did the Vatican. Thousands of the bishop's parishioners gathered to lend their support. The Catholic Church in Brazil had a history of activism during the time of the military dictatorship, but they had been staunch supporters of President Lula's bid to become president.

President Lula sent an envoy with a letter agreeing to reconsider the whole project once more, and urged the bishop to break his fast.

It's easy enough to find the bishop in Barra, once you've got over the journey. It is a ten-hour coach ride from Salvador to Xique-Xique, with frequent stops on the way for the passengers to eat fried cheese sandwiches and drink fruit juices. The road is good for half of the way, then scarred with potholes. By dawn you can make out a flat landscape, where scrub trees, agaves and cacti grow. There is red laterite soil, and a herd of cattle trying to find something to eat. Rather improbably, there is also a flock of ostriches.

At Xique-Xique you change buses. This one is smaller, without air conditioning. The landscape changes too. There is a range of hills to the west, and suddenly, winding across a flat land, the São Francisco River. Between the river and the road is a palm-tree plantation. After an hour's drive you reach the river. To get to Barra, you must first ford the river in a ferry. The river is 680 metres wide, fast-flowing water the colour of drinking chocolate. You wouldn't want to drink it.

In Barra it's nine in the morning, but they are already drinking beer. Men are riding mules. It's market day. There are stalls selling clothes, shoes and plastic buckets. Everywhere is covered in a fine dust that will turn into thick mud once it starts raining. There are more than 20,000 souls living in Barra, a cathedral, and the bishop's palace.

There is something quite Old Testament about the bishop's threat to swap his life for that of the river. An eye for an eye, a tooth for a tooth. You expect to meet someone tall with a long grey beard and a booming voice, but Bishop Luiz Flavio Cappio is a short man with thick grey hair, a friendly demeanour, a soft voice and a quick smile. With his lined face and pinched features, he looks like an engraving of a medieval saint. As you would expect from a man who has just been on hunger strike, he is thin, almost emaciated. His black jeans are fastened tight around his waist, but the bottom hangs down as if they were borrowed from a much larger man.

He was born in Igarachingeta, near São Paulo, on 4 August, 1946. His parents were Brazilian, but of Italian stock. He joined the Franciscan order when he was eighteen years old, and was ordained in 1971. In 1974 he was sent to the region around Barra. In 1997 he was made bishop. His diocese is the size of Portugal. 'From the moment I came here, I realised just how important the river is to the life of the people,' he says. 'It brings life to the dry land. Without it, there is nothing.'

In 1992, together with three colleagues, including sociologist Adriano Martens, he spent a year walking the length of the river, from its source in Serra da Canastra in Minas Gerais, to its mouth at the Atlantic Ocean. The government was still insisting then that there were no problems with the river, but they saw for themselves the deforestation along the riverbanks, the pollution, and the harm that some of the irrigation was causing. Trees were being replaced by vegetables, which in turn needed watering. Every day, the bishop would preach to the local communities, explaining the importance of the river. 'We changed the mind of the people about the importance of the river,' he says. 'Now they realise how important the river is to their lives, they want to preserve it. It brings them water for drinking and irrigating their crops. It also provides fish to eat.'

The São Francisco River runs through five states in Brazil. Each has sought to capture the river's water, from the dams in the south to the Sobradinho Dam near Barra, to the Haparika Dam, the Acuor Dam and the Xingo Dam. 'Everyone in Brazil wants to take water from the São Francisco River,' says the bishop.

The Sobradinho Dam provides hydroelectric power, but also irrigation to Petrolina, a town whose surrounding land has become a powerhouse of agricultural production. With a sunny climate, fertile soil and low humidity, allied to the water of the river, this is one of the most productive and cost-effective places to farm in the world. Grapes mature in 120 days, enough to yield two crops a year. Vegetables flourish in this landscape.

The Brazilian government wants to extend this success story to the north-east of Brazil. This area, known as the *sertão*, is a wild, barren landscape, where drought struck repeatedly in the twentieth century. Even before that, men dreamt of creating an oasis there with the help of the São Francisco River. Dom João VI, who in 1808 installed the Portuguese court in Rio after fleeing Napoleon's troops, was the first to talk openly about re-routing the São Francisco waters. One of his predecessors, Dom Pedro II, promised in tears that he would sell the last jewel of his crown to solve the drought problem. The crown moulders in a museum, with all its jewels intact, but there is still no water in the north-east.

In 1878 around half the population of Ceará died of hunger. This was followed by severe droughts in 1915, 1919 and 1932. Even though the north-east has agricultural potential, especially for fruit trees, it has never been exploited. As one of the best-known experts on drought in Brazil, José Otamar de Carvalho, author of *A Economia Política do Nordeste* (*The North-East's Political Economy*) says: 'The actions of development promoted under the sponsorship of the state have been conceived and executed with a duration determined, in great measure, by the need to mitigate the drought's effects.'

There are two main reasons for the chronic postponement of a solution for the north-eastern drought: resistance by the powerful farmers, who are opposed to changing their traditional way of raising cattle and cultivating cotton, and the fact that in this century the political power has shifted from the north to the south of the country.

President Lula's government's plan is to take water from the river at Cabrobo, and ship it via a network of irrigation pipes to more than ten million people. According to Ciro Gomes, the regional minister of integration, there was more than two and a half years of debate and consultation. Besides, the irrigation project would only take 1.4 per cent of the river's water.

So why is the bishop so opposed to that? 'If that is what

they were really trying to achieve, I would have nothing against it,' says the bishop. 'But there is a big difference between what they say and what they plan to do. They will spend R $4 billion (£1 billion) on taking the water from the river, and it will go to a small group of rich farmers.' Besides, says the bishop, there is not enough water to spare. 'Think of the river as a sick patient,' he says. 'You wouldn't take blood from an ill person would you? But that is what they propose to do. The river is dying anyway. This project would kill it for good.'

The river used to be navigable from Pirapora to Petrolina, a journey of more than 1,500 kilometres. Mississippi river boats paddled up and down its waters. But the deforestation caused the river to silt up, making most of the journey unnavigable. The only boats that still travel along it are small fishing boats.

The government rejected calls from the scientific community, from universities, even from international water experts. They even ignored a call from the Brazilian judiciary for more debate.

On 26 September, the digging machines moved into Cabrobo, a small town by the river, just where it begins to turn south-east towards the Atlantic. Unfortunately for the supporters of the project, Bishop Luiz Flavio Cappio was busy setting up in a small whitewashed church nearby. From here he sent out his message to the world called 'A Life for a Life'.

For eleven long days, the bishop waited in the church. For the first five days he drank only water drawn from the São Francisco River, switching later to filtered water on the advice of his doctor. 'It was very hard, very difficult,' says the bishop. 'The water did not taste good. Now I know what it is like to be poor and hungry. I talked with my soul, and drew strength from the life of Jesus Christ, and his message to me that I should save the river.'

It did not help that the Catholic Church was divided over his stand. The Church considers suicide a sin. However, the bishop says that he did not want to kill himself, even if he was prepared to die. Some in the Church agreed with his interpretation, while others saw it as an act of egoism even to consider killing himself. The Vatican sent a simple message: 'Open your heart to conversation.' The Pope did not want him to die.

President Lula's nerve cracked first, perhaps prompted by the fact that he was due to visit the Vatican himself, and did not want to arrive with a bishop's blood on his hands. He sent two letters to the bishop. Both were rejected. By now many thousands had joined the bishop in his quest, arriving by boat, bus or on foot to support his efforts. Eventually Jaques Wagner, minister of institutional relations, was despatched to negotiate face to face. Five hours of talks followed. Eventually an agreement was signed whereby the government promised to revitalise the river and not to draw any further water from it without extensive negotiation.

'We proved that faith can move mountains,' says the bishop. 'The fight isn't over. The president still wants the project to go ahead, but now knows that there is a strong opposition.'

President Lula has cancelled the commercial contracts, but is talking about using the military to complete the work. Bishop Luiz Flavio Cappio hopes to meet the government soon to outline his plans on how to revitalise the river. These include planting trees along the banks and near the source; stopping effluent and chemical waste from being dumped in the river; and imposing a limit on irrigation. He is also willing to help explore other ways to bring water to the dry north-east. He thinks there should be more emphasis on digging wells and capturing rainwater, rather than kidnapping his river.

We go down to the river in the bishop's white Toyota Land Cruiser. Local women are busy filling buckets with water. What do they think of the bishop's efforts? 'He's the angel of the river,' says Geraldina, a fifty-year-old woman with grey hair and no shoes. 'If he dies, the river will die.'

The Bishop of Barra on the banks of the Saõ Francisco River

The bishop has no plans to become an ecological evangelist, emulating someone like France's José Bové, who has become a rent-an-environmental-militant, travelling anywhere to stir up controversy. 'I am simply inspired to do it for the people,' he says. 'Perhaps if there is something important to fight against in the Amazon. Otherwise I just want to get back to my parishioners.'

But his efforts appear to have inspired a more militant approach to environmental struggle in Brazil. On Saturday 12 November, 2006, veteran activist Francisco Anselmo de Barros set himself on fire to save the Pantanal wetlands. This came at the end of a demonstration by hundreds of people in Campo

Grande, capital of the state of Mato Grosso do Sul, against the proposed installation of a sugarcane processing plant in the Pantanal area. Barros died the following day from ninety per cent burns to his body. He had dedicated thirty years of his life to environmental activism as the founder of the Mato Grosso do Sul Nature Conservation Foundation (Fuconams), one of Brazil's oldest environmental organisations.

Father Luiz Flavio Cappio says the experience of fighting to save the river has been like that of somebody opening a bottle of champagne. 'You take the cork out and the bubbles go everywhere,' he says. 'I made a stand against the decision to try to kill the river and the news travelled far and wide. The truth has killed the lies and propaganda. Everyone has joined the fight now.'

I visited Father Cappio in the spring of 2006. I heard nothing from him and read nothing in the papers, so I assumed that the river was no longer under threat and that the promised regeneration was taking place. But he had been right to be cautious. Just before Christmas 2007 President Lula announced that the irrigation scheme was back on. He himself is from the *sertão*; he wants the water. The sixty-one-year-old bishop went back on hunger strike. His jeans grew baggier. For more than twenty days he sipped water and watched as first one court imposed a moratorium on the project, then another insisted it could go ahead. When the news was relayed to him that the Supreme Court had ruled in favour of the president's wishes, he fainted. When he regained consciousness, he vowed to continue the fight, but he has been suffering from renal failure. It seems that not even the angel of the river can save it now.

Battles such as this for water have become widespread and will only increase as demand grows. The saddest sight you see most nights in the capital cities of Europe is the flower seller who comes into restaurants trying to persuade you to buy a rose for your dinner companion. He or she is normally an immigrant, one step down even from the street cleaners. They barely speak a word of the local language; all they hope is that a gesture on your part might make your evening more successful and earn them enough to eat. It should be a pleasant exchange. But too often they appear shifty, desperate, and you feel that buying a rose for this woman you hardly know – or for a woman that you know too well – will send out the wrong message. Besides, what are you going to do with the rose? Too often they are not even that attractive. They are small, tightly bunched, with no scent to speak of because they are picked too young. Not buying a flower will hardly change your evening, unless your date is anxious or a donkey. But far away in Africa the process that brought that flower to your table is choking life, and has led directly to at least one death.

Joan Root was a film-maker. She was born in Nairobi. Family myth has it that she was conceived during a picnic on an island on Lake Naivasha. She grew up blonde, beautiful and with an instinctive understanding of wild animals. She left school at fifteen and went to work for Shell Oil as a secretary. Then her father set up a photographic safari company and she joined him. A few years later she met Alan Root. He was already a successful cameraman, having worked on a film called *Serengeti Shall Not Die*, which won an Oscar in 1959 for best documentary. They went to the Ngorongoro Crater together, came back to Nairobi and were married.

They started making films together, which were huge successes in America, with commentaries by stars such as Orson Welles and David Niven. They travelled throughout Africa, Australia, New Guinea, South America, with Alan as cameraman and Joan as producer. 'We went straight off on a safari that lasted twenty years,' Joan recalled years later.

When they weren't travelling, they were living in Kenya, in the area known as Happy Valley. It gained this nickname in the 1920s and 1930s, when it was home to a clan of mainly aristocratic English men and women who lived hard and fast, partied late into the nights and didn't worry too much who they slept with. It became so notorious that people would ask, 'Are you married, or do you live in Kenya?'

Alan Root started a tumultuous affair with Jenny Hammond, who had been a friend to both of them. According to Root the affair rocked their marriage, but he had decided to end it. Then Jenny discovered that she had cancer. Thinking that she only had six months to live, he moved in with her, planning to nurse her until she died. Joan must have hoped that Jenny would die soon and that Alan would return to her, but it never happened. Jenny survived another ten years and by then Joan and Alan were divorced.

Back in 1961 they had acquired a house and eighty-eight acres overlooking Lake Naivasha – and the island where she had been conceived. The spot was known in Swahili as Kilimandege – the hill of the birds. It must have been heavenly. Kenya's birds are almost more outstanding than its large mammals. I visited Lake Naivasha in the 1990s, when it was still a wonderful place, full of foliage and birdsong. But change was on the horizon. The catalyst was the appearance of a flower farm. It is the perfect place to grow roses, carnations, tulips and other cut flowers; there is plenty of sunshine and abundant water that can be drawn from the lake. The success of the first flower farm led to others springing up around the lake, and suddenly the shores of the lake were covered in white plastic greenhouses, sucking fresh water out of the lake and replacing it with polluted water. Every day large lorries negotiate the craterous shore roads and ferry the flowers to Nairobi airport, where they are flown to European markets. Kenya is one of the world's major producers of cut flowers, with some eighty per cent of them coming from Lake Naivasha.

It seems such an obvious idea that it is surprising that nobody had thought of doing it earlier. Kenya is a country that knows drought; it has broken many a farmer's heart. Karen Blixen in *Out of Africa* relates the farmer's fear of a lack of water. She writes that to live through a season when the long rains fail is a 'tremendous, terrible experience'. Now living in Denmark with the farm long since sold, she would be woken by the sound of rain on the roof and say: 'At last, at last.'

But the flower farmers on Lake Naivasha didn't need to wait for rain. They used diesel pumps. Joan watched the landscape that she had known so well being wrecked. A key factor in its destruction was the arrival of thousands of migrant workers from all over the country, desperate to work for a couple of dollars a day picking flowers. Because they were poor they were hungry. Because they couldn't afford food they turned to poaching, mainly fish from the lake. Rather than say nothing, she campaigned for action. She was up against big money and ruthlessness. Flowers may be a symbol of peace but she had started a war.

'Naivasha is the perfect microcosm for the larger picture of Kenya: lawlessness, poverty, collapsing infrastructure, corruption, abuse on all levels – the sad story of a displaced society where money talks,' Dodo Cunningham-Reid, another resident, said in *Vanity Fair*. 'If consumers in Europe knew the misery caused by one rose, they wouldn't buy it.'

I had lunch with her at her house Hippo Point when I visited Lake Naivasha. It was a splendid place, with a magnificent library, wild birds everywhere and a swimming pool with steps so that a hippo could walk in – and out – undisturbed.

In the 1990s Joan joined forces with some of the major landowners in the area, including Lord Andrew Enniskillen, to set up the Lake Naivasha Riparian Association, which still meets to this day. The problem is that many of the members are either flower farmers, or rent land to flower farmers; they are concerned about water levels, but not enough to stop pumping water. There was also a lot of research into the effects this activity would have on the lake. In the late 1980s the global environment charity The Earthwatch Institute concluded that, without restraints, the water levels would drop. Today, they say that the lake probably has about another five years' life. The fish will die, the birds and animals move on, and the flowers will wilt.

Joan tried to persuade the poachers to become gamekeepers. She set up an organisation called the Task Force. They were given a boat and a monthly wage, and the blessing of the Kenya Wildlife Services. For a while everything worked. They destroyed a lot of nets. But then there were accusations they were spending money and time drinking and chasing women, not poachers. Joan eventually shut them down, but had made more enemies in the process.

On Friday 13 January, 2006, at 1.30 a.m., three armed men walked down her drive. Her guards, armed only with machetes, melted into the night. The intruders walked up to the house and started banging on the doors. Joan phoned her friend and neighbour on his mobile phone, but he was in Dar es Salaam, Tanzania. John Sutton heard her voice, told her to be calm and to hide in the bathroom. He summoned help then called her back. He heard gunshots. When the police arrived there was a trail of blood and a dead body.

'I've had about eight of my friends murdered in the last ten years, and no one has come to trial,' Alan Root is reported to have said.

Joan Root is buried in Naivasha. There are no flowers on her grave.

The dilemma facing politicians everywhere is this: farmers need water; people need food and water. How to balance this, and what is the best food to grow? Some food production is nothing more than a waste of water. And it is not always the most environmentally friendly thing to do. Chinese, Indian and American farmers are pumping as much groundwater as they can to irrigate crops such as maize, wheat and barley. Groundwater, as its name implies, is any water in the ground. At its most simple, it is rainwater that soaks into the ground and will in time either appear somewhere – as it does from my spring in the garden – or be stored underground. The area where this water resides is known as the water table. Left to its own devices, its level would fluctuate according to the seasons and to rainfall. Large areas of groundwater are called aquifers and these can be tapped to create artesian wells, from which the water can flow out freely. With the advent of the diesel pump, water that has been stored underground for hundreds, even thousands of years has been sent to the surface, to provide for crops and cities.

In America, for instance, the Ogallala aquifer is a vast, shallow aquifer located beneath the Great Plains. It covers some 450,000 square kilometres, under the states of South Dakota, Nebraska, Wyoming, Colorado, Kansas, Oklahoma, New Mexico and Texas. Some of the water dates back to the last Ice Age. It was first tapped in the early years of the twentieth century for watering cattle and growing maize, wheat and soybeans and at the peak of extraction in the 1950s its was said to be falling by a metre and a half per year. In some parts of north Texas extraction is no longer possible. But the figures aren't entirely bleak.

According to the United States Geological Survey, total water storage was about 2,925 million acre feet (3,608 cubic kilometres) in 2005. This is a decline of about 253 million acre feet (312 cubic kilometres) since substantial groundwater irrigation development began in the 1950s, a drop of around ten per cent. Bad, but not catastrophic, particularly if measures are now taken to grow less thirsty crops such as sunflowers. But other bodies claim that extraction is a hundred times greater than the replacement rate and that within a hundred years the Ogallala aquifer will be empty.

There are two types of aquifer: those that can be replenished and those that are fossil aquifers and more like an oil well; once sucked dry they are worthless. Most of the aquifers in India and the shallow aquifer under the North China Plain are replenishable. Fossil aquifers, such as the Ogallala aquifer, or the Saudi aquifer, mean that drills have to go deeper and deeper, until one day nothing comes out. Farmers with aquifers that rely on rainfall could try switching to low-yielding crops, if rainfall permits. But in most arid regions, such as the Middle East or south-west America, the end of water will mean the end of farming. And just to speed things up, billionaire T. Boone Pickens has set up a company called Mesa Water aiming to sell water from the aquifer to anybody who wants it. This is the opening pitch of his website:

Mesa Water represents a group of Texas Panhandle landowners, led by Boone Pickens, who put a lot of stock in two basic things . . . land and family. For generations, these families have lived and worked in the rolling hills they love. God blessed their land with an underground aquifer filled with naturally pure groundwater. And thanks to the Ogallala aquifer, these landowners have more water than they can ever use. With the population of Texas booming and a perpetual drought predicted to hit our area as soon as 2021, water planners, state and local leaders are looking everywhere for a solution. They know the key to secure, drought-proof, long-term water planning is diversity . . . building reservoirs, encouraging conservation, capturing and purifying runoff and buying water from another region and piping it to where it is needed. Today, Mesa Water is ready to sell water to communities that don't have enough for the future.

The whole process sounds almost paternal. T. Boone and his pals are selling on this water because they have so much. They're swimming in it, thank God! Much of the land is hilly and will never be farmed. Luckily for them, Texas law gives the landowner rights over anything under their property, be it oil, gas, minerals or water. But what T. Boone fails to point out at any stage is that once the water is sold, poured into swimming pools, pumped into hot tubs, sprayed over lawns or splashed over cars, it will never be replaced.

We are not there yet, but enthusiastic pumping is happening throughout Africa, China and India. Water is needed to fuel economic growth and farmers are busy pumping as much water as they need. If the pumps suck dry, they get longer pipes. In poor countries such as Mali, economic output is directly linked to rainfall. The attraction of removing this uncertainty is obvious. But at what future cost? In Britain, under the European Union's Common Agricultural Policy, the tendency has been to increase the amount of cereal production and reduce the amount of pasture. This is fine when the weather is good, but even then, it is harmful to the soil. Most of the fertilisers are artificial; pasture farming builds up organic matter, whereas cereal crops reduce it; most of the cattle are housed in sheds, rather than fields, which are used to grow cereals. When there is no rain, the crops don't grow. When there is lots of rain, it skids off the ground and leads to flooding. So if the brightest farming minds in Britain and the European Union with their degrees and laptops cannot get it right, what hope is there for farmers in places such as India, China, Brazil and Kenya? These countries all have young populations, desperate for food or work. Flowers on Lake Naivasha bring employment, even if in the process they ruin the view of people living on the lake shore, disturb the feeding habits of the hippo, and perhaps even ruin the lake itself. Joan Root's story is about to be filmed by Hollywood, with Julia Roberts in the lead role. Hopefully there will still be enough water in Lake Naivasha to make it look convincing.

The most celebrated films concerning flowers and water are *Jean de Florette*, and its sequel, *Manon des Sources*, both directed by Claude Berri in 1986. The films were adapted from *L'eau des collines*, written by Marcel Pagnol in 1962, which in turn was based on his 1952 films, *Manon des Sources* and *Ugolin*. It is a tale of greed and duplicity, hubris and retribution that is reminiscent of a Greek tragedy, of love and jealousy and misdirected letters. But it is really about water. In their search for water, César Soubeyran, a proud, cunning old man, and Ugolin, his nephew, cause the death of a landowner. They hope that they will be able to buy the property cheaply. The men of the village gather in a bar and talk turns to the property.

'It never rains on that land,' says one.

Another agrees but mentions that there is a spring. There was, says César. But it dried up. Another says he saw it and it was big.

'Do you think a spring like that could dry up?'

'Springs are like pretty girls,' says César. 'If you neglect them they leave you high and dry.'

But the owner has left the property to his sister, César's old girlfriend, who in turn leaves it to her son. Jean de Florette is a city man, a hunchback who works as a tax collector. Beside him is his wife, a former opera singer, and on his shoulders, their daughter, Manon. They plan to live there. But water is a problem; Ugolin and his uncle have already stopped up the spring, so they will never find it.

Eventually Jean de Florette decides to dig for water. His plan is to dig a *forage* – a borehole – from which he will draw water. He is working hard, but drinking harder. It doesn't help that he has hit rock. One morning he and Manon light the fuse and stand back. There is a big bang. He is so keen to see what has happened that he rushes to the hole, and is hit on the head by a rock. The doctor is called, but there's no hope. He is dead.

Manon des Sources takes up the story ten years later. It opens with the sound and sight of running water, coursing down through pipes and canals to water Ugolin's field of carnations, which have replaced Jean de Florette's dried maize stalks. César is picking a basketful of flowers. Ugolin is having an aperitif with a flower buyer. The buyer says that he won't be able to keep paying these prices because of all the competition from Italy. This is either the typical banter between buyer and seller, or a presentiment that Ugolin's fortune is taking a turn for the worse. He says nothing, but counts out his money and puts it in a tin jar, already full to the brim.

Manon, now a beautiful girl, has gone slightly wild. Her mother has returned to the opera, but she has stayed behind, tending goats. In a famous scene she dances naked by a pool, playing her harmonica, overlooked by Ugolin, who understandably falls madly in love with her. Manon realises that they weren't so much the victims of misfortune as foul play. Soon afterwards she is chasing after one of her goats that has slipped down a rock face and hidden in a cave. She has stumbled across the village source. Here is her chance to get back at the villagers of Bastides Blanches. And Ugolin. His carnations are in bud, 15,000 of them. Without water they will die within days.

A dog sits in the empty fountain in the village square, while a boy sucks on the pipe hoping to dislodge whatever might be inside. An expert arrives and they call a public meeting. He gives them his verdict. 'The source of your water is some way away,' he says. The trouble may be due to a drop in water supply or to a drop in the water table. Or the water is flowing somewhere else. It may come back in two days, or two years.

It is up to Manon to unblock the spring, by which time Ugolin has gone mad with passion and jealousy. He hangs himself. It turns out that Manon's father, Jean, was César's son. Due to a postal error while he was in Algeria, he never learnt that the girl he loved was pregnant with his child. The disaster that followed was almost preordained.

You could see these films as an extended commercial for Provence. Together with Peter Mayle, they probably did much to inspire thousands of northern Europeans to buy second homes, hoping to run into Emmanuelle Béart in the market or on the hills. Come to think of it, my house has an uncanny similarity to that of Jean de Florette, although we don't have a donkey. Yet. Particularly in the novels of Pagnol, what also emerges very strongly is the combination of a feminine goddess that exists in water, the earth and women. Water is powerful, sensual and essential. Lack of it can drive men mad, just as surely as a pretty girl with a harmonica.

So where does this leave farmers, who want free, plentiful water, and consumers, who want cheap, plentiful food? It is this Hobson's choice that makes water governance so fascinating. Water is essentially a local issue. But it is also a regional issue, a national issue, a transborder issue, a global issue. There is a good reason why the word 'governance' in Chinese is the same as that for water. During the Chinese imperial dynasty, the only thing sure to depose the emperor was if the Yellow River flooded. The 1931 flood is considered to be the greatest natural disaster of the twentieth century, killing anywhere between one million and four million people, a figure which includes all the associated deaths, such as disease from water pollution, famine from lack of crops, even ensuing drought. A few years later, in 1938, the river flooded again, this time killing perhaps another million people. However, the second flooding had another cause. Nationalist troops deliberately destroyed the riverbanks under the orders of Chiang Kai-Shek during the Second Sino-Japanese War, in order to stop the advancing Japanese troops. Some 54,000 square kilometres were flooded. The troops stopped, but at what cost?

The source of the Yellow River was only discovered in 1952, which is curious when you consider what a fundamental role the river has played in Chinese culture for more than 2,000 years. There are now some twelve hydroelectric dams along it, and huge quantities of water are extracted for irrigation. The Yellow River is less likely to flood now, but faces the opposite problem. Since 1972, the river has started drying up once it passes Jinan, and for most of the year, particularly in the summer months, does not reach the sea.

Striking the right balance between having too much and not enough water is as important today as it was in the time of the Chinese emperors, so you would think that a tradition of water enjoying a central importance would persist today. You'd be wrong. Visit any country from Angola to Nigeria to Russia and the story is the same: the oil ministers are Harvard-educated, well dressed and wear Rolex watches; the water ministers – they may be environment ministers with water forming a part of their brief – will be wearing cheap nylon suits, grey plastic shoes with sofas to match and will use their mobile phones to tell the time. The reason for the disparity is clear: oil is money, power and prestige; water is serious, complex, but nobody wants to pay for it and there is never enough money to finance the necessary public works. Occasionally a country will have a big project such as a hydroelectric dam, to which great prestige is attached. But in those cases the water minister will be elbowed aside and other ministries, such as the finance ministries, will take the glory.

How to make people more accountable for their water? How do you stop the waste of water? How do you stop farmers from pumping groundwater or sucking rivers dry?

In Bali there are water distribution councils, known as Krama Subak, which have been sitting for hundreds of years. These control Bali's unique system of water distribution for the island's interconnected rice terraces. In Punjab there is the *warabandi* or rotation system, which in the early twentieth century allocated the distribution of the water of the Lower Chenab Canal system – and is still in use today. There is even one place where they have taken water supply seriously for over a thousand years. In Valencia, every Thursday at midday, eight *síndicos* or magistrates meet under the Porch of the Apostles at the cathedral. Their mission is to ensure that the water from the Turia River is distributed fairly. They are not lawyers and keep no written record of their judgements. Nor are there many punishments, such as prison, that they can mete out. But they aim to settle by argument any disputes that occur between farmers over the right to use the water in the irrigation channels that supply over 17,000 hectares of land known as the Orchard of Valencia. The court first convened in the middle of the tenth century, when Abd-ar-Rahman III was the caliph of Córdoba. It makes the Tribunal de las Aguas de la Vega de Valencia the oldest law court in Europe. The eight magistrates, dressed in black, represent each of the eight main channels of the irrigation system. Each channel waters the farms of some 1,500 farmers. They elect a magistrate to represent their interests. He – it is always a he – must be a farmer and not an absentee landlord or a lawyer. His job is to make sure that the farmers that he represents receive the water they need according to the provisions of a decree first written in the reign of King James I of Aragon that 'everybody shall be entitled to a share of the water in proportion to the amount of land owned'. Common complaints that the court has to deal with include theft or squandering of water, damage to crops by flooding, indeed anything pertaining to water management. It is so obvious, so reasonable and so democratic that it is surprising that there isn't such a court in every country.

But there isn't. In most places it is a question of grabbing what water you can before your neighbour gets it. You might think that farmers should be encouraged or forced by law to grow only certain crops. In the western United States, for example, you need between 305 and 760 millimetres of water to cultivate wheat and barley. In humid regions of the United States, where irrigation supplements rainfall, you could get by with 150–230 millimetres of water. In the Near East, cotton needs up to 915 millimetres, whereas rice may require two to three times that amount. Obviously what you grow has a huge bearing on how much water you use.

Chile has an interesting system of tradable water rights. This is an economist's dream, but something of a tragedy for the common man. In Chile, under the 1981 Water Code, water rights are private property, which can be freely traded distinct from land. These rights are subject to minimal state regulation and are regulated by civil law. Although multilateral agencies have tried to encourage other Latin American countries to adopt a similar practice, none has. In Cochabamba in Bolivia, they tried to introduce the private sector, with the successful concessionaire, International Water, being granted ownership of all water resources. This instantly made other water users illegal, led to widespread protests, the cancellation of the concession, and even an article in the *New Yorker*.

In the Middle East the country that takes water most seriously is Israel. Not that other countries in the region don't talk about water; they do. But it is mainly to complain that there isn't enough, or that it is polluted, or that they feel somebody else is taking their supply. Israel is the one that is most aggressively trying to address the fundamental shortage. For a start, they are willing to accept that they have a limited supply of water. They acknowledge that there have been years of drought, but admit that it is no good ignoring the problem in the hope that it rains soon. As long ago as 1959 a water law was passed, making water resources public property and regulating their exploitation and allocation, as well as preventing pollution and encouraging water conservation. Their main sources are the Sea of Galilee, a coastal aquifer near the Mediterranean and a mountain aquifer under the Carmel mountain range. There are supplies in western Galilee, the Jordan Valley and the Dead Sea Rift. But that's about it. Sensibly, the Israelis have made conservation the first priority. They have encouraged farmers to use low volume irrigation systems, such as *goutte à goutte* – drip or micro-sprinklers – rather than using enormous jets that spray the water up into the air. In the cities they try to manage the resources efficiently, looking out for leaks and exhorting the citizens 'Don't Waste a Drop'. Parks are planted with drought-resistant plants, and watering is done at night.

In addition, they have built desalination plants, tried to rehabilitate polluted wells and treat sewage so that it is clean enough for irrigating. And they have started importing water from Turkey. If you can afford to pay what the market thinks is a generous price, most things are attainable, even water supplies. If all else fails, and it's practicable, rich countries will buy their water from their water-rich neighbours.

'A worm at one end and a worm at the other,' is how his father had described fishing. But, perhaps in the way that children choose to do everything to avoid emulating their parents, he had taken up fishing. It was fly fishing that attracted him. It taught him patience, it got him outside, and it made him forget all the domestic troubles at home. He would always remember catching his first trout. The pull on the rod, the struggle, easing out the line so it didn't break, pulling it in so that the fish didn't escape. Then gradually getting the fish near the net and scooping it up. A four-pound breathing silver thing, slippery to touch, with a metal barb in its mouth. He managed to get it out. He looked at the fish looking at him, then lowered it into the water, and let it go. He watched it swim off up the river. Maybe he would catch it again another time.

8

Water as God

Take me to the river
And wash me down
Won't you cleanse my soul
Put my feet on the ground
Take me to the river

'Take Me to the River,'
Reverend Al Green

THE INDUSTRIAL AGE CHANGED many things. A million horses disappeared from the streets of London, men went from working in the fields to toiling in factories, and the natural world became less important. There was street lighting and tarmacked roads. Food started coming from shops rather than from animals. And while the industrialists built many noble features either to store or carry water, they also industrialised water. Man's intimate and very personal relationship with water was lost, or at least diminished. Water was cleaned and buffed and mixed with chemicals to make it safe. By the beginning of the twentieth century in most of the capitals of Europe, all you had to do was turn a tap and it appeared. In Paris you didn't even have to ruin your hairstyle when you ventured out of doors because of all the arcades that had been built.

In Peter Ackroyd's book *Thames: Sacred River*, he describes how early man instinctively felt that the river and the surrounding springs were spiritual. The source of the Thames in Trewsbury Mead has always been a sacred place. An ash tree now marks the

site. Ash trees are associated with mysticism. Along the length of
the Thames its water and springs were famed for healing: St
Augustine, for example, performed a miracle near the Thames at
Cricklade. But our veneration for the water has diminished over
the years. Ackroyd writes of a spring beside the Thames at
Cricklade, whose water was so clear and pure that for centuries
the inhabitants of Gloucestershire and Wiltshire would come and
fill their water containers. As well as drinking it, they venerated
its healing qualities, particularly for any problems associated with
the eyes. But the spring has now been covered in concrete, and
fills neither water bottles nor eye poultices any more.

Of course, water continues to excite the spiritual crank. A
Japanese man called Dr Masaru Emoto takes close-up photos of
water in his laboratory – first saying words or expressions before
pressing the shutter. When photographed, the water that was
talked to nicely is said to look serene and symmetrical; that which
was shouted or sworn at looks asymmetrical. Scientists have no
hesitation in condemning his work, although his books appear to
have sold well.

Dr Emoto's work, however questionable, plays on the part of
us that feels drawn to the mystical unknown. Early man had no
such qualms. He accepted the divinity of rivers, believed that gods
and nymphs lurked near water, worshipped rainfall and prayed to
end floods or drought. Water was central to most cultures until the
twentieth century. In *A Dragon Apparent* Norman Lewis recounts
a journey in Indo-China to the Mois, a primitive tribe whose respect
for water was central to their culture. Even in England, home of
the Industrial Revolution, its past is remembered in place names
such as Sunningwell and Sittingbourne – both of whose suffixes denote
the presence of water. People still like to be near water, are stim-
ulated and comforted by it. A survey of Glasgow's International

Financial Services District found that the presence of water encouraged staff to work harder, although they were unable to put their finger on quite why this should be.

One of the challenges facing Judaism, then later Christianity and Islam, was to make water central to religion, while reducing its spirituality. They appreciated the cleaning and purifying aspects of water, as well as its role in creating life – and at times destroying it. But they wanted people to worship God, not water.

In Judaism, for example, the Torah stresses the importance of ritual washing and purification, particularly in running water. Priests had to wash their hands and feet before conducting religious services. Jews are also encouraged to wash their hands before and after meals.

In Christianity, baptism symbolises both the Israelites being led out of slavery in Egypt through the parting of the Red Sea and Jesus' immersion in the Jordan River by John the Baptist. Catholics believe that baptism washes away sin. Holy water, which has been blessed by a priest, is kept in the font. In the ninth century the custom of sprinkling worshippers with water at Mass was introduced.

In Islam, water is used for both cleansing and purifying. Muslims must wash their hands and feet before praying and there is always water in the mosque – partly because many mosques are built on the sites of springs.

The two books that arguably say the most about water are the Bible and the Koran. This is no coincidence, because water is at the very heart of spiritual and religious life. And the books are set in the Middle East, where water has always been precious. At times, parts of both read like manuals on animal husbandry, with plenty of advice on how to water sheep.

At the beginning of Genesis, there is no rain, but a vapour rises from the earth, a fine dew, or an automatic sprinkler system like you'd find on a golf course. A river that flows out of the Garden of Eden to water the plants and flowers splits into four, two of which are called the Tigris and the Euphrates. All is well until Eve is tempted by the serpent and they are all thrown out of the garden. Then Cain kills Abel. And the earth is filled with degenerates, except for Noah and his family.

Water's next appearance is as a terrible flood. It rains for forty days and forty nights. The water swells, covers the highest mountains by more than twenty feet, and kills every living thing except those in the Ark. Eventually the waters recede; a dove is released and flies back with an olive leaf. The voyage is over. They all get out and multiply.

Things return to normal. Water is used for feet washing and there is a dispute between Abraham and Abimelech over a well. Abraham claims that Abimelech's servants had seized his well, even though he had dug it. He gives Abimelech seven lambs as witness that he had dug the well, and the two settle their differences and name the place Beersheba.

Wine's first entry in the Bible is less salubrious. Lot's daughters find themselves in a deserted place with their father and with no chance of meeting any men. So in turn they get their father drunk on wine and persuade him to have sex with them so that they can fall pregnant.

Not long afterwards, Isaac, the son of Abraham so nearly sacrificed to God on an altar, is in need of a wife. Abraham sends his servant to Mesopotamia, telling him to wait by a well for the girls who come out to draw water. This was clearly a well known pick-up joint. The girl that offers him – and his camels – water will be the perfect wife for Isaac. Luckily for Isaac it is the lovely, virginal Rebecca who comes with a full pitcher of water on her shoulder and offers it to the servant.

Here is one largely unremarked aspect of water: going to collect it is a way for women to leave the house and escape their controlling spouses. As well as a chore, it can also be a pleasure. Places where you can get water – rather like the legendary water coolers in American offices – are places to catch up on the latest gossip and talk to your friends, even meet a lover. In Chinua Achebe's *Things Fall Apart*, going to fetch water is the catalyst for a meeting between the hero and the woman who becomes one of his wives:

> As they stood there together, Ekwefi's mind went back to the days when they were young. She had married Anene because Okonkwo was too poor then to marry. Two years after her marriage to Anene she could bear it no longer and she ran away to Okonkwo. It had been early in the morning. The moon was shining. She was going to the stream to fetch water. Okonkwo's house was on the way to the stream. She went in and knocked at his door and he came out. Even in those days he was not a man of many words. He just carried her into his bed and in the darkness began to feel around her waist for the loose end of her cloth.

Back in Genesis there is a famine, caused by drought. There is more bickering over wells, and the Philistines fill in Isaac's well because they are jealous he has grown so rich. In other books there are more elaborate water proverbs, such as the mention in Ecclesiastes, 'That all rivers run into the sea, yet the sea is not full; unto the place from whence rivers come, thither they return.' In fact the Bible overflows with water. Recently I was at a wedding. The couple had picked Psalm 23, which was a curious choice, one normally heard at funerals, but it remains one of the loveliest verses in the language:

> The Lord is my shepherd, I shall not want.
> He maketh me down to lie
> In pastures green; he leadeth me
> The quiet waters by.

It struck me as I stood in the church that the last line, 'The quiet waters by', is as ambiguous as some of the lines in Shakespeare's best sonnets. Does it just mean, by quiet waters? Or is 'waters' used as a verb, as in 'washes over'? Or is there a sense – as there is in the King James version when 'quiet' is replaced by 'still' – that the water current is powerful, but imperceptible, as in the phrase 'still waters run deep'? Perhaps it is all of these. At least it shows that as a shepherd Jesus appreciates the importance of water.

If anything, the Koran puts more emphasis on water than the Bible. While man is fashioned from clay by Adam's God, Muhammad's Allah makes man from water:

> In the name of Allah, Most Gracious, Most Merciful
> Who made from water every living thing.

The god of the Koran is a rainmaker, who sends rain down to water the crops and to help the people he has made from water. Water is a gift of Allah. The importance of water in Islam does not derive from the climatic realities in the Arabian Peninsula, but directly from the revelation of Allah. The Koran states that water is a source of life, and discusses the importance of water in more than one hundred places. Allah asks, 'See ye the water which ye drink? Do you bring it down from the cloud or do We?' The prophet Muhammad forbade the wasteful use of water, even when one is at the side of a river. Water plays an important role in Islamic rituals, and Islam also teaches its followers other aspects of water such as pollution, conservation, ownership, endowment, distribution and territorial prerogatives – not all of which are scrupulously followed in Muslim countries. The Koran describes the water cycle, the separation of fresh water and seawater, the promotion of agriculture, sources of foods and jewellery, and means of transportation.

Likewise sharia law, the legal framework that governs most aspects of Muslim life, originates from the concept of sharing water. In Arabic 'sharia' means the clear, well-trodden path that leads to water. It is said to have been laid down by the prophet Muhammad, with some of the commands stated in the Koran, and has become a code of living among Muslims, even formally adopted by the courts of some countries. Under sharia law, water is Allah's property – but can be used by all and is free to all. However, like many things in the Koran, it is not clear whether payment is acceptable or not. Arabists say that the linguistic meaning of sharia reverberates in its technical usage: just as water is vital to human life, so the clarity and uprightness of sharia is the means of life for souls and minds. In other words, water's purity has a divine analogue.

The teachings of the Koran inspired Muslims to honour and cherish water. They built some 400 steam baths among the fountains of Granada. Within a hundred years of their expulsion from Spain only one survived. But if there is one place where religion, art, architecture, spirituality, even gardening – and water – are combined it is at the Alhambra in Granada. For me it is one of those few places where the reality exceeds expectation. I remember being distinctly underwhelmed by the pyramids, and as a child disappointed by a visit to the Tower of London. It probably helps that the rest of Spain has become so overbuilt in the last twenty years. As one of my friends says: 'Most of Spain looks like it has been half-built by a Moroccan in a hurry.' But the Alhambra is proof that give a Moroccan – or an Arab at least – enough time, and they will produce something exquisite, even if the layout is chaotic on first sight. But even this seems deliberate, like the intricate design of a carpet or a tile.

The Alhambra's origins are surprisingly uncertain – some reports say it was originally a Jewish stronghold, others that its name refers to a 'red fort'. What is not in dispute is that Ibn-Nasr, the founder of the Nasrid dynasty, was forced to leave Granada to escape persecution by King Ferdinand and his followers. He moved into the Palace of Badis in the Alhambra outside the city walls. According to an Arab manuscript published as the *Anónimo de Granada y Copenhague*: 'This year 1238 Abdallah ibn al-Ahmar climbed to the place called the Alhambra, inspected it, laid out the foundations of a castle and left someone in charge of its construction.' His tomb in the Alhambra cemetery is inscribed with these words: 'In times of war he was as invincible as a lion; in times of peace he was as generous as water over the dry earth.' The Alhambra's early water supply relied on cisterns that would fill with rainwater. And, in common with most castles, even monasteries, built in arid lands, the roofs were sloping and connected to a series of pipes to capture any falling rainwater. After Ibn-Nasr's death, a series of irrigation canals were built – the main one known as the Sultan's Canal – to bring colossal quantities of water to the city. One consequence of this is that its purpose shifted from being a fortress to a pleasure dome.

But what a place! The patio features a fountain with twelve lions. Nobody knows their exact significance, although it is possible that since the fountain was a gift from the Jewish community, the twelve lions represented the twelve tribes of Israel. During Moorish times the fountain functioned as a clock, with a different lion spouting water each hour. Conquering Christians took the fountain apart to see how it worked, and it has never told the time since. Water is carried from the fountain to many parts of the palace, along pathways that bubble with life, into yet more fountains, and still courtyards such as the Court of the Myrtles, where the water is contained in a long rectangular basin rather like a swimming pool. Two fountains splash lazily at either end, but the main purpose of the pool is to act as a cooling and reflective device, showing the buildings by day and the moon and stars by night. 'This is a place of transparent crystal,' said poet Ibn Zamrak, whose words are inscribed on the walls of the Nasrid palaces. 'Those who look at it imagine it to be a boundless ocean.' Not only did the builders understand light and shadow – the windows with their honeycombed apertures are a perfect example of this – but they also realised that water, particularly in a dry land, lent a place unity, serenity, even spirituality.

Nor were practical issues overlooked. There is a hammam in the Alhambra, though this is out of bounds to most visitors. It was remodelled by the Christians when they took control of the place on 1 January, 1492, the main change being the introduction of a bath allowing full immersion in water, something prohibited by the Muslims. The baths were places to relax, to gossip, even, according to some reports, a place for the sultan, sitting on a balcony, to check out the naked bathers. The benefits of bathing were widely appreciated by Muslims. Ibn al-Khatib, author of *The Book of Hygiene*, wrote that: 'There are those who maintain that bathing produces in the body the same effects that wine does, in other words happiness and pleasure. This explains why so many people sing in the bath.'

On the way to the Generalife, the rather strangely named garden and villa that is a part of the Alhambra complex – literally the word means 'noblest of villas' – you pass through the Patio de la Acequia, or Courtyard of the Water Channel. It was through here that water coursed on its way to the Alhambra Palace. There are now fountains here, a nineteenth-century addition. Above the courtyard is a long staircase of about thirty steps, the Escalera del Agua, on either side of which the two balustrades contain open pipes down which water flows. This is an original feature, and an exciting one, greatly admired by many who saw it.

The screech of a peacock is often heard when rain is approaching

In 'Tlön, Uqbar, Orbis Tertius', Jorge Luis Borges writes of a particular Islamic night called the Night of Nights, when the secret portals of heaven open and the water in the jars is sweeter. In the Alhambra you can imagine that the heavens open every night, and that the water is always sweet.

It was a spring day during the war. The wind was shaking the trees, blowing the clouds over the Downs so they looked like young lambs, fluffy and full of life. There was blossom on the trees, the flowers were in bloom, the cow parsley was already tall and thick. The writer pushed through it and walked slowly towards the water. She took off her shoes and stepped into the river. But she kept her clothes on; the water was cold, after all. She had been hearing voices for a few days now, and was sure she could take no more. Her message to her husband had made that clear: 'I feel certain that I am going mad again. I feel we can't go through another of those terrible times. And I shan't recover this time. I begin to hear voices, and I can't concentrate. So I am doing what seems the best thing to do . . .' She began to fill her pockets with stones. She walked into the current of the cold River Ouse and felt the water lift her and carry her downstream. Did she sing a little, like Ophelia, as she went? The body was not found until some twenty days later. She was buried under a tree at the foot of the Downs.

9

Pour Pour Not Jaw-Jaw

> Although many Africans are poor, they are willing to pay for
> what they need. The plentiful creativity and entrepreneurship in
> the informal economy can be harnessed to cater to them. Prepaid
> telephone cards and soft drinks, often distributed via informal
> networks, can be found in tiny stalls in the most remote corners
> of Africa, despite all the difficulties with transport.
>
> *The Economist*, 7 September, 2006

ON THE CORNER OF 18th and H Street in central Washington
DC, just a short stroll from the White House, is a steel and glass
building. Critics say the glass is the only transparent thing about
the place. Its benign, nondescript exterior hides the fact that its
inhabitants inspire fear and loathing in equal measure. Protestors
have even set themselves alight over its activities.

They are digging up the pavement outside so that it looks
as barricaded as the American Embassy in London, though
whether this is to deter terrorists or just double-parking is not
quite clear. This is the headquarters of the World Bank, which
is not quite as despised as its sister organisation, the International
Monetary Fund – known by some as the International Misery
Fund – but it comes close.

People dislike the World Bank's power, its arrogance, its
love of lending money to finance the construction of white
elephants in developing countries, even its stand on trying to

encourage the private sector to play a role in water development. Its mission statement, carved into the brick, reads 'Our Dream is a World Free of Poverty', and for most of its employees, this dream has come true. How well they have done in the rest of the world is a moot point.

The development world is certainly a strange place: one imagines that it is full of people trying to save the planet, but you quickly realise that most of them are trying to make a living. It has helped alleviate my poverty at times, for I have worked as a consultant for the bank on a number of occasions. I spent some time helping to persuade journalists in developing countries that they should write more – and more intelligently – about water. You might think writing about water is relatively no harder than writing about fashion or sport. A meeting with Nick Kotch, then Reuters' bureau chief in Africa, soon put me straight: 'The most courageous journalist I ever met wasn't a war correspondent or a political reporter. He was covering the Turkwel Dam project in Kenya.' Water reporting, if it's any good, is a mixture of personal and political. In Africa, if you are going to ask the difficult questions, it can also be dangerous.

So I know and like some of the people who work at the World Bank. Individually they are intelligent, well educated and well meaning. However, its charter – which governs how it lends to its own shareholders, some 185 nations in total – makes its job difficult. It cannot criticise member-countries' institutions, even when they are corrupt, useless or dumb. It is an easy target. Even some of its own staff, such as economist William Easterly, who worked there for many years, are scathing about the place and conclude that few, if any, of its projects do any good at all. And like all institutions it can itself be intransigent, even downright foolish. One friend who works at the bank says that they get blamed for everything: blamed if they do nothing, and blamed if they do something. So why do they lend for white-elephant projects such as dams and aluminium smelters in inappropriate places? It is a bank, he says, it's their job to lend money.

I am in Washington for Water Week, an annual gathering of the World Bank staff who work on water issues, along with a smattering of interested parties, most of whom seem to be consultants hoping to pick up some juicy contracts, although with the weakness of the dollar a European would probably be better off busking on the London Underground. I make my way through security – there's very little, just a man who asks for photo identification and a scanner for the briefcase. I am given a name badge, and a programme. The title is *2007 Water Week. Water Futures: Sustainability and Growth, February 28–March 1*. Given that water is one of the most sustainable things on the planet – it is almost impossible to get rid of it, boil it and it turns into vapour and comes back somewhere else – this strikes me as a particularly vacuous title.

I take a bottle of water from a choice of Poland Spring or Perrier – there is no trouble getting hold of water at Water Week – and head into the auditorium. It is filled mainly by men in grey suits, with the occasional woman in a flash of colour. At the microphone there is a woman talking. I see from the programme that her name is Kathy Sierra and that she works for the bank. Like most people who work at the bank, she uses the bank's special language. She is talking about synergies and how the bank is 'bringing sustainability as a core value'. Sierra tells us that the bank is adapting to a changing environment. In the 1980s the bank worked mainly on large hydro projects. 'This was not always very well done, we ignored sustainability,' she says. In 1987 the bank introduced the concept of sustainable development, then at the beginning of the 1990s abruptly started pulling back from infrastructure projects. Why?

'It is all down to a paradigm shift,' she explains. 'The private sector was expected to move into the water sector and there was also pressure from civil society to get involved. We had a concept of "Do No Harm". This was an error on our part. In the twenty-first century we have set about rebuilding the business. While it is important to do no harm, we were missing opportunities. We can bring value to the poor. We will need hydropower.'

I suddenly realise what she means by hydropower. She is talking about dams. So why not call them dams? Maybe civil society doesn't like it. I see that all the hydropower sessions are scheduled for Friday, when only bank staff are allowed to attend.

'This is an exciting time to be thinking about sustainability. An exciting time to be thinking about a paradigm shift. We want you – all of you here – to push us this week. We want you to take us out of our comfort zone.'

There is a polite ripple of applause, although I see that a few people sitting next to me have already nodded off, obviously in an impressive display of synergy. Then it's time for Jamal Saghir, director of the Energy, Water and Transport group, to speak. 'We shall be talking this week about the importance of human water security,' he says. Then he is off on a reminiscence of his own. He tells us how the 1980s was the age of bricks and mortar for the bank. Then the 1990s brought risk aversion and a decline in lending by the bank. But, good news this, things are changing: 'In 2000 we are starting balancing infrastructure and lending and a water pipeline came on stream,' he says. 'You realise how the bank changes.' Nobody can fail to be moved by this talk, except the few who are sleeping through it. 'A local private sector is emerging. Some private projects have been cancelled, ten to be precise, but sixteen new ones have been launched, including in Russia.' I am not sure why Russia is being lauded – personally I would be sceptical of anything happening there – but apparently this is a good sign.

'We need more hydropower to stop carbon emissions. Africa is using less than ten per cent of its hydro potential. There are many deaths from waterborne diseases in sub-Saharan Africa, south Asia and east Asia. We want to push irrigation.'

And here he paused. And added: 'We want to encourage everyone here to think outside the water glass.'

Was I the only one trying not to laugh? Thinking outside the glass? I looked around. Those that weren't napping were clapping.

I have a copy of the *Financial Times* with me, in case I need something to read. Flicking through surreptitiously, I chance upon an ad from UNDP, the United Nations Development Program. It reads: 'Where does water cost more per litre than in central London? In a developing-country slum.' Frightening, and true. But why isn't anybody saying this during Water Week?

There is a pause for coffee. I feel I need something stronger. Then it is time for the next session called Water Futures: Sustainability and Growth (a panel discussion). It is chaired by Margaret Catley-Carlson, a formidable and sharp woman whose job title is Chair, Global Water Partnership.

There are five speakers. Juan Lozano, the Colombian minister of environment, housing and territorial development, is the first to mention the issue of water as a 'human right'. Lynn Lawry works at the International Medical Corps: she says that 2.6 billion people are at risk from waterborne diseases, 'that's one in two in the developing world'. She says that 'water is a human right'.

What do people mean by this? Is water a human right any more than electricity, mobile phones or thick curly hair? I would suggest that few things have been as unhelpful to the development of the water sector as dubbing it 'a human right'. There are many human rights – you can see them on the United Nations website. It is rather chilling to read the original thirty articles of the Universal Declaration of Human Rights, first published in 1948 in post-war euphoria, because one realises that for most people in most of the world, few of them are available.

Water came later, being adopted in November 2002 as part of the Committee on Economic, Social and Cultural Rights. According to the UN, 'All the 145 countries which have ratified the international CESCR will now be compelled to progressively ensure that everyone has access to safe and secure drinking water, equitably without discrimination.'

These strategies should:

1. Be based on human rights law and principles.
2. Cover all aspects of the right to water and the corresponding obligations of countries.
3. Define clear objectives.
4. Set targets or goals to be achieved and the timeframe for their achievement.
5. Formulate adequate policies and corresponding indicators.

All well and noble, but how feasible is this?

'A violation of this right has grim consequences,' says Ms Lawry. I couldn't agree more, but why, exactly, is it a human right? I understand that one cannot live without water, but nor can one live without food. A teenage girl cannot live without a phone and my wife insists she couldn't exist without Philosophy Exfoliating Cleanser, although I suspect she might be able to muddle along. But should they all be human rights too?

'Water is a human right,' says Jamal Saghir. 'But it is not free. Somebody has to pay for the delivery.'

Again, I couldn't agree more. My objection to it being dubbed a 'human right' is that this attitude encourages paralysis. When I was in Ghana in 2002, employees of the Ghana Water Company told me that they opposed private water supply because water should be a 'human right'. Later that day I saw them setting off in tankers to deliver water to the poor in the slums, and selling the water by the bucket. A private company would have connected people to the mains and charged them less in the process. In my book, not being ripped off by your water supplier should also be a human right.

If the concept of 'water as a human right' is one factor that stops the poor from getting water by encouraging inertia, the other is price. The emotional bond that we all have to water makes it tempting to view it as something special, not as another simple commodity. The Greek poet Pindar called water the 'most special of elements' and that view, even if water is no longer regarded as an element, persists to this day. But the market can cope: as things become rarer, so they rise in price. Adam Smith, the eighteenth-century moral philosopher and political economist, noted that diamonds were expensive because they were both beautiful and hard to find. (It is interesting to note that diamonds were once graded according to their transparency, with the three highest grades known as first, second and third water. That practice has now been stopped, although it still occurs colloquially.)

So if water is now scarce, should the price not go up? That would also encourage people to conserve it. When I was in Johannesburg in 2002, I discovered that the largest users of water in the city are not the rich, filling their pools and watering their lawns, for they have to pay for it. The thirstiest consumers are in Soweto. There it's free, so when it gets hot they put a hosepipe on the corrugated iron roof. You can't blame them; it's quite an efficient form of air conditioning. But they wouldn't do it if they had to pay for it.

Nobody in Washington DC, however, wants to discuss price. Finally Mrs Catley-Carlson pipes up: 'Where do we get the money for water?'

There is a man on the panel called Lloyd Timberlake, representing the World Business Council on Sustainable Development. 'We think that in terms of water, all ideology is dead,' he drawls. 'The powerful people in every community have the water. The poor don't.'

The Chair poses another question. 'What technology would help water?' she asks. Mr Timberlake likes the idea of water purification – maybe there's work in it for some of his members. He also likes the idea of water bills in some cities doubling as lottery tickets, with non-paying customers excluded from winning.

Lynn Lawry comes up with a suggestion that gets a lot of interest in the hall. 'I think we should create a talking book to encourage illiterate people to appreciate the importance of water and how to conserve it.' I agree with her. The Chair agrees with her. Most of the people in the room seem to agree with her, even those nodding off for a well-earned sleep.

I have a flashback to a March day in 2005, when I was sitting under a jacaranda tree in Addis Ababa talking to members of the

World Bank's Water and Sanitation Program. The head of the Africa operations was Piers Cross. Piers is a charming South African in his early sixties, with sharp, clear features and grey hair. He always seems to be rushing off somewhere, but before he goes he comes up with good ideas, expressed so quickly they almost come out in a stutter. During the United Nation's Summit on Sustainable Development in Johannesburg, he had short facts about the poor state of sanitation printed on every piece of lavatory paper in the place. Delegates couldn't fail to see the message.

Piers introduced me to Anthony Waterkeyn, a veteran of water projects in Africa, who has the look of a man who has spent years in the field. Anthony was working in Uganda, in an area called Busia, where a new health chief was achieving spectacular results. Since independence the district health workers had gradually been fired or retired and Ugandans living in rural areas forgot the basics of hygiene. They didn't wash properly after going to the toilet. They didn't wash their hands before cooking or eating. Would I be interested in going to Uganda with him, visiting the rural areas, and perhaps coming up with something innovative that he could use to help other people in rural Uganda to follow the same strategy?

I have to confess that 'yes, sure' wasn't my first thought. When I think back to how I saw my adult life progressing, I assumed I would one day score a hundred before lunch at Lord's against the Australians, then go on to write the great English novel in the afternoon. Persuading Ugandans to wash their hands after wiping their bottoms was not what I saw myself doing in my thirties. But maybe it would be a good thing to do. And perhaps ultimately more useful. If not a Nobel Prize for Literature, perhaps one for Bottom Wiping?

I went to Uganda. Anthony met me in Kampala and the

next day we set off in his Land Rover for Busia. With us was his daughter, Tammy, who had been in the north of Uganda. Uganda has endured one of the longest – and least reported – civil wars in Africa. The country has been effectively divided in two for more than twenty-five years, with the southern-based government forces fighting the Lord's Resistance Army. This quaint-sounding outfit is ruthless and unpleasant, using child soldiers to capture young girls and put them to work as cooks, cleaners and sex slaves. Tammy had been spending time with some of the girls who had managed to escape to a refugee camp. She showed me some of the drawings she had made of them, designed to act as a form of therapy. They were simple line drawings, more Matisse than Rembrandt, but effective. I began to get an idea.

But first, because it was the weekend, we were heading to the Nile. If your vision of the Nile is of a long, straight, lazy river slipping past fields and temples and carrying feluccas that hardly seem to have the energy to make it home for dinner, then you should go to Uganda. The Nile here, at its source as it leaves Lake Victoria, is a wild angry beast. We stayed at a campsite on a hillside overlooking the river. From our tents, drinking whisky in the sunset, we could see the river below, a large, swollen angry mass. Even 300 metres above it you could hear the sound of the water.

Anthony and his daughter set off early in the morning, planning to swim through some of the rapids wearing flippers and holding on to small bodyboards. But I opted to go in one of the inflatable boats. Piers had also shown up, and he joined me, entering fully into the spirit of the event, hurling himself out of the boat during the practice session. Our guide, a local called Patrick, was showing us what to do if the boat capsized. I had been rafting down the Zambezi and our boat didn't capsize once, so I was fairly confident that we would be all right. I didn't think much of the practice efforts, getting mouthfuls of water and being stuck under a dark rubber boat.

Practice over, we hit our first rapid. You could hear it before you could see it, a deep ominous sound like the roar of a lion on the high veldt. But it wasn't too bad, just choppy water, which made the boat bounce about. The second and third rapids were equally pleasant, almost exhilarating. The sun was warm, the water was cool. This was a good place to be. We pulled into the side of the river to wait for Anthony and his daughter. There was a group of local Ugandan women washing clothes in the river and laying them out on the rocks to dry. They looked at us in our lifejackets, sunglasses and helmets and must have thought we were mad. Didn't we have any washing to do?

Anthony and his daughter appeared. I thought he looked a little less chipper than normal. His only comment was that it was 'exhausting'. There were three inflatable rafts now, and a couple of kayaks. They would show us the route through the rapids. We set off again. A few rapids, then it would be time for a cold beer and lunch. Everyone was feeling happy and it was good to be travelling in a group. So it's safe to say that I wasn't prepared, either physically or mentally, for what happened next. As we came round a corner, the roar of the rapid ahead became louder than anything we had encountered so far. This was an angry lion, perhaps even a pride.

'Hold on,' said Patrick.

Then we hit the mass of swirling spume and the world turned upside down. The boat flipped, we were a mass of legs and arms, paddles and elbows. I was under the boat and unable to breathe, managed to swim clear, but I was in a wall of foam carrying me downstream and every time I bobbed up to breathe,

I swallowed more water. It was horrible. Eventually, maybe 200 metres later, I slowed down and was able to breathe. I looked around. The boat had gone one way. There were some heads in the other direction. No sign of Piers.

After bobbing along for a while and enjoying the sensation of breathing without having water forced into my mouth, the boat came to pick me up. I managed to haul myself on board and we went looking for other bodies. We found Piers, looking dishevelled but smiling.

We picked up our paddles and moved on. The water was calm again now and what had happened seemed like a distant memory, like a childhood Christmas. We all looked at each other and smiled. It could not get any worse.

Then we heard the next rapid. It made the one before seem insignificant. I wondered if I could get out of the boat, scramble ashore and make my way back to the campsite on foot. Then we struck the first wave. I don't remember much of what happened next, but I saw the video that evening. Our raft hit one of the ten-foot high waves head-on then lifted vertically in the air. As if in slow motion the boat paused, then fell backwards, upside down. Again we were trapped beneath it, fighting an enemy fiercer and crueller than we could imagine. In those situations you simply react, but I felt sure I was going to drown. People always say drowning is one of the nicest ways to go. It was like being simultaneously suffocated and washed by a pressure hose.

There was one set of rapids on the way that we didn't attempt. This was Bujagali Falls, where the water descends in a series of cascades through rocks and trees. It was deemed too dangerous, although a couple of the kayaks made it through. We went up on the bank, walking on the red laterite soil to watch. As I was sitting watching, one of the locals started talking to us.

He was prepared to give us a display. Clutching just an air-filled plastic jerrycan, he was ready to leap into the foaming water and show us how the locals go down this river. Only the very brave and very poor.

'My name is Michael,' he said. 'Give me $10 and I'll show you. Give me $5.'

Anthony explained that a few months earlier the local champion bodysurfer had taken the wrong line, gone too deep and drowned. Many of these surfers cannot even swim. His body was fished out miles downstream. I gave Michael $10, but explained that I did not want him to go in the water on my behalf. I was happy to sit on the rocks and sketch the falls in my notebook that I had carefully concealed in our waterproof bag.

If the Ugandan electricity company has its way – together with financing help from the World Bank – the shady spot where I was sitting and the falls themselves will soon disappear. They are backing a plan to build a 200 megawatt hydropower dam. There is one higher upstream, where the Nile leaves the lake, called Owen Falls. This was built in 1954 but is now inadequate for the country's electricity needs. When Jamal Saghir was talking about Africa using only ten per cent of its hydropower potential, this is the sort of project he wants to see happen.

It will mean some of the Busoga people who live on the riverbank will be forced to move. It will mean that a waterfall that has existed since before memory will be drowned. Local NGOs and international ones such as the International Rivers Network are fighting the proposal, arguing that the electricity generated will not help the more than ninety-five per cent of the population who are not connected to the local grid. They say that there should be more emphasis on renewable energy sources – biofuels, solar, geothermal – and on reducing the losses in the system, estimated at thirty per cent. Meanwhile the water of the Bujagali Falls continues to flow, but for how much longer?

A figure was waving to me from the shallows. It was Michael, wearing only swimming trunks and holding a plastic container. Where he was standing the water was eddying calmly, but then he took two steps forward into a foaming mass and was tossed downstream. I watched as his head bobbed, sinking and rising under the wild water. If he lost grip of the plastic float he would probably be sucked under, only to emerge later downstream, dead. I hoped he hadn't gone on my account. Somebody else must have given him some money to make the trip. Or maybe he was just bored. He disappeared from view behind some rocks, then later, much later, I saw a hand waving from the calm water away in the distance.

Next day we drove to Busia. Piers had disappeared so it was just Anthony and Tammy. We drove through a dry, barren landscape. Busia is a busy, dusty town in eastern Uganda near the border with Kenya. We had a lunch of stringy chicken in a restaurant and discussed the fortunes of Chelsea Football Club with the owner. Then we went to see the district officer. As we drove along one of the earth and gravel roads, dodging the giant potholes made by lorries in the wet season, Anthony told me what he knew about Busia.

'Busia is a relatively new district,' he said. 'It used to be part of the Tororo district until 1997. There's a population of about 250,000 people who speak a lot of different languages, including Samia-Lugwe, Ateso, Swahili, Lugisu, Japadhola, Lusoga, Luganda, Lugwere and Ngakarimojong.'

'And English?' I asked.

'The administrators will speak English,' he said. 'But in the rural areas you won't hear much English spoken. And most of the people live in the rural areas. It is poor, generally subsistence farming.'

'And the water situation?'

'The district has around 250 working boreholes and more than a hundred springs. Water coverage is about fifty per cent in the towns, dropping to closer to forty per cent in rural areas. Those people will have to walk an average of three kilometres each way to get water in the dry season. This comes down to around half a kilometre in the wet season, although the water quality might not be as good.'

'And what if it's bad?'

'Diarrhoea, cholera, dysentery,' he said.

We parked beside a low grey building. We were due to meet Dr Oundu, the district director of health services. Dr Oundu was of medium height, with glasses, a small moustache and an orange and white striped shirt made of cheesecloth. He ushered us into his small office and started outlining his department's achievements. The statistics tripped off his tongue like a child reciting his times table.

'Dabani sub-county lifted sanitation coverage from less than forty per cent to more than ninety per cent in a twelve-month period between 2003 and 2004,' he said. 'In Dabani there are five parishes with fifty-two villages, and a population of around 15,000 living in nearly 3,000 households. They were eating fresh shit every day because they did not have latrines nor did they wash their hands after defecating. We wanted to change this.'

Dr Oundu explained that forcing change wasn't difficult, but it required effort. 'We pointed out that open defecation and lack of hygiene were the reasons that so many of them were sick and dying. So we introduced five key measures: building pit latrines; encouraging hand washing and building handpumps; introducing use of pot racks to dry cooking utensils; covering drinking water supply to avoid contamination; and keeping compounds clean and using refuse pits. If they failed to build a pit latrine they would be fined.'

'How much?'

'5,000 Ugandan shillings.'

'That's about $3, right?'

'Yes. It may not sound much to you, but it's a lot of money for them. More than 340 people were arrested, of whom 225 were fined. We used the fines for prize money for a competition to find the most hygienic homestead.'

'Everyone always says doing things like this costs a lot of money. Did you need much money from either government or multilateral agencies?'

'No, not at all. We used our existing resources, borrowing bicycles and motorbikes so that we could go around checking the properties. But really it was a matter of will rather than money.'

'Could other people do this elsewhere?'

'Of course. But they have to want to.'

We began a tour of some of the prize-winning homesteads, to see for ourselves the realities of life in Busia. Poverty is always surprising, often unpleasant. I have visited a number of slums in Africa. During one conference in Abidjan we were all driven to the middle of a slum where somebody – probably the World Bank – had helped pay to install a water supply. We were led out of our minibus and walked past open sewers and surprised children to view the tap. Unfortunately, the man who had taken charge of the tap – obviously as a means of making money – thought we were coming to take his tap away, so as we got out of the minibus, he unscrewed the tap and scarpered. All that fifty delegates got to see was a bit of metal hosepipe, through which water was reputed to flow.

There was more to see on this visit to rural Busia. We drove over dirt roads, past scrubby acacia trees and into small fenced encampments. They reminded me of the places one imagines early Britons living in, before the Romans arrived and civilised them. There were a couple of small houses, with round walls made of mud and thatched roofs. In some of the compounds there was a separate kitchen. Women and children stood around, the children often naked. There would be some chickens, perhaps a goat or a pig. In one place we saw a small field, no bigger than an allotment, of cotton. I had never seen it growing before.

Anthony was magnificent. After peering down a couple of pit latrines, examining the hand-washing devices they had made and the pot racks, I had seen enough. But Anthony patiently inspected every last detail – and looked interested to the end. He would have made a splendid district officer in the days of the Empire. That afternoon, before it grew dark, we drove back to Kampala.

My idea was to produce a small booklet that the mothers would read – or show to their children if they couldn't read. I had learnt that the Ugandans have a euphemism for going to the toilet, 'to help myself'. We would use this phrase, and we would try to show that even if they did use a toilet, they would have to wipe their hands. We would show a pit latrine and say, 'This is not a toilet', rather like René Magritte's picture of a pipe and underneath the caption, *'Ceci n'est pas une pipe.'* I persuaded Anthony's daughter to illustrate the book and had it designed with simple writing and bright colours. Within a month we had it finished. Anthony declared himself 'delighted' with it. He would take it off to a World Bank retreat they were all having somewhere in the South African bush.

The first sign there was something untoward was when I received a call from the communications department of the World Bank's Water and Sanitation Program. They wanted to know what the terms of reference for this booklet were. Had we written an Advocacy Approach document, outlining the concept and the target audience? I explained that this had been a rush job, conceived under a tree in Addis Ababa and researched and written within weeks.

'You will need to write an Advocacy Approach document,' said the functionary from the communications department. 'We have to explain to our donors what you are up to.'

When I had done that, she phoned me again.

'I am not sure about the narrative arc,' she said. 'I don't think this is in the right order. The head of communications certainly doesn't think so.'

'I don't give a shit what the head of communications thinks. If he could write, he wouldn't be in communications.'

I heard no more from her, but heard from Anthony that our project was not going well. Even though they had received the disk, ready for printing, it looked like nothing would happen, that the booklet would never get distributed. In despair I phoned Piers. I explained as quickly and as patiently as I could that the publication of the booklet was being frustrated by petty office politics. We might be able to save lives – or at least improve them.

'I'm not sure,' said Piers. 'Sometimes these one-off efforts make very little difference at all.'

Back in the conference hall in Washington DC it occurs to me that over the years I have sat through countless lectures on water. Death by PowerPoint, they call it. Ten years of writing about water and nothing seems to have changed. The whole of Africa has started using mobile phones but comparatively few households have been connected to water. I should have written about wars, sport or wine. In wars, people do great deeds or die, but at least the war comes to an end. In sport, people win trophies or lose, sulk or resign, get injured and retire. You may get shot at while reporting, but at least there is some action. In wine, every year there is a new vintage to consider, to sip, slurp or swallow. But in water, nothing changes. The same empty words; the same broken promises. Different locations but the same platitudes repeated over and over like a Chinese water torture. It is five years since I visited the 'flying toilets' of Kibera, one of Africa's biggest slums on the outskirts of Nairobi. People shit in plastic bags then hurl them away. If you are lucky they tie the ends first. None of the well-meaning NGOs has managed to put an end to this disgusting practice.

I had been to the World Summit on Sustainable Development in Johannesburg in 2002. I had been to the Third World Water Forum in Kyoto in 2003, where proceedings were enlivened by the invasion of Iraq and everyone stood in the corridors watching CNN. I had been to the Cannes Water Symposium in 2003 and to World Water Week in Stockholm in 2004. I had interviewed Dr Anna Tibaijuka, head of UN Habitat, who had said all the same things that the World Bank was saying in Washington during Water Week in March 2007. 'There is room for the private sector in water,' she told me. 'We need to make sure they don't lose money, but also that they don't make excessive profits. The notion that water is free is a dangerous myth. Water is not free. You have to fetch it. Air is free.'

If I have heard all these arguments before, surely everybody else in the room, whose job it is to try to develop water projects, has heard them too. Does nothing change in the world of water? I was reminded of that joke about the English climate. 'Everybody complains about the weather, but nobody does anything about it.'

Why are we so reluctant to pay for water? Why does it take so long for anything to get done? At the risk of sounding didactic, here is what I have garnered from hours and hours of sitting in conference rooms and talking in corridors. All you need to know about water projects can be summarised in ten commandments:

1. Safe water and waste-water provision is best carried out by the local municipality, if it's big enough. If not, small municipalities should club together. Hold the elected officials responsible.

2. If the municipality or region cannot do it, because they are bankrupt, corrupt or just inefficient, then look to get the private sector involved.

3. On no account give an unregulated monopoly to a large private company. Private companies by definition are out for a profit and will screw you if they get a chance. Give them a concession contract, preferably a joint venture with a local company. And watch them carefully.

4. People will have to pay for their water. Enough to cover the cost of delivery and to stop them from wasting it. People are happy to pay for good quality, piped water. It is cheaper than buying it from tankers and carting buckets. But charges need to remain affordable to all.

5. Anyone who isn't going to pay the water bill doesn't have a say in the procedure.

6. Beware of NGOs carrying slogans.

7. Watch out for development bankers bearing prescriptions.

8. Think carefully before you dam or drain.

9. Animals, fish, birds, insects and plants share this planet with us. Leave them enough good quality water.

10. Ignore any of the above rather than do something downright barbarous.

And that's about all you need to know. The European Union rarely gets any praise, but it deserves credit for introducing the EU Water Framework Directive in 2000, which aims to manage the quality and quantity of Europe's water. The document states that: 'Water is not a commercial product like any other but, rather, a heritage which must be protected, defended and treated as such.' With the possible exception of Spain, which has developed beyond its water capacities, most of the original member states of Europe have spent billions on their water infrastructure and river basins, and the water is drinkable, swimmable and fishable. You might argue that Europe is rich and can therefore afford to spend money on hydrology. I would counter by saying that it is rich precisely because it continues to focus on important matters such as water. Other countries should do the same, before, say, equipping their navy or sending rockets into space. There may be engineering difficulties to overcome and finance to raise, but neither of these problems is insurmountable. And the task is as nothing compared to Rome's nineteen aqueducts or the *qanats* in Iran. There will be interested parties to convince and placate, but that is possible too. As I look through the stack of notebooks I have been keeping over the last decade, I see the same message recurring on just about every page: 'There was a lack of willingness from the authorities to solve the problem,' this from a spokesman for the European Investment Bank talking about Polish municipalities; 'There's a lack of political will,' this in a conference on African water utilities in Abidjan; 'We must mobilise political will and build awareness,' this from a politician in Kyoto.

There are no votes in building water treatment plants or piped connections. If you consider the few countries in the developing world that have a coherent water policy – Chile, South Africa, Israel – you can see that special cases apply. Chile's water reforms were organised by Pinochet, who brooked no opposition. South Africa is richer than just about all the other sub-Saharan countries combined and gets rich users to subsidise the poor – one of the few examples of a country where subsidies actually reach those who need them. Even so, many of the rural areas remain unconnected. And in Israel they make everyone – including farmers – pay a market rate for water. This might seem like a common-sense approach, but common sense, like water, is often in short supply.

But I at least was ready to vote with my feet. It was time to leave these conference rooms and get some fresh air. I needed to find some people who would actually do something. But first it was time for lunch.

The afternoon sessions at the World Bank were, if possible, a little less enticing. I could have attended the session at two o'clock: Update and Lessons from Output-based-Aid (OBA): Innovative Approaches for Reaching the Poor. (Here's a suggestion: connect them to the water mains. You can pay for it by selling the presidential jet.) Or I could have hung around for Balancing Brown and Green Interests: Total Water Quality Management. I looked in out of duty, but couldn't face it. I went to Kramer's bookshop up by Dupont Circle, then to the Smithsonian Institute and the National Gallery. When Henri Matisse was too old and ill to paint, he made a series of cut-outs using coloured paper. One of his best is a blue woman carrying a jug of water on her head. Both she and the jug have the same sensual shape, offering both life and fecundity. Later on I went back to the bank for the cocktail party, a swell affair. It was set in the massive atrium, which reaches up more than ten storeys high. There were tapestries on the walls and kilims from the Caucasus, ferns and red flowers in plant pots, and plenty to drink. We were given a choice of Budweiser, Amstel Light or Pilsner beer. There was a white Australian wine, Lindemans Bin 70, and a Chardonnay Riesling from California, and a Cabernet Sauvignon from Pepperwood Grove. And the food was good too. Tables were piled high with *pissaladière* of roasted shallots and gorgonzola with grilled fennel, leeks with roasted tomato compote, miniature crab cakes, salmon en croûte with cucumber dill sauce.

Romans in the swinging '60s enjoy natural air conditioning at the Villa d'Este

Between mouthfuls I got chatting to Dr Hussein Mansour, an Egyptian minister. He told me that the three main problems facing Egypt were water, water and water. But when the population was asked to name them in 2006, most came up with different answers, ranging from education to terrorism to food. Only five per cent said water.

Remembering that I had left something in the conference room, I went to go and get it. But on the way in I was stopped by a security guard, who objected to my bottle of Poland Spring.

'There's no water allowed in the conference hall.'

'No water during Water Week?' I asked.

'Very funny,' he said, not smiling.

Back in France, I decided that Mael and I should follow the course of our own water supply. A Chinese proverb says when you drink water, think of the spring. I was worried about what we would do if anything happened to it. What would become of my peach trees? What would happen to my swimming pool? What would happen to my marriage?

So one morning in May we went down to the spring to see if we could find out where it came from. Its source is plain to see: it comes out of a small fissure in the limestone. Left to itself it would join the stream that flows through the garden in the winter. In the summer it dries up. But before the spring was tapped to supply water to the house, the local children used to come and swim here.

But where does the water come from? The problem is that it emerges directly from the side of a hill and climbing it is difficult, but for a small path that we have cut through the thyme, lavender, rosemary, cistus, Spanish broom and pine trees. Each pace is a scented step. Butterflies flit about with their idiocy of flight. Later in the year the air will be crazy with the sound of cicadas.

Trouble is, I don't expect the watercourse to follow our path. It doesn't. Mael, brandishing his divining rods, is veering off course, through the thick brush. It is hard going and the vegetation, designed to withstand the hot, dry summers, is hostile. I suspect he wants me to follow him. Everything seems to pinch or prick. He is weaving around, not to avoid the undergrowth but because this is the direction that the water is flowing underground. By that trick of his of tapping his feet, with each tap being a metre's depth, he can tell us how deeply the water flows. Here it is seven metres below, there eight. We get to the top of the hill, some 200 metres above the house. Below I can see one of my daughters heading for the swimming pool and the dog lying in the shade of the palm tree. To the north I can make out the blue hills above Faugères and, beyond, a darker line of higher hills, almost mountains. At what point do hills become mountains? But Mael's copper rods are twitching, so there is no time to think or enjoy the view of the Espinouse Mountains. We are off again, almost overcome by the pungent thyme. The dog has heard us and run up the hill. He is now beside me, almost tripping me up.

The view is now towards the sea. You can just make out a thin line of blue in the distance. But our water isn't coming from there. The trail seems to be leading due east, on a plateau dense with impenetrable shrub. There is a track that the wild-boar hunters occasionally follow, but mainly this is overgrown. I am pleased to see that the water comes from uncultivated ground. Around here there are many vineyards which most of the winegrowers treat with just about every chemical known to man.

We decide to turn back. We know where the spring is. We don't know where that water comes from, but it is somewhere deep underground where we cannot follow. Water, like God, moves in a mysterious way.

The boy didn't expect to find the cave. He had been following his dog up the hill when the dog disappeared. He called the dog, 'Timothy! Timothy!' but there was no sight of him. Then he heard a muffled barking. He pushed his head between a gap in the rocks and heard the barking get louder. He was only ten, so was able to squeeze through the rocks and down the same tunnel that the dog had taken. It was dark but there was still a little light from the hole he had come in by. The place was wet, there was water underfoot. The tunnel narrowed so he had to bend, then opened up into a large space the size of his school gymnasium. It was full of giant columns of coloured rock. He remembered from geography lessons that they were stalactites and stalagmites. 'The mites go up and the tights go down,' Mr Robinson had said, laughing so they could see down his throat. Thousands of years of raindrops had created this. He called his dog again. He found the place creepy. It reminded him of a cathedral.

10

Waiting with an Empty Bucket

New Delhi: water scarcity in the capital is a problem that gets compounded by 'improper management' and 'careless implementation of plans', according to Delhi Jal officials. Preparing to face one more hot summer, the Jal Board is banking on a 'carrot and stick' policy to get its employees to fall into line. After several rounds of meetings, the board has cautioned the employees that 'strict action' will be taken against 'non-performance'.

'Drawing up schemes and laying plans is not enough. We need good management skills and proper implementation of schemes. The Summer Action Plan for the year 2007, if implemented efficiently, will leave the city with no water problems,' said a senior water official.

By a staff reporter, *Times of India*, 18 April, 2007

EVERY MORNING OF THE year, around six o'clock, a crowd gathers at the entrance to Bindusar Camp, east of Kailash in New Delhi. This is a middle-class area, with grand houses on both sides of the road, some three or four storeys high, worth up to 40 million rupees (£488,000). But between the Shri Ram Temple and an open space of grass, said to contain archaeological artefacts and precious ruins, there is a small V-shaped piece of land, no more than half an acre. More than 750 people are crammed into this tiny area, having illegally built a hundred or so small brick and corrugated iron-roofed dwellings. Each home is not much bigger than a dog kennel. There is also a shop, a small restaurant, and two open sewers running down either side of a narrow path.

One standpipe provides water to all the residents, but supply is erratic and strictly controlled by those who live nearby. The quality of the water is not even that good. This is why the group of people is waiting: not for a bus to take them to work or school, but because at some point a water tanker is scheduled to appear. They are armed with thick hosepipes, an inch or so in diameter, some of which have metal ends that will sink down into the tanker to suck out the water, and an assortment of plastic containers, metal buckets and jerrycans to carry it away. It is already a warm day and will soon get hotter, forecast to reach up to forty degrees. But now it's pleasant. The air is fresh and there is even birdsong in the trees.

At ten to seven a shout goes up. Everyone gets up and looks eager, crowding into the road. A water tanker has appeared. But the cries of joy turn into despair. The tanker has turned off and gone another way. The group sits down again. It is a mixed bunch: mainly men and boys, with some women and children in the background. The men are wearing old shirts and trousers or *lungis*, the Indian word for a sarong. Some are barefoot. The women are in saris or dresses. They return to the side of the busy road, allowing the buses full of schoolchildren, motorbikes and cars to pass. A cow saunters past and lies down in the shade. Then another tanker appears. This time everyone pushes to see, and the road is blocked. The vehicles honk impatiently, but what can they do? That tanker follows the earlier one, and there are groans, similar to the noise a football crowd makes when a favourite striker misses a sitter.

Third time lucky. This tanker doesn't turn off but is heading our way. Already ten to fifteen young men are clambering on the tank, poised to drop the hosepipes into the water. The lorry pulls off the road and shudders to a halt. There are now more than a hundred people clustered around, aged from five to fifty. The pipes, some joined together in a bundle, are thrust deep into the water. On the ground men are becoming breathless as they try to suck water through the thick pipe. Then the water starts to flow. Some wash their hands in it, others stick the pipes straight into the containers. There is little pushing or shoving, there's a calm to the chaos. Each time a container is filled a woman or child brings it to the side of the road and places it on the pavement. A girl aged around ten catches my eye. She is struggling with a big bucket, dodging honking motorbikes, and puts it down beside where we are standing, then goes back into the fray. There seems to be no threat that somebody else will come along and take their water. Soon she and her family have around six or seven containers, all filled with water.

Inside the lorry, the driver and his mate wait, head in hands. They don't lift a finger to help but just sit, until their cargo has been emptied, like a cow being milked, passive and compliant.

Twenty minutes have passed, and the last drops are being eased out of the tanker. There's a tap at the bottom of the tank, and a man is helping a woman drain the last of the water into her bucket. Then, when the tanker is sucked dry, someone signals to the driver. He starts the engine, and in a cloud of diesel smoke, the orange lorry with brown doors and an empty blue water tank disappears down the hill.

The only sign of what has taken place is some spilt water washing down the hill, and a few families still moving buckets. On the other side of the road two men are fixing a pole between three jerrycans, large metal containers originally designed for petrol, which they then hitch onto their shoulders and carry up the hill.

The young girl who had caught my eye earlier comes to pick up her buckets. She is about four feet tall and wearing a yellow T-shirt – my middle daughter's favourite colour – embroidered jeans and flip-flops. Her hair is scraped back from her face and tied with a blue ribbon, frayed and dirty. She is dark, pretty, and appears bright. We ask her name.

'Manju,' she says, speaking in Hindi. She understands not a word of English. *Manju* is a Sanskrit word meaning 'sweet' or 'pleasing', quite a common girl's name in India. It is also the name of a Japanese confectionery.

'How old are you?'

'Nine, I think.'

'Have you ever been to school?'

'No.'

'What do you do all day?'

'Household chores.'

The water smells strongly of chlorine, so it has been treated and should be safe, if unpleasant, to drink. Even so, she says that she and her siblings sometimes fall ill and have diarrhoea, but she thinks this is probably due to something in the food. In the monsoon, they come out to collect water with umbrellas. She likes it when it rains; she bathes in it. She has never been to the sea, nor has she swum in a river. She has only once been outside Delhi, to visit her family village, a day's drive away.

Her face is eager, she is happy to talk to us, but she has work to do. She lifts one of the fifteen-litre containers and places it on her head. Her back arches under the weight. We watch her cross the road and go up the steep hill and out of view. When she comes back to get the next container, five minutes later, I notice beads of sweat on her nose and upper lip. There is a gold ring in her nose. Every day they do this, she tells me. They wait for an hour or so for the tanker to appear, and it takes about another half an hour to get the water to the house. In total they manage to collect around a hundred litres every day, which they use for cooking, cleaning and drinking. There are six of them in the family, two adults and four children. Sometimes the tankers come three times a day. Occasionally they don't come at all.

Manju's mother, Sunita, joins us. She tells us that Manju is not nine but fourteen. If so, she is badly undernourished. Sunita is late for work. At seven o'clock she is supposed to be at a house, where she works as a maid. She earns around £15 a month. She will be scolded because she is late, but what can she do?

At least the water is free, although Sunita says that they would rather pay for it and not have the chore of waiting for a tanker every day. When the water doesn't come they have to go out looking for it. Sometimes they find a tanker elsewhere and they scramble to get water. This can lead to clashes. The water may be free, but it comes at a cost. The family is already paying the greatest price that an Indian family can pay: the lack of an education for one of their children. Sunita runs up the hill to her work, while Manju takes the last container and ushers her brother across the road. Although he is probably less than five years old, he has small containers of water in each hand. She does not look back; she has work to do.

Back at my guest house, I sit on the terrace and order a glass of water. It comes in a plastic bottle with a pink label, proudly proclaiming 'Himalayan, packaged natural mineral water, discovered by Dadi', whoever he is. The label tells me that the water is sourced at the foothills of the Himalayas. 'It has a perfect balance of natural minerals, and no traces of any harmful chemicals or bacteria. It traverses a journey of twenty years through layers of clay and rock, acting as natural filters, from the catchment area to our deep underground reservoir where it is bottled at source in its natural form.'

Twenty years those drops take to filter through the clay and rock. In twenty years' time Manju will still be standing by the side of the road in the early morning, waiting for a tanker, dodging the traffic, with two or three children of her own.

The previous day I had visited Ashish Kundra, an assistant to the finance minister, at his office in Parliament House. It is in the red-brick style that is emblematic of New Delhi, Lutyens' most lavish achievement that was completed just in time for the English to leave, so it almost became a parting gift. Up here it is calm and peaceful, for private cars are banned. In one direction is the president's house; in the other India Gate, the arch designed by Lutyens as a memorial erected by the British to commemorate the Indians who died fighting for the Empire in the First World War.

We go to Ashish's first-floor office with a minimum of fuss. We want to take the stairs but are directed to the lift. Inside, a man jerks himself awake by flinging himself forward onto his stool, and takes us up the one floor. Ashish's office contains a sofa, a couple of chairs, photographs on the wall of the prime minister, two of the president, and a map of the world, partially obscured by a cupboard. And the man himself: he is younger than I had expected, in his early forties, with dark hair, wearing a striped shirt, expensive glasses and a face that is just beginning to go slightly fat around the jowls.

Ashish, a high-flying member of the India Service, used to

be in charge of the Jal Water Board, and devised an audacious plan to shake up the water company. It has 27,000 employees, most of whom have been there for decades, and many of whom are completely worthless. There is no need for 27,000 employees; it should be able to make do with 5,000 at most.

Ashish explains the problem. 'Delhi gets its water mainly from the Yamuna River and from groundwater. We think there is a possibility of 670 million litres a day, with the potential for a further 140 million litres if agreements are signed with other states such as Uttar Pradesh,' he says. 'This works out at about 230 litres per person, per day. However, some sixty-five per cent of water supplied is not paid for. This includes physical leakage of forty per cent, lost through the pipes.'

In that time-honoured phrase, management believed that 'something must be done'. So as well as recommending the construction of fifty new reservoirs, Ashish cooked up a daring plan to bring in private companies to run two pilot zones in the city. They would be chosen by international tender and would be awarded a management contract for five years. This would give the Jal Water Board time to formulate a firm plan to manage the city's water. The private company would be compensated through a performance contract, linked to increasing the hours of supply (few homes enjoy continuous running water in Delhi; just like every city in India, water only runs for a couple of hours a day in the morning, and a couple at night, if you are lucky), losing less water, collecting more revenue, and passing on technical and managerial skills to the existing Jal Water Board staff.

On paper this sounded like a feasible scheme. It wasn't a question of privatising the water supply, nor did it create a monopoly, as there would be two companies involved, although each company would be given a separate part of the city. One problem that the private sector has failed to solve is that involving it normally entails awarding a monopoly, even if you split a city in two. This is what happened in Jakarta, Paris and Manila.

The plan for Delhi was bold in that it might solve the problem and at least buy time for the company. But they were not ready for the objections from civil society. An alliance of different parties came up with a series of different complaints, objecting to the involvement of the World Bank, claiming this was a first step towards full privatisation, that the poor would be disconnected. 'Complaints about the bank were not completely unjustified,' says Ashish. 'But it has many checks and balances and helps reassure international bidders. As for everything else, it is just not true.'

Also ranged against the proposal were a number of NGOs, the most outspoken of which was Parivartan, which means 'change'. This is ironic, when you consider that change was the one thing they didn't want. 'If you want things to change, you have to take bold steps,' says Ashish.

Delhi's chief minister, Sheila Dikshit, a grey-haired woman with the face and demeanour of a grandmother, has long been willing to take courageous steps to transform the city. She introduced a ban on diesel bus engines, forcing them to switch almost overnight to compressed natural gas, and privatised Delhi's electricity supply and distribution network. But a combination of bad luck and bungling by the World Bank brought the project to a standstill. They were perceived to be favouring the bid of Price Waterhouse Coopers.

The chief minister lost her nerve. With a shrug of her *chunni* or scarf, she cancelled the whole process, something most see as a lost opportunity. Ashish certainly does. He does not want to dwell on the failure but says: 'Nothing now will happen for a number of years. They will just try to dream up more ways to pump water into a leaking system.'

It is a short drive from Ashish's grand office to the Yamuna River. We stop the car on a bridge and look down. The water is a dull, grey-brown colour, about a hundred metres wide. It smells like a drain. There are few things uglier than a dirty river: where it should sparkle, it glowers. There is no light, no movement. It is as sad as an empty swimming pool or a half-empty bottle of champagne the day after an all-night party, without bubbles but with a cigarette floating in it. I am with Sanjay, my friend and guide. 'The Yamuna is a sewer,' says Sanjay. 'We take a perfectly good river and turn it into a sewer.'

We watch as a middle-aged man walks along a path to the river. He is followed by a woman and two young children. In his hand is a clay pot. He bends and places the pot in the filthy water. It floats for a minute, then sinks. The man dips a coloured cloth in the water and wipes the face of one child. Then the group faces the water and prays, hands together below their chins. Then they walk back up the path, away from the river.

Once they are out of sight, a man, naked except for a loin-cloth, goes in the water after the pot. He pulls it out and opens it. There is a puff of dust and ashes, one of the first man's ancestors, possibly his mother. The man searches around in the pot for some money and appears to find a coin. Then he puts the pot back in the water and, empty now, it floats away down the Yamuna. If it can stay afloat for long enough it will eventually reach the Ganges. Rivers have always been regarded as holy. The Romans used to think that each river had its own goddess. In the third part of his poem *Four Quartets*, T. S. Eliot writes of a nameless river:

I do not know much about gods; but I think that the
    river
Is a strong brown god – sullen, untamed and intractable,
Patient to some degree, at first recognised as a frontier;
Useful, untrustworthy, as a conveyor of commerce;
Then only a problem confronting the builder of bridges.
The problem once solved, the brown god is almost
    forgotten
By the dwellers in cities – ever, however, implacable,
Keeping his seasons and rages, destroyer, reminder
Of what men choose to forget. Unhonoured, unpropitiated
By worshippers of the machine, but waiting, watching
    and waiting.

Waiting and watching for what exactly? For revenge perhaps? The Yamuna had better strike soon before it is too late.

'The Yamuna is one of our most sacred rivers,' says Sanjay. 'Its source is in the Himalayas. It is like a god. Not quite as powerful as the Ganges, but important nevertheless. People pray to it, call it a goddess, we are supposed to revere it like a mother. But look how we treat our goddess.' The wind, which was blowing away from us, turns slightly into our faces, a smell like a blocked drain. It is time to leave. Annual rainfall is higher in Delhi than in Paris. 'If we only had more water, we could at least dilute the pollution,' says Sanjay. But there is no more water.

Sunita Narain is a short, dark-haired woman in her forties who works for the Centre of Science and Education. By luck her group, a committed NGO, has just produced a report on the river, which they are launching in the amphitheatre of the India Habitat Building. I go along. There is a good turnout for the tea and biscuits at 6.30 p.m. Then, in the presence of the chief minister, the head of the Jal Water Board and a minister who makes no sense at all, Sunita presents her findings.

'The Yamuna is the most polluted river in all of India,' she says. 'Up to eighty per cent of the water that arrives in Delhi leaves as sewage. It is criminal. Dirty water is still the single largest cause of child mortality. It should make us all very angry. This isn't just about a river: it's about the future of India.'

She is a good speaker, doing her best to get the crowd excited; they seem tired, but they are listening.

'The river is dead,' she says. 'It just hasn't been cremated. What goes for Delhi is the same for every city in India. We always believed that the river is polluted not because of us but because of somebody else. Every city in India thinks it is New York, Shanghai or London. We think we can bring water from miles away and send sewage miles in the other direction. We can't. And we subsidise the rich, not the poor.'

If you are connected to the mains the cost of tap water in Delhi is around two rupees for a 1,000 litres. In contrast, you have to pay twelve rupees for a plastic litre bottle of water. With a series of maps and charts, Narain shows that even with all the money that the city has spent on building sewage treatment plants, efforts to clean up the river have not been successful. Her findings suggest that the treated water ends up being mixed with raw sewage. The effluent goes back into the river, and the shit drifts downstream.

When she has finished, Chief Minister Dikshit goes to the microphone. 'All this is true,' she says. 'But what can we do? The experts told us that sewage treatment plants were the answer. Now Sunita tells us that they are not working properly.'

Almost in mid-sentence she switches from English to Hindi,

so I miss large chunks of her speech. But she ends with a suggestion, in English, that I do understand: 'My humble solution is to say, give us your expertise and we implement the plan. We have tried everything we can think of!'

In the summer of 1858 the residents of London had to deal with a phenomenon dubbed 'The Great Stink' by *The Times*. The smell was so bad that curtains soaked in chloride of lime were hung in the Houses of Parliament. It wasn't very effective. The smell both penetrated the curtains and affected the spirits of all Londoners. The Thames had been turned from a river into a sewer, and the smell that was so upsetting to parliamentarians was the smell of their – and their neighbours' – shit. The weather was hotter than usual, which encouraged the bacteria to thrive.

It is quite an achievement to turn a large tidal river into a cesspit, but the Londoners of the 1850s managed it. Part of the blame belongs to the flushing toilet. Prior to that, people used chamber pots. Their contents were tipped into cesspits that were emptied every so often. Flushing toilets sent down greater quantities of water into the cesspits, which then overflowed and emptied into other drains, finally washing into the Thames. This polluted water was then pumped back into the water supply, leading to cholera and other illnesses. To deal with the crisis a body was set up called the Metropolitan Commission for Sewers, whose chief engineer, Joseph Bazalgette, came up with a plan to build an eighty-mile network of sewers to prevent raw sewage from running into the Thames. His pipes ran under the Embankment, which was built to accommodate them. He took the sewage to the east of London, where it could be flushed out into the river with minimal effect on the population. This system involved three major pumping stations, at Abbey Mills in the Lea Valley, at Deptford and at Crossness on the Erith marshes. Abbey Mills is still operational. At Crossness you can see the spectacular building and engines and pumps that meant that you could breathe freely in the Houses of Parliament.

Water in London has always been provided by a mixture of private and public bodies, with control and ownership changing hands as frequently as the tide. The Romans were the first to mechanise the drawing of water from the river, using both fixed and floating waterwheels. It is thought that the wheels were powered by slaves, who would walk about ten paces to turn a treadmill. Each turn would raise a hundred litres of water. A few years ago a Roman waterwheel was reconstructed and displayed outside the Museum of London.

When the Romans left Britain, their water supply remained the core infrastructure until the Middle Ages. The Church took over some water supply activities and in Cambridge in the fourteenth century, for example, Franciscan friars laid a pipeline from a spring into the city. Then in the 1570s, Peter Morris, a Dutchman, installed an ingenious pump near London Bridge that used the force of the current to push water a hundred feet up into a cistern. The authorities were so impressed that they awarded him a 500-year concession – which still has another seventy-five years or so to run. Although neither he nor his waterwheel, nor even the bridge itself, still exist, there is one legacy. In 1701 Richard Soame bought the waterwheels. When legislation prohibited water from being drawn from the Thames, his descendants were given shares in the New River Company, which became the Metropolitan Water Board, which became Thames Water. The shares will continue to pay a dividend until the lease runs out in 2082. Morris' original waterwheel was destroyed in the Great Fire of London, but subsequently rebuilt. By 1809 there were five waterwheels lifting four million gallons a day from the river.

Other private companies invented different schemes. At the beginning of the 1600s Hugh Myddleton, a goldsmith and entrepreneur, built the 'New River', a forty-mile channel running from springs in Hertfordshire to London. It was privately financed and operated. Even King James I took a stake. By the 1800s there were twelve different private companies competing for business in the boroughs of London. Just like their modern counterparts, they were more interested in connecting their pipes in rich areas. Then, as now, the poor were neglected. In 1904 most of London's water companies were nationalised to form the Metropolitan Water Board, a move deemed necessary to finance the huge investments, as well as rationalising the water supply. In addition, private companies were not held to provide a good or safe enough service.

In the 1950s and 1960s England's water supply was integrated with sewage treatment. In the 1970s ten regional water authorities were created in England and Wales. This made good sense. In the 1980s they were privatised, which made less sense. Water was sold, although riparian rights were granted. This meant that if you already used the water from rivers, you could continue doing so, provided you said how much you used. Understandably, people wildly overestimated their usage and needs, which when added together, came to more water than there was available. Moreover, the City of London seeks short-term gain and was rewarded: at times some of the water companies, thanks to the laid-back regulators, were more profitable during the 1990s than Microsoft.

At the start of the twenty-first century, many customers are complaining that their water bills are too high. Investment is low and there are no new ideas. There is a lack of water in the south-east, but endless water in Scotland. Why not send it south? The latest step has been Welsh Water abandoning its corporate structure to become instead a not-for-profit organisation, a move some people are calling a 'deprivatisation'. And so it goes on, with fashion dictating the way that water is supplied, sometimes private, sometimes public, but more often than not, chaotic.

I decided to visit Abbey Mills. I contacted Thames Water's archivist, Matthew Wood. Thames Water was sold by its German owners, RWE, to a consortium led by Macquarie, an Australian bank, for £8 billion in 2006. We agreed to meet on a Friday in October in 2007. I took the Tube east to West Ham. It was one of those grey London days when the sky and the earth seem to be one. I had a good cup of coffee in a small café run by a Chinese man opposite the station, then set out on my quest. I passed the Channel Sea building. Beside it was a grey lagoon that looked like it contained the sewage of generations of Londoners. Matthew later confirmed this to be the case. It was not just the air quality that made living in west London more salubrious; as well as the smoke, Londoners sent their shit to the east. I could smell it in the air that day, even though nowadays it is piped and treated. Years ago it would have smelt foul.

Beyond were rooftops, pylons, industrial buildings and, shining out among the detritus, the gold dome and weathervane of Abbey Mills. It was like seeing a marble in a bag of cement. I turned right at the sundial – there was no possibility of a shadow today – and went down the slippery wooden stairs, where Matthew was waiting for me. He is a thin, cheery figure with cropped blond hair and blue eyes. Company policy insisted that we wear yellow jackets. Suitably attired, we went outside and over to a corner of the site where the coal bunkers used to be situated. Originally the pumping engines were powered by coal, which would arrive by boat, then travel via a small-gauge railway, to be dumped in these bunkers. From there it would be carted into the boilers. Until the 1940s there were two giant chimneys, each 190 feet high, though all that remains is the base of one of them, still a good-sized structure. When they were first built, they had ornate tops and looked like the towers of a minaret. These were taken off, or fell off, and the coal fires were subsequently decommissioned and replaced by electric engines. What hastened the end of the towers was the suspicion that the Luftwaffe was using them as a navigation aid during the Blitz. After a bomb had fallen and destroyed part of the boiler house, the towers in turn were demolished.

We turned to face the building. By any standards, it is an impressive housing for a series of engines and pumps whose sole purpose is to pump shit some forty feet up, sufficient elevation for a final transit towards Beckton. Bazalgette explained it thus: 'The fall in the river isn't above three inches a mile; for sewerage we want a couple of feet *(so that the sewers are self-cleansing)* and that kept taking us down below the river and when we got to a certain depth we had to pump up again. It was certainly a very troublesome job.' At Beckton, Bazalgette had built a series of lagoons that would filter the waste water and contain it until the tide was right, and the sewage would be swept out to sea. Nowadays there is a waste water treatment plant at Beckton. Matthew has been there and watched the water joining the river.

'It was as clear as water coming out of the tap,' he told me. 'I could have drunk it, only I didn't fancy it.'

The effort that went into the design of Abbey Mills is striking. It is the work of Charles Driver, who specialised in engineering-based projects, especially railways. I was surprised to learn that he designed Tunbridge Wells West, a station that I passed every day on the way to school in Tonbridge. Abbey Mills is the size of a decent French provincial church, not as large as a cathedral, but bigger than a parish church. However, in style it is more Greek Orthodox than Catholic. At the top, the gold weathervane and lantern, the glass dome that looks like a watch-tower in a folly, burnished in the pale light. The weathervane no longer points north. It was restored after the great storm of 1987 and the restorers obviously couldn't read a compass. Below that are grey tiles and a line of patterned lead sheet. Then an orna-mental guttering, encaustic tiles manufactured in Minton. And everywhere a mix of light yellow Suffolk brimstone bricks, woven into which are decorative red bricks. The final effect is a mixture of Venetian architecture – particularly the arches – a Greek Orthodox church, and even a mosque. 'It's been nicknamed the "Mosque in the Swamps",' says Matthew. 'But we're not supposed to call it that.'

Over the porches are elaborate stone carvings of flowers such as foxgloves, lily in the valley and hops. There are a number of large wooden doors, like the entrance to a Florentine church, with brass and copper florets for decoration. Matthew believes they built such an elaborate building to show the taxpayers where their money was going. Most sewerage work, after all, is under-ground, so there's nothing to see. Here was a chance for the mayors who backed the project to get a sense of the scale and grandeur of the works. But Abbey Mills is not a mausoleum to the Victorian age. It is still in use, acting as a back-up when there is a storm.

'I can't see it ever being decommissioned,' says Matthew. 'There are too many pipes coming into it.'

Some years ago Thames Water even cleaned one wing, and restored some of the brickwork at a cost of £2 million. They either lost heart or wanted to save money, but the effect of the gleaming yellow bricks in the renovated wing is to make the older part look even more neglected. In 2012 the Olympics will be nearby and Matthew is hopeful that this will encourage the

With its dome and minarets, Abbey Mills was soon nicknamed the 'Mosque in the Swamps'

company to finish the job. There is quite a lot of activity on the site today, he explains, much more than usual. On Monday the new CEO is coming to visit.

We walk round the corner to where the new F pumping station stands, which came into service in 1997. All the pumping stations at Abbey Mills are known by their initials. This is the sixth on the site, so it is known as F. It is made of grey metal, on a smaller scale than Abbey Mills, and certainly less decorative.

'It won an architectural award,' says Matthew.

'I can see why. It looks good.'

'It looks like a metal shed to me.'

Matthew, although probably no more than forty, is not a modernist. He makes no secret of his admiration for Bazalgette.

'The man was a genius. He saved more lives than Florence Nightingale. If there's one obvious candidate for the fourth plinth in Trafalgar Square, it's him. He and his team worked out that the sewer pipes should fall an eighth of an inch every hundred yards from central London until they get here. Genius. They built everything out of brick. The sewers are built to last; they will probably still be in use in another thirty years. And what do we do now? We build on the cheap. We put iron pipes in the ground that rust. It's all down to the cheapest tender.'

Across from Pumping Station F, we could make out the tops of the towers of Canary Wharf opposite us. The developers of Canary Wharf were very keen to ensure that their project never flooded, so they paid Thames Water to put in a connecting sewer.

We enter Abbey Mills through one of the ornate doors. The place is quite empty. A fern grows in the wall ten feet in the air. Parts of the complex are used in films: Norwegian pop band A-ha shot a video here; it was a location in one of the Batman films, and Jeffrey Archer's film on life in prison was set here, the bare whitewashed brick walls serving as a convincing backdrop. Before we enter the main pumping area there is an arresting exhibit. Two elm logs, each ten feet in length, are fitted together, the middle hollowed out by a corkscrew of some kind. Until the eighteenth century these were used as pipes to carry water. They must have been very prone to leaking. Sometimes they weren't even buried underground, but just placed in a row on the ground. Matthew shakes his head. 'To think that the Romans made beautiful, waterproof clay piping. Once they had gone, we were reduced to this.'

The interior of the pumping station is full of ornate metal columns, and as you look up, there's a white banister railing and above, the glass of the lantern. Again, it is reminiscent of being in a church. According to Matthew, the dome with its glass windows was there to act as a flue: when the engines were coal-fired you needed somewhere for the smoke to go. Looking down, and you can see forty feet down, large black pipes appear bearing sewage. Penstocks operate like doors to stop the flow if necessary. Once there would have been eight beam engines clattering in this space. Now there are eight electric engines, encased in metal grilles and looking a little like daleks. They are operated remotely from Beckton.

We go for a cup of tea: it is quite cold in the pumping station and on a day like this you could do with those coal fires. Then we go down into the archives: row after row of handsome leather books, some two feet square in size. There are 142 of these volumes containing all the original drawings and designs for Abbey Mills, Beckton and the northern outfall, the pipe that takes the waste water to Beckton. Inside some are letters to or from Bazalgette, while some of the drawings have been signed off by Bazalgette with a swirling 'JWB' and a date. On the other side of the archive stack is a similar number of books dedicated to drawings of the London sewerage system. Matthew is sometimes called on to check a detail on these plans, when the digital maps in use today don't correspond with what the workers have found in the ground. There are a million photos in the archive. The Victorians might be accused of many things, but not of being slapdash.

Back in Sanjay's house he shows me some of the systems that ensure that he and his wife don't go short of water. He freely admits that they are amongst the lucky ones, 'spoilt' in his words. Their house is in one of the best parts of Delhi, near the government and World Bank offices. It is a white, airy building, one of forty or so properties built around a grass square. Inside it's cool. The air conditioning is switched off because Sanjay has a cold, but the fan is turning slowly like an aeroplane propeller when the engine has been shut down. Sanjay has lived in England and America. There are prints on the wall to commemorate these travels: Millais' *Corn Gatherers*, Van Gogh's couple asleep on a hayrick, and a pointillist painting by Henri-Edmond Cross of the Iles d'Or.

He takes me to the back of the house, pointing on the way to the parallel plumbing. One tap, which is connected to the mains, only produces water twice a day. The other tap is connected to his water storage system, a large black plastic container that holds 500 litres. Inside one of his landlord's back rooms is a Z pump, which bores down fifty or more metres into the ground and extracts water at no expense to the householder. These pumps are supposed to be registered – new ones are banned – but it is thought that many people are still installing them, and few are registered. His landlord has also fitted a suction pump.

'The idea is that you start sucking as soon as you think water is about to come down the pipes,' says Sanjay. 'That way you get more water than your neighbours. The problem is that nine out of ten households have these pumps, so nobody really benefits. In fact, it's more of a drawback because they suck up a lot of rubbish.'

Most water meters in Delhi don't function and there is little incentive to fix them. Meters are designed to work on a continuous-flow basis, but the stop-go nature of Delhi's water supply means that most things connected to the system don't work properly.

'I would say that trying to get hold of water occupies a lot of people's time in Delhi,' says Sanjay. 'Many people get up at five o'clock in the morning to turn their pumps on.'

I tried to reach Arvind Kejriwal, the head of Parivartan, the NGO most vocal in its opposition to the plan to introduce the private sector to help with water in Delhi. I phoned his office on numerous occasions. Mostly there was no answer. Once I heard a voice.

'Can I speak to Mr Kejriwal please?'

'He is not here.'

'His mobile doesn't seem to work either.'

'His mobile only works at night.'

But it didn't work for me at night either. I wanted to ask Parivartan why they had been so opposed to change. Did they believe they had won a victory by maintaining the status quo? Did Manju or her mother care who supplied the water? They would be happy to pay for it, if only somebody would supply it.

The Javanese have a saying: water on the moon. They use it to refer to something that is unattainable or out of reach. The Indians could adapt it to this: like water at midday in Delhi. Who ultimately is to blame for the water situation in Delhi? Is it the British, a final subjugation from the Empire? Is it the poor, for refusing to pay, or the middle class, for snaffling whatever subsidy is on offer? Or maybe it's the World Bank, for bungling – or

being perceived to have bungled – two small private management contracts in the city? Could one blame the press? Should
local editors have done more to convince the population that
running water will only come when you pay a realistic amount
for it? Should we slate Parivartan, the NGO whose name means
'change', but which seems reluctant to accept any? It fought the
World Bank's plan, and won. But since then, what has it achieved?
Is there now piped water running in every household thanks to
its efforts? No.

I know who I blame. I blame the government. I blame the
voters. I agree with Sunita Narain that India should be ashamed
of the water situation in Delhi – and by definition, ashamed of
the situation throughout the country. They should hang their
heads in shame that the country's greatest asset, its children, are
waiting at street corners with buckets of water rather than going
to school. A whole generation – Manju and her contemporaries
– will remain illiterate and innumerate just for the lack of running
water.

Could the effort that Manju's family has to expend in
collecting water be replicated across the world if the water
situation becomes more acute? Possibly. Governments, whose
main aim is to be re-elected and can rarely think beyond the next
opinion poll, are failing to address the problem. India as a nation
is more obsessed with sending a rocket to the moon than water
through the pipes of Delhi. The world is more obsessed with
climate than the fact that one billion people do not have clean
water. There are no votes in water. The topic is too nebulous.
And besides, it will rain soon. But what if it doesn't?

As I write this, the television news is all about floods in England.
Tewkesbury is marooned. It's ironic that floods lead to water

shortages, but 130,000 homes in the town have no running water. They are distributing bottled water from supermarket car parks; there are 1,000 bowsers dotted around the county of Gloucestershire. And are the English demonstrating their habitual sangfroid in a crisis? No doubt some are, but the papers tell tales of greed and stupidity. MINDLESS YOBS POLLUTE WATER SUPPLY screams the *Daily Mail*; apparently the yobs were peeing in the bowsers, pouring bleach in them, or merely tipping them over. Brigadier Jolyon Jackson, the man leading the army operation in Gloucestershire, downplayed reports and called for a 'sense of proportion'. A retired accountant and his son were overcome by diesel fumes as they tried to pump water out of the cellar of Tewkesbury Rugby Club. 'He lived for the club,' commented a neighbour.

It has been the wettest May, June and July since records began, and according to the *Guardian* it is all our fault. And it is going to get worse. But rain in one place doesn't necessarily mean rain everywhere. Some months later I turned on the television and watched the bizarre spectacle of Governor Sonny Perdue standing on the steps of the Georgia Capitol, head bowed, praying for rain to end the region's historic drought.

'Oh Father, we acknowledge our wastefulness,' Perdue said. 'But we're doing better. And I thought it was time to acknowledge that to the creator, the provider of water and land, and to tell him that we will do better.'

Hundreds of Georgians, from ministers to office workers, landscape gardeners to truck drivers, had gathered in downtown Atlanta for the prayer vigil. Some held bibles and crucifixes. They linked arms and sang 'What a Mighty God We Serve' and 'Amazing Grace'. 'We have come together, very simply, for one reason and one reason only: to very reverently and respectfully pray up a storm,' said Governor Perdue.

Dressed in a green suit and brown cowboy boots, Governor Perdue might be accused of leaving it a little late, as well as having a dodgy dress sense. Metropolitan Atlanta's aquifers have sunk to a record low, while the city's Coca-Cola plant keeps producing bottles of Coke and golf courses keep getting sprayed.

'We've been so busy industrialising that we've forgotten how to spiritualise,' Gil Watson, senior minister at Northside United Methodist Church in Atlanta, told the crowd. 'We've been so busy with our economy and what we can have and what we can possess that we've forgotten that you possess it all. Great God, this is your land. We till it for you. We are entrepreneurs for you, dear God.'

A neighbour of mine in France is sceptical of the prowess of water diviners. He thinks they are all con men who poke around with pointed sticks, making up nonsense about underground currents and watercourses. When he first built a borehole in his garden he employed one. 'He ran this way and that with his divining rods,' says Marcel. 'Eventually he decreed that we could dig in this place. It's about the most inconvenient place possible, but we did as he directed.' After a few years the water supply grew clogged with limescale, so Marcel decided to call in a hydrologist from Béziers. 'He gave us geological data and maps,' says Marcel. 'It's not a matter of witchcraft but of fact. This area of France was once under sea. There is still an underground reservoir of water below ground. If you dig deep enough, you will find it.'

It is like the old argument between Church and State, fought so fiercely by the French at the beginning of the twentieth century. Rationally it is hard to believe in *sourciers*; but their magic is compelling. Marcel, a rationalist, chose science. He dug a hole near where he wanted it, close to the house, and uses it to water his lawn, which is green and rolled like a cricket square.

I telephoned the hydrologist and he agreed to come and see me. On the appointed hour he showed up, in a blue Peugeot and a smart suit. He wore a hat, something I thought people only did in films. We discussed the weather. It hadn't rained for three months. Then he began walking round the garden, describing the different rocks, talking of schist and lignite. He told me that the water would come from there – pointing to the site of the spring.

'That hill is a water tower,' he says. 'Drill in there and it would be like tapping an enormous sponge.'

The heat has been building all summer, and her memory is of the dust blowing down the streets like an angry woman. The dust creeps into the eyes, the hair and the bedroom, even the food. People get moody for no reason. Every evening there are raised voices, angry people. Waiting for the monsoon is like waiting for a birthday: it seems it is never going to come. Then one morning she hears banging on the corrugated iron roof, a drumming like a round of applause. It should be light by now but it's dark. She gets out of bed and goes outside. It is as if people are throwing buckets of water at the door. It reminds her of the Holi ceremony, when water fights erupt throughout the country and she fills balloons with water. But it has been so long since it rained that she has forgotten what it's like. She feels the water streaking down her face, penetrating her thick brown hair, moistening her scalp. She feels her body revive. It is as if she is a flower that hasn't been watered all summer. Her father sees her outside and shouts, come in, you'll get cold, but she doesn't want to hear him, she runs off to an open space where the water is rushing across the ground, turning the dust into a swirling watercourse. This is luxury. This is money.

Water For War Or Peace?

> Perhaps the truth depends on a walk around the lake.
> Wallace Stevens

IT IS A COMMONLY held belief that all the wars of the future will be caused by water. If I am foolish enough to mention to anyone that I am writing a book about water, I am asked: 'What, as in, soon we're all going to run out and start fighting about it?' Flaubert's *Dictionnaire des idées reçues*, one of the most deliciously subversive works of the nineteenth century, lists the received wisdom of that age, the clichés of the bourgeois middle class. For example, that the English are 'all rich'; that you should never eat apricots without pointing out that 'we won't be having any more of them this season'; and my favourite, his take on architects: 'all idiots. Always forget to put in the stairs.' For water the entry is: 'Paris water gives you colic; sea-water is good for swimming; Eau de Cologne smells good.' If he were writing his dictionary today he would probably add : 'Can't live without it. Best drink of the lot. Oil of the twenty-first century. Soon we will all be fighting over it.'

But there is always an element of truth in a cliché. And we are of course right to be concerned about our water supply. When Frank Johnson interviewed the dancer Sylvie Guillem, he asked her why she hadn't had any children. Her reply was that she did not want to bring children into a world in which one day they might turn on a tap and find that no water came out. Aside from this being a typically quixotic French reply to a question – there were probably many places in France even when she was born where water did not always come out of a tap when you turned it on – it shows a high degree of concern, shared by many others. Barely a day goes by without an invitation to a conference on water and security arriving at my house. Where once we were worried about having enough to eat, now it appears we worry about having enough water to drink and to nourish our crops.

This is a relatively recent reincarnation of an old concern. Just as modernism made us unable to appreciate art, industrialisation made us lose touch with water, where it came from and how we might best use it without exploiting this precious substance. Before then, water was at the heart of every civilisation. Once it was simply a matter of turning on a tap, all the mystery disappeared. Although even early on, back in the nineteenth century, some enlightened souls had their doubts about the quality of industrialised water. If you leave The Berkeley Hotel in London, cross Knightsbridge and walk towards Hyde Park, you come to the Albert Gate. Beside this is a six-metre granite drinking trough, carved along one side of which is 'Metropolitan Drinking Fountain and Cattle Trough Association'. What strange thing is this? It turns out that in 1859, Samuel Gurney, a Member of Parliament, and Edward Thomas Wakefield, a barrister, founded an association to provide free drinking water to city inhabitants. In 1867 it changed its name to include cattle troughs, which would include drinking water for animals, especially horses which were the main means of transport. These troughs carried inscriptions such as 'Be Merciful To God's Creatures'.

The first fountain was at Holborn Hill by the railings of

St Sepulchre's Church on Snow Hill. In the next six years 85 fountains were built, often located near public houses: in those days, as it often is today, beer was the more popular drink. Back then it was also safer. But the association guaranteed the purity of its water. There was also a religious stance, with many inscribed with quotations from the Bible, such as 'Jesus said whosoever drinketh of this water shall thirst again but whosoever drinketh of the water I shall give him shall never thirst.' It was the great age of philanthropy: Queen Victoria donated money towards a fountain in Esher, Baroness Burdett Coutts paid for elaborate fountains in Victoria Park, while the Maharajah of Vizianagram footed the bill for equally splendid fountains in Hyde Park.

The association was a great success. By 1879 it had erected and was supplying more than 800 drinking fountains and troughs in the capital. Granite troughs became the standard design, as earlier examples of cast iron or wood lined with zinc proved to be less hard-wearing. As well as supplying water, the fountains were built to encourage temperance and support a muscular Christianity. But with the launch of the motor car and the disappearance of most of the horses, it lost some of its *raison d'être*. It started building water fountains in schools, and changed its name to the Drinking Fountain Association. In 2000 it received a lottery grant to build more fountains, and has expanded some of its operations abroad, in places such as India and Nepal. Nevertheless one can't help thinking that it has lost some of its grandeur. The sums it disburses are small. For example in 2005, it disbursed a total of £17,256, including donations for twenty-eight drinking fountains to schools, giving £2,000 to improve water sanitation in a village in Nepal, and another £2,000 to Karen hill tribes in Thailand. All eminently worthy, but quite insubstantial when you consider that American philanthropists are doling out billions of dollars every year. It celebrates its 150th anniversary in 2009. Maybe that will help its fund-raising effort.

For the latest fear is that the gloomy warning of Thomas Robert Malthus, a nineteenth-century English political economist, who prophesied that the population would soon grow faster than the food to feed it, might yet come true. However, it will occur due to a lack of water – and thus not enough to water the crops – rather than just a simple lack of food. Farmers, with the help of scientists, were able to produce more food to feed the hungry mouths caused by the population explosion of the twentieth century. It is ironic that the sudden shift to biofuels is hitting the production of food. We may not be depleting oil supplies, but now we'll all die of starvation on the way to the petrol station.

Malthus made his prediction in 1830 when the population of the world reached around one billion people. His gloomy prognosis has turned out to be incorrect, so far. A hundred years later, the world's population had doubled. People were being fed, even if there were probably more poor, most of whom struggled along on a subsistence diet. And there were some serious famines in that time, although these were mainly caused by incompetence, or – as in the case of the Irish famine – malice. But food supply, if properly managed, was not a problem. And lack of food was not stopping population growth. By the end of the twentieth century there were six billion people on the planet, with a further 73 million appearing every year. By 2014 we should be seven billion.

To date, water supply has not been a problem. But it could be. Which is why so many believe that we will all soon be going to war over it. Already in the nineteenth century, Mark

Twain was clear what he thought: 'Whisky's for drinking, water for fighting,' he said. In addition, there is now the threat of climate change. The received wisdom is that the south is going to get hotter and drier. Australia's drought will be prolonged indefinitely; the country may produce good cricketers but soon they will have no grass to play on. Much of Africa will become a dust bowl, one large Sahara. Southern Europe will get hotter and hotter. If we had any sense we would all move to Scandinavia. Plenty of water, fewer people, and soon a balmy climate.

Malthus might after all have the last laugh. Agriculture is already the biggest user of water, absorbing seventy to eighty per cent of most countries' supply. In many places, especially China and India, groundwater is where farmers find water for their crops. Day and night, diesel pumps suck faster and deeper into the ground. The groundwater level is sinking. There are warnings, mostly unheeded. But what are you supposed to do as a farmer? Stop pumping? And why should the developing world listen to doomsayers from the West? They are just doing what just about everybody else has been doing for years. California has managed to win a court case guaranteeing its water supplies from the Colorado River; in other words, the state of Colorado has lost the right to its own water. Worried lest the same thing happens to them, the states of the Great Lakes have signed an agreement refusing to share their water with anybody else in the future.

There are numerous places where a lack of water could conceivably lead to political trouble. Think of the Nile, the Jordan Valley, the Tigris and Euphrates. All are in areas where water resources are scarce. Egypt, which relies entirely on the Nile for its water supplies that flow from the Ethiopian highlands, has a strong army and air force and has sworn to attack if anything is done to restrict the flow of water. If conflict is likely to happen anywhere, you would expect it around the Nile. It is the longest river in the world, passing through the territory of ten countries, five of which are among the poorest in the world. Four are land-locked. And seven of them are involved, or have been until recently, in internal or international conflicts. All rely to a lesser or greater degree on the waters of the Nile for their economic growth. For most of them, the Nile's water is central to their survival.

Water has been a useful weapon. During the Herero Wars in Namibia in 1904, German troops seized the few wells and water supplies in the desert area of Omaheke in the western Kalahari. They were ordered to shoot any approaching Herero on sight. Many died, although a few were able to escape to neighbouring British territories. In Germany during the First World War there were fears that reservoirs might be destroyed or poisoned. During the Spanish Civil War General Franco made plans to destroy the Ordunte Dam near Bilbao. The Germans made similar plans to attack the Aswan Dam during the Second World War, while the Soviet army succeeded in blowing up the Dnieper Dam in 1941. But the most dramatic attack of the Second World War came when Barnes Wallis, the engineer and inventor, developed a way to cause devastation to the industrial heartland of Germany. The mission was to puncture four major dams, the Möhne, the Eder, the Sorpe and the Ennepe, cutting the supply of hydroelectricity, causing colossal flood damage, but also weakening German morale.

Not surprisingly, the dams were well protected, with torpedo netting to prevent them being attacked by conventional weapons. So Barnes Wallis designed a bouncing bomb, which worked on the same principle as the children's game of ducks and drakes, when you send stones skipping over a body of water. The drum-shaped bombs would be dropped already spinning backwards. When they hit the water they would skip in a series of jumps until they reached the dam wall; then, still spinning, they would run down the wall and be detonated by a hydrostatic fuse. Royal Air Force 617 Squadron was chosen to carry out the operation. To make the bombs work, they would have to be dropped from a very low altitude, just eighteen metres. The Lancaster bombers would be flying in the dark, over unknown terrain, while the dams' defenders would be shooting at them. The Dambusters, as they became nicknamed, practised dropping the bombs over open water in England, including the Eyebrook Reservoir in Rutland, the Derwent Reservoir in Derbyshire and the Fleet Lagoon at Chesil Beach, Dorset. There were two principal technical problems to overcome: first, they needed to know how far they were from the dam before they released the bouncing bomb, to ensure that it neither fell short nor bounced over the dam wall; second, they needed to know that they were flying at exactly eighteen metres above the water. The first problem was solved by making a special aiming device that measured the distance from the dam; the second dilemma was overcome by mounting two spotlights on the plane, which, when they converged on the surface of the water, indicated they were flying at the right altitude. But the spotlights acted as a useful target for the German gunners.

On the night of 17 May, 1943 nineteen Lancaster bombers left RAF Scampton, five miles north of Lincoln. The forecast was good, with clear skies and little wind. Two of the planes didn't make it to the target, being shot down over the Dutch coast. Others failed to find the target in the mist – the weather forecasters got that wrong – some were shot down by anti-aircraft fire, some bombs fell short, others jumped over the wall, some even hit the wall but failed to breach it. Three bombs, however, hit their mark, exploded the walls, and caused serious devastation and loss of life downstream. The Möhne was still pouring water twelve hours after the wall was breached, leaking at a rate of more than 8,000 cubic metres a second, much greater than the flow of a normal flood. When the waters reached the Rhine a day later, the river level was raised by four metres.

How successful were the attacks? It was unfortunate, to say the least, that one of the largest losses of life was a camp full of Russian and Ukrainan prisoners of war, who had been captured and kept in a building just below the Eder Dam. Hydroelectric production was disrupted. Probably the biggest benefit from an Allied point of view was the realisation, both in Germany and Britain, that the Germans were no longer invincible. In addition, the devastation caused by the flooding badly affected food production in the area that year. Barnes Wallis was in no doubt of the success of the mission, even though 53 of the 133 aircrew that set off did not make it back to base. 'I feel a blow has been struck at Germany from which she cannot recover for several years,' he wrote. 617 Squadron still exists. Its badge shows a dam being struck by three flashes and water gushing from the hole, with the motto '*Après nous le déluge*'.

It is unnerving that one of the major British successes of the war – made into a popular film in 1956 starring Michael Redgrave and Richard Todd and remade in 2007 by Peter Jackson with a script by Stephen Fry – was an attack on a civilian population. In 1977, Protocol I to the Geneva Convention prohibited attacks against installations such as dams, dykes and nuclear power stations 'if such attack may cause the release of dangerous forces and consequent severe losses among the civilian population'. The United Kingdom ratified Protocol I in 1998, but with an important caveat: 'The United Kingdom cannot undertake to grant absolute protection to installations which may contribute to the opposing party's war effort, or to the defenders of such installations, but will take all due precautions in military operations at or near the installations referred to in paragraph 1 of Article 56 in the light of the known facts, including any special marking which the installation may carry, to avoid severe collateral losses among the civilian populations; direct attacks on such installations will be launched only on authorisation at a high level of command.'

In these examples, water is merely a tool in a war, not the cause of the war. To start a war, because another country is either denying you water or flooding your land, is quite different. If water is a potential source of conflict, it is also one of cooperation. David Grey, the World Bank's senior advisor on water, has spent much of his professional life trying to resolve water conflicts. The work is not straightforward, but he views water primarily as a thing around which people gather. 'About ninety-five per cent of the world's nation states share a river,' he says. 'When you share a river, there can be tension, maybe large or small, but this is perfectly rational. If you have your own river, it's a wonderful thing. You can manage it from source to sea. You can increase fish stocks, energy, navigation, even plant trees on the river banks.' What happened in Germany, when the eighty-odd regional states along the Rhine worked together to make the Rhine navigable, is a classic example. They all had something to gain from the Rhine being a viable waterway. Grey, however, argues that cooperation along rivers is not inevitable: 'It's a win-win situation. If you don't do it, everybody loses. But you might argue for a country such as Turkey, which sits upstream on the Euphrates from Syria and Iraq. What's in it for them? The answer is a basket of benefits, such as cross-border tariffs on trade and energy and many other issues.'

For those who live upstream, scarcity of water is not a problem. Their issue is normally one of oversupply. In Ethiopia, for example, which is the source of much of the water in the Nile, the rain falls heavily in two or three months a year, which washes away as soon as it can, wreaking havoc en route. Some ninety per cent of Ethiopia's roads are 'dry roads', made of soil and clay. In the rainy season, when the farmers want to get their goods to market, there is no way of getting there. Building roads that would withstand such weather would cost three times as much. So Ethiopia's problem is what to do with all the water they receive; how to manage it. If you live upstream, you can irrigate, generate power, you can conserve forests and reduce the sediment that would otherwise flow downstream. Egypt's problem, meanwhile, is to make sure they get the water they need. The answer can only be dialogue: 'According to the Egyptian ambassador to Ethiopia, trade has increased by fifty per cent year on year between Egypt and Ethiopia in the last few years because of increased dialogue between the two countries, mainly regarding the waters of the Nile,' says Grey.

It is no surprise that the issue of water is a preoccupation of Egypt's rulers. The Nile's failure has caused the downfall of the ruling party before. According to Professor Fekri Hassan, the non-appearance of the Nile floods back in 2200 BC was responsible for the collapse of the Old Kingdom. Hassan studied the records of the Nile's floods but he discovered that there were none for 2200 BC, the year that the first great civilisation in history disintegrated. The pharaohs, who had built the pyramids of Giza, and ruled supremely for more than 1,000 years, lost control of their people without warning. Hassan found a hieroglyph in southern Egypt in the tomb of a regional governor called Ankhtifi which read: 'All of Upper Egypt was dying of hunger to such a degree that everyone had started eating their children.' What had caused this? According to Hassan and his colleagues there was a mini Ice Age that year, which caused, among other things, lakes that normally supplied the Nile with water to dry up. The people starved; the rulers fell.

So why do I not think water will be the spark for future conflict? Partly because water, by definition, is not an incendiary element. Water soaks things, dampens events and douses expectations. About the only aggressive use that it can be put to is in a pressure washer such as a Kärcher water jet, used to disperse rioters in Continental Europe and South America. The word *karchériser* has even become a verb in French, meaning to 'sort someone out' or 'get rid of them'.

The Mekong basin, which is shared by Cambodia, China, Laos, Burma, Thailand and Vietnam, is a good example of how water encourages harmony. None of these countries is wholly stable – all have had disputes with their neighbours over the last twenty years – but there have been no incidents concerning the river itself. Even during the years of conflict between Laos and Thailand, Laos' hydroelectric dams supplied power to Thailand, and Thailand paid the bills.

For most people, assuming they have access to it, water is a source of joy. Look how children react when they are taken to the swimming pool. They jump, they splash, they enjoy themselves. Laughter travels further over water – and so do the screams. Babies can be introduced to swimming before they can walk. Kids also love having a bath. They can play with their ducks, splash their siblings, wash their hair, practise their swimming strokes and upset their parents by emptying the contents of the bath onto the bathroom floor.

In addition, water itself has rarely been a commodity that has been appropriated by a single section of a community. It is true that in the developing west of America, farmers and businessmen stole water supplies to suit themselves. It is a hard to seize as a monopoly, perhaps because of its slippery nature and democratic style of delivery – it never rains diamonds or oil, for example. In India it is fashionable to do your own rainwater harvesting. For years in the Caribbean every house has been built with a storage tank in the cellar, filled every year by water that falls on the corrugated iron roofs. Controlling water is a community activity. In the darkest days of the Israeli–Palestinian conflict, representatives of both sides would meet to discuss water issues though this pragmatism has now been rather superseded by Ariel Sharon's aggressive seizure of most of the land with a reliable water supply. The latest news from Gaza is that the Israelis are refusing to supply the Palestinians with steel sewage pipes, which they claim will be used as rocket launchers. The lagoon at Um Al Nasser is now filled to bursting. In March 2007 one of the walls was breached and stinking sewage engulfed the village, killing five people and drowning goats, sheep and chickens. As more waste enters the lagoon every day than is discharged, there is a real fear that it might happen again.

As a race, the Jews have always appreciated the strategic importance of water. King Herod, although not a Jew but an Idumean, had an impressive fortress built in Masada, overlooking the Dead Sea. He intended it as his own refuge, but had no cause to use it. It contained giant cisterns built into the rock, which filled when it rained and were sufficient to supply the 968 Zealots with water throughout the four-year Roman siege, which eventually ended in a mass suicide.

Given its importance to the well-being of a nation, you would think that water would spark many wars. That is what President Anwar Sadat had in mind when he said that Egypt would never go to war again unless it was to protect its water supplies; and the same holds for the king of Jordan, who said that he would not go to war with Israel unless water was involved. The then secretary general of the United Nations, Boutros Boutros-Ghali, joined in, confirming that the next war in the Middle East would be about water. Except it wasn't. They were all speaking in the early 1990s: the next war, and the one after that, was about oil not water, about neoconservatism against Islamic fundamentalism, about Saddam Hussein's humiliation of George Bush Snr and revenge.

Journalists, of course, like talk about water wars, recalling the old newspaper adage that 'if it bleeds, it leads'. Middle Eastern leaders saying that they think there is a realistic chance of peace because of a joint interest in sharing the water resources of a watershed that crosses both boundaries, is not news. It is boring.

But more often than not, water has led to cooperation rather than fighting. In fact there is only one war that can be definitely linked to water in the history of mankind. There have been more wars over salt. The first water war took place in what was Sumeria – now Iraq – more than 3,000 years ago. There have been as many wars over football, as when El Salvador and Honduras went to war, partly because of the result of a World Cup qualifying match. Honduras won the first leg at home 1–0, but El Salvador destroyed them 3–0 in San Salvador.

Then the fighting broke out. In the hundred hours of fighting it is estimated that 4,000 people died, with casualties equally shared between both sides.

Very little is known about the water war in Sumeria. Sumeria is part of what was dubbed the 'Fertile Crescent' by James Henry Breasted, an archaeologist at the University of Chicago. If you look at the area on a map, it also looks like a boomerang, with one tip extended down the Nile River, the elbow extending up towards the Jordan River, with the right hand tip at the mouth of the Tigris and Euphrates rivers, where it empties into the Persian Gulf. Western civilisation began here and the ancients called this area Mesopotamia, literally 'the land between the rivers'. In the book of Genesis, the Tigris River is one of the four rivers that flow out of the Garden of Eden. Gradually the Fertile Crescent became sterile. A build-up of salt reduced productivity. But before it silted up the inhabitants were ready to fight over access to water.

The World Bank's David Grey regards the hypothesis that nations won't fight about water in the future as absurd. Besides, he asks, how do we know what causes a war? He gives an interesting example to illustrate his argument. In 1981 a brilliant agricultural economist called John Garang wrote his PhD thesis at Iowa State University on the proposition that if the marshes of southern Sudan were drained and the waters diverted into the Jonglei Canal running between Malakal and Bore, it would lead to war. In 1983, back in his job in the Sudanese army, he was sent to the southern region of Bore to quell a mutiny. He was probably the wrong man for the job. Rather than dealing with the mutineers, he took control of them, and started the war that he had prophesied would occur. French contractors working on the Jonglei Canal were taken hostage and the project halted. By

1986 Garang had an army of 12,500, known as the Sudan People's Liberation Army, and support from Mengistu Haile Mariam, the Marxist leader of Ethiopia. When Mengistu was overthrown, Garang turned to the Christian Right in the United States for support. After aid and lobbying from Washington, a peace accord was finally signed in 2005. Garang was made vice president of Sudan, but three weeks later died in a helicopter crash.

Was this struggle really about water? There is no doubt that the Jonglei Canal project is divisive. It was designed to bypass the Sudd swamps where, according to water experts, much water is lost as the river flows through a series of channels, lakes and marshes. But who can say whether water is truly wasted? Wildlife thrives in the Sudd swamps when the water flows, but at times, when there is too much water, cattle can be drowned. The canal would make communications with Khartoum much shorter, as well as making southern Sudan accessible at all times, rather than cut off during the rainy season. Are these sufficient reasons to launch a twenty-two-year war? Probably not. And besides, this was a civil war, not an international campaign, although it shows how emotive water can be, particularly if you plan to divert it from a community. The BBC's obituary of Garang says that he 'spent his early and middle life in the bush planning to blow up oil wells'. It is perhaps a coincidence that southern Sudan is where most of the country's oil lies. But water – or the proposed diversion of the river into the canal – may well have been the trigger that turned Garang into a mutineer. And now with Garang dead, either by accident or design, there are fears in southern Sudan that the canal project may be revived.

Nothing better illustrates the relationship between oil and water than the Great Man-made River project. If you have enough oil revenue you can do anything you like: in the 1950s,

American firms such as Occidental Petroleum were given licences to search for oil in the Sahara Desert in Libya. They didn't find oil, but they did find water, lots of it. The Great Nubian Sandstone aquifer accumulated during the last Ice Age. Some of it collected around 38,000 years ago, while in other parts it is just 7,000 years old. Besides being bitterly disappointed, the engineers did not know what to do about their find, until one bright spark had the idea of selling President Qaddafi the idea of a giant pipeline, taking the water from the desert towards the coast, where most of Libya's 5.5 million inhabitants live. Their endeavours would be paid for in oil. Qaddafi jumped at the idea, claiming that he would turn the desert as 'green as the country's flag', turning the desert into a garden being every Arab's dream. He even produced a *Little Green Book*, modelled on Mao Tse-tung's *Little Red Book*, outlining his aspirations.

A team of construction workers was driven to the desert and put to work. Technically it is quite a feat: two million cubic metres of water are piped every day along a 1,200 kilometre stretch of pre-stressed concrete, from As-Sarir and Tazerbo to Benghazi and Sirt, via the Ajdabiya Reservoir. Another pipeline supplies Tripoli. A drop of water takes nine days to pass from source to tap. The aquifer is said to be the size of Germany, and many hundred metres deep. The project produced many challenges, not least when the United States government imposed sanctions on Libya in 1986 and the work passed to a subsidiary of Halliburton's called Brown & Root, conveniently based in England. Work continues on a second phase of the project, and a third pipeline is planned, another 1,200 kilometres in length. But then another dilemma occurred, one that nobody had considered. What to do with the water? For it soon transpired that much of the soil of Libya is calcitic. Add water, and it turns into rock. For the moment the flow has just been added to the Benghazi water supply, although Qaddafi has talked about extending the pipeline through Chad and into Egypt.

It is hard to imagine a more wasteful or ridiculous water project. Qaddafi wanted to use the water to grow crops, but in the desert, some sixty per cent of the water evaporates before it does any good. One day – nobody knows quite when, but the water is unlikely to last more than fifty years – the tap will be turned on but nothing will come out. The pipes will be the longest skateboard park in the world. It is hard to know the exact cost of the project, but some estimates are as high as $27 billion, which makes the water in Libya the most expensive in the world. It would have been cheaper to buy bottles of Evian for every Libyan than pipe the aquifer water from the desert. Better still would have been to build desalination plants on the coast. And while Qaddafi insists that 155,000 hectares of land will be irrigated, and calls the river the 'eighth wonder of the world', it is nothing of the sort. The Great Man-made River is really a Great White Elephant.

Libya should enjoy its desert water while it lasts. For elsewhere in Africa the situation is grave. The Egyptian geologist, Farouk El-Baz, thinks that much of the present conflict in Darfur, the region in the west of Sudan, has its origins in the competition for water. More than 200,000 people have been killed since the troubles began in 2003, and more than two million displaced. The geologist claims to have found the lost lake of Ptolemy, once an enormous body of water about the size of Lake Erie in America that disappeared hundreds of years ago. The water may have evaporated, or just gone underground. El-Baz wants to dig wells to exploit it. Those who pay for the boreholes will 'have their names on the wells forever'. He wants to build irrigated farms in the desert. In time, towns would be built to service the farms. It is a noble aim, though the discovery of Lake Ptolemy is not the revelation that some are claiming. Its existence has been noted for many years; the dilemma has always been how best to exploit it. But is the conflict in Darfur really about water? The secretary general of the United Nations, Ban Ki-moon, says that one of the underlying causes of the killings is 'climate change'. The droughts of the 1980s certainly led to disagreements between nomads and farmers – a dispute that is almost biblical in its origins. But to say that water is the root of the problem is disingenuous and overlooks the Sudanese government's backing of the nomads, encouraging them to form militias and carry out ethnic cleansing. Once again it is race or religion, not water, that is the root issue.

Those who start wars invariably have enough water. But as water security becomes more of an issue – whether countries have enough water at an affordable price, and not so much that it's destructive – the possibility of conflict increases. Commodities alone do not make a country rich. Look at Singapore, the Netherlands, Japan, even Britain: for centuries they have made their living through trade. But none of them is water poor. Holland, at times, has had too much, but that is largely seawater. David Grey points out that whereas most rich countries have no problem with water, many poor countries are also poor in water resources. When there are favourable rains, their GDP increases; when it fails, so do the crops. 'Water security is more difficult than food security,' he says. 'What is enough? What is an acceptable level of risk? What about drought, desertification and flood? Whenever we see variations of water supply we see poverty. There is a strong correlation between poverty and variable rainfall.' Rather than sending Africa food supplies, should we be shipping them icebergs?

To illustrate how either too much or too little water can affect an economy, Grey cites the example of Kenya in 1998. Heavy winter rains in 1998 damaged roads, bridges, and railways to the tune of some $2.5 billion. This was followed by two years of drought. Cattle died; crops failed. GDP fell by nearly twenty-five per cent. 'The economic costs were much higher,' says Grey. What happened then? Socially the country fell apart. Politicians, policemen, even postmen were accused of corruption. But what would you do in those circumstances? Better to steal than to starve, surely. And perhaps the looting can be directly linked to lack of rainfall – and flooding.

In the past, Africans coped with climate change by migration. It is only the inhabitants of strong and rich kingdoms, such as the kingdom of the Inner Delta in Mali, the Luo of Lake Victoria, the Meroitic or Nuba kingdoms of the Middle Nile or the Bartose of the Upper Zambezi who could stay in one place. The weaker, with poorer water resources, tended to move. The Bantu, for example, travelled from the west of Africa to the east. In the Americas, native Americans such as the Opi planted floodplains and when the land was exhausted, moved elsewhere. But there is nowhere to go any more: everywhere is taken.

In some areas, massive investment in water projects has transformed the economy of a region. At the beginning of the twentieth century the Americans raised millions of dollars in capital to dam rivers, create reservoirs and provide water for irrigation. In one generation the Tennessee River Valley went from an area of real poverty and deprivation to one free of malaria and with a thriving economy. Similar things happened in

Colorado. President Lyndon Johnson, looking back on his career, wrote: 'Of all the endeavours I have worked on in public life, I am proudest of the accomplishment in developing the Lower Colorado River. It is not the damming of the streams or the harnessing of the floods in which I take pride, but rather in the ending of the waste of the region. The region – so unproductive in my youth – is now a vital part of the national economy and potential. More important, the wastage of human resources in the whole region has been reduced. Men and women have been released from the waste and drudgery and toil against the unyielding rocks of the Texas hills. This is the true fulfilment of the true responsibility of government.'

Most politicians, regrettably, don't think like this. Most have no idea about the importance of water, or if they do, anticipate that projects will be too expensive or too long-term. Not that every water project is a success. What began as a way of developing the American west and alleviating poverty in the south has turned into an endless search for more water and forever more elaborate means of getting it from the source to the consumer, without recouping a fraction of the cost. Likewise, the Chinese authorities are already expressing doubts about the adverse environmental impact of the Three Gorges dams. And China's leader should know something about water: Hu Jintao began his career as a water engineer.

The impact of water on an economy is something that should not be overlooked. When Rebecca West visited Yugoslavia in the 1930s, she fantasised about buying a small plot of land on the island of Korchula and building a house. But she was advised against it, as she relates in her epic on Yugoslavia *Black Lamb and Grey Falcon*: 'One thing you will not have in abundance. That is water. But then you could afford to build yourself a big cistern, and it always rains here in the winter. That is the trouble, things work in a circle. People here need water if they are to make money. But because they have no money they cannot build cisterns to store water. So they cannot make any more money.'

One further factor suggests war over water is unlikely anytime soon. Who really suffers when there is too little water or too much? Who walks long distances through the dust to a well? Who waits by the side of the road as the temperature soars above forty degrees in the hope that a water tanker will appear? And who failed to get out of New Orleans when Hurricane Katrina hit? The poor. And who starts wars? The rich and the powerful, who have enough water to bathe their children, water their gardens, and fill their swimming pools. What does it matter to them if others walk long distances to carry silver water jugs on their heads? It is rather picturesque. An enlightened leader might care that his people would be better off in some sort of revenue-generating activity, but for the most part, they don't care. A lack of water keeps them docile. Keeps them grateful if the leaders choose to share some of their precious resources. Politicians in water-sensitive areas, like the south of Italy, have long recognised the efficacy of campaigning around election time and promising to deliver new water systems. The poor might occasionally riot, but that will die down. And they certainly won't have the energy or the desire to go to war with another country. The poor don't start wars; they are too busy collecting water.

Rather than arguing over the last drop, perhaps we could find water elsewhere? For the first time ever, water has been conclusively identified in the atmosphere of a planet outside our solar system. We might find life; but perhaps finding water is even more important. Like something out of *Le Petit Prince*, the French fantasy by Antoine de Saint-Exupéry, planet HD 189733b is located sixty-three light years away, in the constellation Vulpecula. It is a gas giant slightly larger than Jupiter, and orbits its star once every 2.2 days.

The researchers, who made the discovery using NASA's Spitzer space telescope, say the discovery lays the ground work for detecting water, and possibly life, on more familiar, rocky worlds like Earth. Dr Giovanna Tinetti, an ESA fellow from the Institut d'Astrophysique de Paris and UCL explains: 'The Holy Grail for today's planet hunters is to find an Earth-like planet that also has water in its atmosphere. That discovery, when it happens, will provide real evidence that planets outside of our solar system might harbour life. So the discovery that water exists on an extra-solar gas giant is a vital milestone along that road of discovery.'

There is no shortage of water in space; but it is often in the wrong state to encourage life, being either frozen or gaseous. What is needed is liquid water. The researchers, led by Dr Tinetti, found that the planet absorbs the starlight in a way that can only be explained if it has water vapour in its atmosphere, dimming at two infrared bands: 3.6 and 5.8 micrometres. If the planet were just a rocky world with no atmosphere, both bands (and a third at 8 micrometres) would respond the same way. But in this case, the atmosphere absorbed less radiation at 3.6 micrometres than at either 5.8 or 8 micrometres. Water is the only substance that can explain this behaviour. As for finding water on smaller planets, first we have to find the planets. Today's telescopes are not able to detect the gravitational wobble exerted by smaller, rocky worlds that will be so much more interesting to us. But when the James Webb Telescope launches in 2011, some smaller planets might well become targets for this kind of analysis.

Of course, even if we find water on Mars or anywhere else, it will not be the slightest use to us. More water is not the issue.

We have enough of it, although not always in the most convenient location. But it is how we manage our water resources that
will be the key to our success and survival.

As I am pondering whether or not my house needs more water,
I decide to visit a German friend of mine, the owner of a former
wine domaine west of Béziers. It is what they call a 'Château de
Pinard', which translates literally as Plonk Castle. The winegrowers of the Languedoc made so much money at the end of
the nineteenth century that they could afford to build enormous
castles. They were able to produce six or seven times as much
wine as growers from the north, and with the appearance of the
railways they had access to northern markets such as Paris. But
the wine was poor and the boom didn't last long; by 1907
there were riots in Montpellier and Béziers and the dream of red
gold had turned sour. Prices fell so low that the fire brigade in
Carcassonne used wine to dampen blazes in preference to water.

    As I drive down through the plane-tree-shaded roads,
crossing and criss-crossing the Canal du Midi, which wends its
way from the Atlantic to the Mediterranean and is itself a master-
piece of engineering, I wonder how much water my household
actually needs. We have a spring that can keep the swimming
pool full, the flowers watered, the children bathed. We also have
a well. I used it in the summer of 2003 to create a vegetable
garden. By mid-August the well was dry and I had to use the
water from the spring. True, it would be pleasant to have fountains and water cascades, a green lawn that you could walk on
rather than our grass that turns brown in July and is covered in
prickles, and pots of daisies. But is it necessary? Is it moral? If
I take the water from the ground, am I not depriving somebody
else downstream? Mael would say yes.

Georges Barbier knew why the fishes flew

At my friend's château he shows me the enormous domed structure that houses the spring. You descend a flight of stone stairs and in a space about five metres square is a pool of water, like a plunge pool at a spa. The top layer of the water is grey and slimy, but further down the water is good. A further flight of stairs leads down to the spring, but it is underwater. The water level starts to rise in October, at times reaching another ten or fifteen feet higher, covering the stairs that we had just come down. The spring used to supply all the water for the wine domaine, and for the first five years that my friend had the house, it supplied him too. The property is semi-detached. He owns the main house, but there is a series of outbuildings next door, one of which houses the spring, which is owned by somebody else. One day that man phoned my friend.

'The authorities are about to start banning the digging of boreholes,' he said. 'I plan to dig one immediately and suggest you do too. I will arrange everything.'

My friend agreed. He has access to town water and to the giant spring, but clearly felt he needed more. He took me over to his borehole. There is nothing to see but a small electric motor. If you flick a switch it starts pumping water. But the process to get it working was more complicated. First, a water diviner appeared, who, just like Mael, had a set of dowsing rods. He paced around the garden, took off one shoe then ten metres later, took off another. Between the two shoes was an underground river, some ten metres deep, beneath the ground.

'Dig anywhere there and you will find water,' he said. His previous job had been to find water in Narbonne. He found it on the site, but warned that they would have to dig fifty-five metres deep through rock. They dug and dug. Eventually they reached fifty-five metres but found no water. They phoned him. What should we do, they asked. 'Dig another two metres,' he said. They did as he instructed and hit water, 'cold enough to put straight into pastis'.

Having marked a spot, the next step was the arrival of the *forage* diggers. They use hollow metal rods about an inch in diameter. The first one that goes into the ground is pointed like a spear and has holes in it. Then they start banging in the rods using a heavy weight operated by an engine. When the first rod finally reaches water it moves easily because there is no resistance. They keep pushing the rods until they hit earth again, then insert a high-pressure hose through the rods to blow out the earth. The water can now seep in through the holes. All you need to do then is put a hose down through the rods and attach it to a pump. Of course, this depends on the depth of the hole. It was Newton who first discovered that you cannot pump water more than 9.8 metres; any more than that and gravity, friction and water's loose molecular structure makes it fall back down. To get it up from lower in the ground, you need a pump down the hole.

'The first bit of pumping produced sandy water,' says my friend. 'Now it's so clear you could drink it.'

They use it for filling the large plastic swimming pool and for watering the garden. My friend says there is one thing to remember.

'Never let the hose fall down,' he says. 'If you do that, it's finished and you have to dig another hole.' His son-in-law, who is Argentinian, agreed.

'I did it once on one of our farms in Argentina,' he says. 'The only problem was that the borehole was eighty-five metres deep and there were 1,000 cattle to water that day.'

As I make my way back through the vineyards, over the Canal du Midi and the River Orb, I consider all the benefits that man has derived from water: its use in washing, in construction as the fixer for cement and limewashes, all the mills that have been built and still today power stations that use coal or gas to heat water which then turns the turbines, and in transport on rivers, canals and the sea. When John F. Kennedy went to watch the America's Cup yacht race, he said: 'All of us have in our veins the exact same percentage of salt in our blood that exists in the ocean, and, therefore, we have salt in our blood, in our sweat, in our tears. We are tied to the ocean. And when we go back to the sea, whether it is to sail or to watch it, we are going back from whence we came.'

I thought of the millions of fishermen that every day stand by the riverbank and cast their bait or fly into the unknown water. How sad the fate of the Chaobai River, that once flowed through Beijing, but is now just a dry channel. Water will be piped in especially for the Olympic rowing, but once the oars have been unshipped the dam will be breached and the water will disappear like the cheers of the crowd. I recalled some of the memorable swims that I had made, particularly in the rivers of France, where the water seems softer, the current more benign, or in the lakes around Munich, where I swam as a teenager for hours alongside a beautiful blonde girl called Jutta.

There is much we can learn from water. A friend of mine, a water expert, became a banker. For a while he was bewildered. Then he realised that, just like hydrology, all you had to do to understand banking was to follow the flows. Water takes the path of least resistance, but it is persistent. Given enough time, it will erode the hardest stone. When it gets together in sufficient quantities, it can extinguish fires, move mountains and destroy anything. Likewise, when people collaborate, they can build amazing things. People, like water, are happiest when there is movement. In cooking – how could one live without steamed vegetables or boiled eggs? You can even put it in a mattress to make a waterbed. And of course, there is nothing better to quench a thirst. *Cha-no-yu,* the Japanese tea ceremony, translates as 'hot water for tea'. It isn't just an elaborate ritual, but a celebration of the simple pleasures of life, infused with calm and dignity. Water is the secret ingredient in wine-making. The most famous wine of the last century, the Cheval Blanc 1947, was created by dumping huge lumps of ice in the vats. 1947 was a notoriously hot vintage. If wine gets too warm, fermentation stops. Modern wine makers have sophisticated techniques to chill the wine, such as air conditioned wine cellars and stainless steel tanks with built-in refrigeration. In those days nothing like that existed. But they made beautiful wine. Astronauts train in water; coping with diving masks and oxygen tanks is considered to be the best preparation for Space. And even if the scientists are correct that one day Europe will be powered by massive solar panels in the Sahara, the electricity will be generated by steam-driven turbines.

I also thought of the uses that I could put the water to in the garden. I could have tomatoes, courgettes, aubergines and melons;

I could have a field of carnations like Ugolin and sell them in the market. I could have fountains spraying jets high in the air, staircases cascading water like those in the Alhambra, and a lawn fit for croquet matches, cucumber sandwiches and afternoon tea.

That evening I go down to the spring and listen to its steady flow. There is magic in that sound and that place. This is where we christened Bea, my youngest daughter, and my son Leonardo. This is where the water has chosen to rise from the ground. If we dig elsewhere and force it up we are treating it as a commodity, not a gift. Furthermore, we may well be depriving somebody else. My dreams of fountains and lawns will have to be abandoned. I shall plant geraniums and lemon trees rather than weeping willows and hydrangeas. I have come back to the source. It is sufficient, provided we use it wisely.

The water is lukewarm, but the woman flinches instinctively as she puts her foot into it and lowers her body into the pool. This water will transform her life. The pool is about twice the size of a bath. All she can think of as she sinks into the water is that it will ease the pain. She turns, writhes in agony, the water caresses her back, giving her some relief, like the hand of a loved one.

'This really hurts,' she tells the midwife. Inside she is cursing herself for opting for a natural birth.

'You need to push,' the midwife tells her softly. She tries to push. It feels like the right thing to do; her body responds well. She breathes as she's been told to in antenatal classes. The deeper her breath, the less her pain. She sinks further into the water; it touches her mouth, it tastes of nothing. Outside a lawnmower starts.

'Please tell them to shut up,' she shouts. 'How can they be mowing at a time like this?' Is this the anger one feels just before the birth that the irritating antenatal teacher described? What will

happen if the baby comes out now? Will it drown? An unbearable pain and then another push. And another. Will this never end? Now there are shafts of lightning searing down her back. She wants to die. She turns over, hoping the water will comfort her. She hangs on to the edge of the pool, pushing as if her life depends on it. Of course it doesn't, but another one does. Suddenly the midwife is in the water with her. She feels a burning sensation in her groin and then – release. It's over. She turns around and relaxes like she does in her bath at home. The midwife hands her the baby. It is covered in a white substance. Gently she washes it off with the tepid water. The first of a million baths.

'It's a girl!'

Acknowledgements

LIKE WATER, WRITING THIS book threatened to be a source of both conflict and cooperation. It risked turning all the people I met into a collaborator: everyone has a water story.

Hugh Goldsmith acted as godfather, giving me crucial leads, sources and encouragement. I am most grateful for his help and guidance. Patrick Cameron, James Dorsey, Simon Fletcher, Norrie Hearn, Kim March, Stephen Medcalf, Patrick Pinettes and Nick Sole provided a variety of invaluable services such as suggesting quotations, reading chapters or just realising when a glass of wine would be a suitable substitute for water. Jonathan Miller lent me his summer house in which to write much of it, and came up with some useful editing suggestions. I have been lucky to count Tracey Osborne as a friend for more than ten years; she is responsible for getting me involved in the murky world of water in the first place. Water professionals including Dr Felix Franks, David Grey, Vandana Mehta and Anthony Waterkeyn were generous with their time and knowledge. Sanjay Gupta was an invaluable guide in New Delhi, as in her own inimitable way was Iona Fergusson. My old friend Ewerton Oliveira da Silva helped me track down the Bishop of Barra. My thanks also to the librarians at the Institute of Civil Engineering and at the British Library.

This book was the idea of my lovely agent, Lucy Luck. Her other brainwave was introducing me to Stuart Williams at

Harvill Secker. A better editor one couldn't wish for: his subtle ideas have transformed the book, while his keen eye has saved me from a bucketload of basic errors. Finally, as always, I am indebted to my wife Helena. As the poet said, I love her like water.

Illustrations

Index